MORE
who knew?

Thousands of Money-Saving Secrets for Cooking, Cleaning, and All Around Your Home

MORE
who knew?

Thousands of Money-Saving Secrets for Cooking, Cleaning, and All Around Your Home

Bruce Lubin & Jeanne Bossolina Lubin

CASTLE POINT
PUBLISHING

Castle Point Publishing
58 Ninth Street
Hoboken, NJ 07030

ISBN: 978-0-9832376-5-5

Printed and bound in the United States of America

10 9 8 7 6 5 4 3 2

Dedication

For Jack, Terrence, and Aidan, as always

Acknowledgments

We couldn't make our books without the generous support of many people, who we'd like to thank here. First, thanks to our families and friends for cheering us on and providing us with millions of tips over the years, long before we started writing down who submitted what. Thank you, too, for putting up with us when we're on a deadline.

We owe great gratitude to Jennifer Boudinot, who is a tremendous partner and friend, and Brian Scevola, who has continued to be an all-around good guy and fight our fights for years now. A big thank you to Joy Mangano, whose vision and enthusiasm inspires us. To Beth, Maureen, Andrea, Joanie, Wendy, Monica, Marianna and everyone else at Ingenious Designs, we owe you a drink! And a nice big bottle of white vinegar. Thanks to all of the designers we have worked with to make Who Knew? books wonderful to read, including Richard Pasquarelli, Christine Heun, Jatin Mehta, and of course, Lynne Yeamans, who proves that old coworkers are the very best kind. We've also been blessed with some great editors over the years, including Heather Rodino, Lindsay Herman, and Rachel Federman. And we have Carol Inskip to thank for all our wonderful indexes! Special thanks to Todd Vanek and Melissa Glover of Bang Printing, who make it possible for us to print all our books in the USA.

We're also grateful for the help we've received from Anthony "Sully" Sullivan and David "Drunkle" Runkle. Arwen Saxon, Pete Donegian, and everyone else at the Billy Mays Memorial Studio, you don't have nicknames yet, but we will come up with some for next time! To Lynn Hamlin, thank you not only for your support, but for your insight and know-how. Mindy McCortney is always amazing, and we are never luckier than when we get to work with her!

Last but not least, thank you to our readers! We couldn't do it without you, and we're humbled by the number of people who have brought our books into their homes! A special thanks to all our readers who have given us their families' time- and money-saving tips, either though the mail, on our Facebook or Twitter pages, or through our website, WhoKnewTips.com. This book is for you!

Contents

PART ONE

CHEF'S SECRETS

Whether you're preparing a huge meal for a holiday get-together or just whipping up a snack for the kids, cooking conundrums can be some of the most frustrating. Mix your pancake batter just a bit too much and the pancakes will be flat; add the barbecue sauce too soon, and your ribs will burn. Simple mistakes like these can turn cooking into a chore. But in this section, we'll not only give you the how-to for improving your favorite dishes, we'll also provide tips and tricks to make the little things (and few of the big ones) quicker and easier, such as helping your food last longer, turning every mealtime into a success, and making the most out of your trips to the grocery store.

CHAPTER 1

Cooking Basics

What Is Meal Planning?

Meal planning is as simple as it sounds. Figure out what you're eating for dinner a week or two in advance, then plan your meals around similar ingredients so that they are quicker, easier, and cheaper to prepare. To make life even less stressful, try to make several meals at one time, so you can freeze or refrigerate them for later. Here are some tips to get you started.

✦ Begin with what you know: pick five to seven meals your family love and that you could make with your eyes closed. Try to include some that you can easily stretch to two meals—for example, a giant pot of soup or chili, a large casserole, or a big batch of pasta.

✦ Write your meals for the week (even if they are leftovers or if you have plans to eat out) on a white-erase board or a post-it note tacked to the wall. You'll not only be more motivated to follow through, but you'll hopefully get your family more involved.

✦ Make a list of the ingredients you'll need and buy them all in one shopping trip. As meal planning becomes ingrained in your everyday routine, you'll be able to plan your meals around what's on sale at the grocery store or what you have on hand.

✦ The more meals you can make out of the same ingredients, the better. Cut up a bunch of veggies, for instance, and use them in both a casserole and a stew.

✦ It's ideal to make a whole dish and freeze or refrigerate it ahead of time, but unfortunately, you won't always have the time or the space. So think about little things you can do to make preparing dinner quicker and easier later. For example, roast a whole chicken, then break apart the meat into bite-sized pieces that can easily be thrown into pastas, soups—or anything, really!

✦ Save your menu and use it again later. This will save you some thinking time, and will be especially handy when the meats you used last time are on sale again.

✦ One of the great things about meal planning is that it makes it easier to accomplish your food-related goals. Want to eat healthier, organic, or less meat? With these meal ideas ready to go, you'll be less like to resort to your usual less-than-healthy options.

Learn to Love Home Cooking

If you're used to eating out a lot, it's hard to break the habit. Since dining out eats up a lot of money (please excuse the pun), it's worth it to try to cut back. Make it easier on yourself by doing your shopping on a different day than when you actually prepare the food—that way you aren't stacking up the chores of buying groceries and making dinner. Plan ahead and try to make enough food to take to work with you for lunch the next day, thus saving even more. Encourage yourself by inviting over a friend for dinner; then have dinner at her house the next week. Once you see all the money you save, it will be much easier not to order in.

Save on Heat

When meal planning, think about multiple dishes that you can cook simultaneously in the oven, such as a roast and a casserole. Better yet, turn a pot lid upside-down while cooking, then place veggies wrapped in foil on top. This will save time—and money on your gas or electric bill!

Your Freezer Is Your Friend

Remember, your freezer can be used for more than just frozen casseroles and steaks. Every time you make something, ask yourself if it's worth it to double the batch and put it in the freezer. Examples of foods that can be frozen are cookie dough, pancake batter, cooked French toast, spaghetti sauce, pizza dough, and burritos. See the "Making Your Food Last Longer" chapter for more ideas!

Putting Parsley Through the Ringer

Unfortunately, when you're chopping parsley ahead of time, you'll find it quickly wilts. Solve this problem by getting out as much of the water as you can. This is easily accomplished by wringing it in a kitchen towel.

Who Knew? Readers' Favorite

Before using a measuring cup for a sticky liquid like honey, coat the inside with vegetable oil or nonstick cooking spray. The liquid will pour out easily.

Prepare for the Unexpected While Cooking

Professional cooks keep small plastic bags nearby in case both hands are covered with dough or food and they need to answer the telephone. Or, you could put your hands in plastic bags before mixing meatloaf or kneading dough, and then take them out to answer that urgent call.

Conserve Cooking Utensils by Planning Ahead

To use the fewest cooking utensils possible, first measure out all the dry ingredients, then the wet ingredients. This way, you can reuse the measuring spoons or cups without having to wash and dry them first.

Improvised Spoon Rest

Who needs a spoon rest when you're at the stove cooking? Just rest your spoon on a piece of bread; it will catch all of the juices and bits of food. Toss the bread when you're done cooking.

Tidy Tongs

You've figured out that putting tongs on a spoon rest often creates more mess than it saves. We got this idea from a barbecue party we went to last summer. Use a mug. So perfect and easy you're sure to have an "A-ha, why didn't I think of that?" moment.

Make the Kitchen Towel Switch!

If you use them a lot, paper towels can end up being one of your most expensive (and wasteful) grocery items. To encourage yourself to use a kitchen towel rather than its paper cousin, install a hook above the counter that you can hang a towel on. Having it close by will remind you of this cheaper, greener alternative and will cut down on your paper towel usage.

Dental Floss in Your Kitchen

A must-have for your kitchen tool-kit is unwaxed dental floss! (No, really.) Not only is it useful for trussing a turkey, but it's also great for baking. Dental floss is perfect for cutting a cake without making too many crumbs, and if your freshly baked cookies are stuck to the baking tray, simply hold a length of dental floss taut and slip it underneath the cookie. It works better than a spatula!

Who Knew? Readers' Favorite

We love hot-pressed sandwiches! And we were tempted to buy an expensive sandwich press to make ours at home until we learned this ingenious trick. Simply fry the sandwich in a pan as you would a grilled cheese, but place a piece of foil on top and weigh down the entire sandwich by pressing a kettle full of water on top.

Cuts Like a Knife

You've finally saved up enough to buy a brand new knife set (or, better yet, you're compiling a gift registry). So which knives should you get? The three basic knives everyone should own are a chef's knife, for chopping and slicing; a paring knife, for deseeding and other small jobs; and a boning knife, for cutting meat and poultry. Additional cutlery items you may want to have are a serrated knife for slicing bread, a cleaver, a fish-filleting knife, and a pair of kitchen scissors.

Storing Knives

Two of the best places to store knives are on a magnetic rack or in a wooden countertop knife block. Never store knives in a drawer with other utensils. Not only do you risk injury, but the knife blades may become nicked and dented.

On the Chopping Block

Studies continue regarding the safety of plastic cutting boards versus wood ones. Most cooks have their favorite, and many use both. No matter what kind of cutting board you prefer, here are some safety and cleaning tips.

+ Reserve one cutting board for raw meats, poultry, and fish; use other cutting boards for prepping vegetables, cheeses, and cooked meats.

+ Wash all cutting boards immediately after use in very hot, soapy water. If you have a plastic cutting board, run it through the dishwasher, which reaches higher temperatures than the water in your sink does. To make sure you get every last bacterium, you can also wash the boards in a weak bleach solution.

✦ Remember that it's harder to scrub bacteria out of nooks and crannies, so you should discard cutting boards whose surfaces have deep knife marks.

✦ Avoid setting hot pans on wood cutting boards or butcher-block countertops. Bacteria love heat, and the hot pan may serve to activate them or draw them to the surface of the wood.

✦ To quickly disinfect a plastic cutting board, wash it thoroughly, rub half a cut lemon over it, and microwave it for a minute.

✦ Another way to make sure you're getting the germs out of a wooden cutting board is to cover it with a light layer of salt to draw out any moisture from the crevices. Leave the salt on overnight before scraping it off. Then treat the wood with a very light coating of mineral oil. Make sure it is only a light coat, because mineral oil may affect the potency of a number of vitamins in fruits and vegetables.

✦ Do you have a cutting board that has a lingering odor that just won't quit? Remove the smell by rubbing the board with very salty water or some white vinegar.

Clean Cutting Boards

Cutting boards and breadboards need only simple soap and water to get clean, but you can make them look newer by rubbing salt over them with a wet cloth. After you rinse, plastic ones can be left to dry, but wooden ones do best if you towel them dry so they don't warp.

Fridge Hygiene

Store cooked foods above uncooked meat in your fridge. This minimizes the risk of food poisoning caused by drips from uncooked meat and other foods. Wrap any food with strong odors and avoid storing it close to dairy foods, which can become easily tainted. And throw away that slimy lettuce at the back of the vegetable drawer!

Who Knew? Readers' Favorite

The next time you defrost your freezer, spray it with a thin layer of cooking oil afterwards. The oil repels water (and ice), which will prevent it from frosting over. If it does ice up, you should easily be able to chip away the ice without having to defrost the entire freezer.

Freezer Facts

You can freeze any food except canned or preserved food and whole eggs. Some foods, however, do not freeze well. High-fat products like cream and mayonnaise tend to separate when defrosted, and high-water content vegetables such as lettuce and cucumbers will go soggy. Freezer temperature is critical for maintaining the quality of foods. Keep it set at 0°F.

Ice Rinsing Remedy

When ice cubes stay in the freezer tray more than a few days, they tend to pick up odors from other foods you have stocked away. Give them a quick rinse in cold water to avoid altering the flavor of your beverage.

Cook It Through

Contrary to popular belief, freezing doesn't actually kill bacteria or other food microbes, but what it does do is put them in a dormant state so they won't be active or reproduce until the food is thawed again. This is why it's important to cook food thoroughly after defrosting. If you defrost raw meat and then cook it, you can freeze it again, but remember you should never reheat foods more than once. If you want to use a meaty sauce like Bolognese for several meals, reheat individual portions when you need them rather than the whole pot.

The longer a food is frozen, the more nutrients it loses. Seal all foods to be frozen as tightly as possible to avoid freezer burn and the formation of ice crystals. Ice crystals cause thawed food to become mushy.

Slow Cooker Safety

Many people question whether a Crock-Pot is safe for cooking foods, or if it's a breeding ground for bacteria because it cooks at low temperatures. Most slow cookers have settings that range from 170–280°F, and most bacteria die at 140°F, so you should be safe. However, to minimize the risk of food poisoning, follow these tips.

✦ Don't attempt to cook frozen or partially thawed foods, and don't use the cooker to reheat leftovers. (Uncooked foods at refrigerator temperature are safe to use.)

✦ Cook only cut-up pieces of meat—not whole roasts or poultry—to allow the heat to penetrate fully.

✦ Make sure that the cooker is at least half to two-thirds full or the food may not absorb enough heat to kill bacteria.

✦ Cover the food with enough liquid to generate sufficient steam.

✦ Always use the original lid, and be sure it fits tightly. Never use the cooker with the lid off.

✦ When possible, cook on the highest setting for the first hour, then reduce it to low if necessary.

Deodorize the Disposal

A quick and easy way to deodorize your in-sink garbage disposal is to grind an orange or lemon peel inside it every so often. It will get rid of grease and smell wonderful!

Vanquish Smells with Vinegar

To help control unpleasant cooking aromas, dampen a cloth with a mixture of equal parts vinegar and water. Drape it over the cooking pot, taking care that the edges are far from the flame or intense heat.

Who Knew? Readers' Favorite

Remove strong food smells from your hands by running them under cold running water while rubbing them with a stainless steel spoon. Rinse with soap and water.

Toothpaste Trick

You've been cooking with garlic, and now you can't get the smell off your hands! To get rid of this or any other kitchen odor, just rub some white toothpaste between your hands and wash off.

Stop the Stink

Don't throw away used coffee grounds—instead, keep them in a can near the sink. Rub a small amount over your hands after handling fish, or chopping garlic or onions to get rid of odors on your hands.

Check the Temperature without a Thermometer

If you suspect your oven's temperature isn't in line with what it reads on the dial, but don't have an oven thermometer to test it, use this simple trick. Put a tablespoon of flour on a baking sheet and place it in a preheated oven for five minutes. If the flour turns light tan, the temperature is 250–325°F. If the flour turns golden brown, the oven is 325–400°F. If it turns dark brown, the oven is 400–450°F. And an almost a black color means the oven is 450–525°F. Figure out the disparity between what the temperature is and what it reads, and make sure to set your oven accordingly in the future.

Who Knew? Readers' Favorite

Save a lot of cleanup time by lining the bottom rack of your oven with aluminum foil when cooking something messy. But beware—you should never line the bottom of your oven with foil, as it could cause a fire.

Foil Foible

Never wrap foods that contain natural acids—like tomatoes, lemons, or onions—in aluminum foil. The combination of the foil and the acid in the foods produces a chemical reaction that affects the taste of the food.

Protect Silver from Acidic Foods

Some foods are particularly harsh on silver: Olives, salad dressings, vinegar, eggs, and salt will all cause silver to tarnish quickly. Wash your silver as soon as possible after it's had contact with any of these items.

Cooking with Wine

When cooking with wine, try not to use too much, or the taste may well overpower the dish. Wine should only be used to improve the flavor. If you want to assure that you taste the wine, just add it to the recipe about five to seven minutes before completion. And don't forget a little sip for the cook!

Avoid a Boiling Blunder

To keep a pot from boiling over, stick a toothpick between the lid and the pot. Other tricks include placing a wooden spoon across the top of the uncovered pot or rubbing butter around the inside lip of the pot.

Perfect Pasta Water

Stop your pasta water from spilling over with this trick: Add a long metal spoon to the pot, and it will absorb the excess heat and let your pasta cook at the correct temperature.

Canola Cure

To sauté or fry with butter, margarine, or lard, add a small amount of canola oil to raise the smoke point. This will keep the solid fat from breaking down at higher temperatures.

Who Knew? Readers' Favorite

When sautéing or frying, always heat your pan for a couple of minutes before adding butter or oil to ensure that nothing sticks and that the food will cook evenly. It's also a good idea to sprinkle a little salt in your pan before frying—it will keep the oil from splattering.

Important Tips for Deep-Frying

Sometimes food sticks together when you're deep-frying it. To prevent this, lift the basket out of the oil several times before leaving it in for good. And don't try to fry too much at once—the oil may bubble over from the temperature difference of the cold food and the hot oil. And speaking of hot oil, be sure it's 300–375°F before you add the food.

A Lighter Coat for Fried Foods

When making a batter for foods for deep-frying, try adding ½ teaspoon baking powder for every ½ cup flour. The coating will be lighter.

Frying Temperatures Are Critical

Oil needs to be at the proper temperature whether you're sautéing or deep-frying. If the temperature is too low, the food will absorb too much oil and become greasy, not crispy. If the oil is too hot, the food may burn on the outside and not cook through. Most breaded foods are normally fried at 375°F, but check the recipe. Chicken should be fried at 365°F for 15–20 minutes for white meat and 20–25 minutes for dark.

When Cooking with Oil

In terms of fat content, less oil is always better than more! So if you have to coat food with oil before sautéing or baking it, use a spray bottle rather than a brush to reduce the amount of fat that ends up on your food.

Unsalted Butter Is Best

If you sauté with butter, be sure you use the unsalted kind. When salted butter melts, the salt can separate from the butter and impart a bitter taste to the dish.

Tips for Breading

Keeping breading on foods can be a challenge, but there are a few tricks to try (other than using superglue, which we don't recommend). First, make sure that the food to be breaded is very dry. Use eggs at room temperature, and beat them lightly. If you have time, refrigerate the breaded food for an hour, then let it sit at room temperature for 20 minutes before cooking. Homemade breadcrumbs adhere better than the store-bought kind because of their uneven texture.

Who Knew? Readers' Favorite

When changing the yield of a recipe, don't increase the seasonings proportionately, or the recipe will taste wrong. If you're doubling the recipe, increase the seasonings only by one and a half; if you are tripling the recipe, double the amount of seasoning.

Crushing Spices

Don't have a mortar and pestle? A great way to mix and crush spices is to place them in a pan and press with the bottom of a smaller pan. A coffee grinder works well, too.

Herbal Flavor Booster

Crushing dried herbs before using them will boost their flavor, as will soaking them for a few seconds in hot water. This technique also works well with dried herbs that have lost their flavor.

Great Garlic Tips

Garlic is one of our favorite seasonings, and we find it's much better fresh than in powdered form. If you love garlic too, here are some tips for cooking with this delicious ingredient.

✦ To make garlic easy to peel, soak it in very hot water for 2–3 minutes, or rinse it under hot water to loosen its skin.

✦ If your head of garlic sprouts, some of the flavor will go into the sprouts; however, the sprouts can be used for salads.

✦ If you have added too much garlic to your soup or stew, add a small quantity of parsley and simmer for about 10 minutes.

✦ Mincing garlic can be a sticky mess, but it doesn't have to be. Sprinkle the garlic with a few drops of olive oil beforehand. The oil will prevent the garlic from sticking to your hands or the knife.

More Than One Way to Skin...Garlic?

Here's another easy way to remove the skins from garlic! Just break the cloves off from the head and place them in a bowl or mug. Place another bowl on top and shake heartily. The skins will start to come off, making the garlic easy to peel.

Save Some Zest for Later

Don't discard the rinds of limes, lemons, oranges, or other citrus. Grate them, then store in tightly covered glass jars in the fridge. They make excellent flavorings for cakes, and can be sprinkled over chicken and fish as well.

Make Seasoning Easy

Keep a shaker filled with a ratio of 75 percent salt and 25 percent pepper (or whatever ratio you usually use) next to the stove or your food-preparation area, and it will be even easier to season foods.

Who Knew? Readers' Favorite

If you're preparing a recipe that calls for crushed ginger, don't bother with your knife. Simply peel the ginger and put it through a garlic press.

The Baking Powder Test

Did you know that baking powder loses potency over time? If you can't remember when you bought yours, test it before using it. Here's how: Put ½ teaspoon baking powder in a small bowl, then pour in ¼ cup of hot tap water. The more vigorously it bubbles, the fresher the baking powder. Try this test first on a fresh box of baking powder so you will be familiar with the activity level of fresh powder. Once opened, baking powder will remain fresh for about a year.

The Baking Soda Test

If you are not sure how old your baking soda is, you can test its activity level. Stir ¼ teaspoon baking soda into about 2 teaspoons of white vinegar; it should bubble vigorously. If it doesn't, throw it out.

Cooking Substitutions

Preparing a recipe and realize you forgot one essential ingredient? Use the chart below to find a proper substitution. Unless otherwise noted, use the substitution in equal measure to the ingredient called for in the recipe.

INGREDIENT	SUBSTITUTE
Active dry yeast (one ¼-ounce envelope)	1 cake compressed yeast
Allspice (for baking only)	1 part ground cinnamon + 2 parts ground cloves or ground nutmeg
Anise seed	fennel seed
Apples (1 cup chopped)	1 cup firm chopped pears + 1 tablespoon lemon juice.
Arrowroot	use 2 tablespoons flour for every 4 teaspoons arrowroot
Baking powder (1 teaspoon, double-acting)	⅝ teaspoon cream of tartar + ¼ teaspoon baking soda *or* ¼ teaspoon baking soda + ¼ cup sour milk or buttermilk (lessen other liquid in recipe)

Basil (dried)	tarragon *or* summer savory *or* thyme *or* oregano
Bay leaf	thyme
Black pepper	cayenne pepper (use much less; start with a pinch)
Brandy	cognac *or* rum
Bulgur	cracked wheat *or* kasha *or* brown rice *or* couscous *or* quinoa
Butter	hard margarine *or* shortening *or* oil if it is not a baked good
Buttermilk (1 cup)	1 cup milk + 1¾ tablespoons cream of tartar *or* 1 tablespoon lemon juice + milk to make 1 cup (let stand 5 minutes) *or* sour cream
Cake flour (1 cup)	1 cup minus 2 tablespoons unsifted all-purpose flour
Capers	chopped green olives
Caraway seed	fennel seed *or* cumin

Cardamom	cinnamon *or* mace
Chervil	parsley *or* tarragon *or* ground anise seed (use a bit less)
Chives	onion powder (small amount) *or* finely chopped leeks or shallots (small amount) *or* scallion greens
Chocolate, baking, unsweetened	3 tablespoons unsweetened cocoa powder + 1 tablespoon (one ounce or square) butter *or* 3 tablespoons carob powder + 2 tablespoons water
Chocolate, semisweet (6 ounces)	9 tablespoons unsweetened cocoa powder or squares + 7 tablespoons sugar + 3 tablespoons butter
Cilantro	parsley and lemon juice
Cinnamon	allspice (use less) *or* cardamom
Cloves (ground)	allspice *or* nutmeg *or* mace
Club soda	sparkling mineral water *or* seltzer
Cornmeal	polenta
Cornstarch	flour, as thickener

Corn syrup, light (1 cup)	1¾ cup granulated sugar + ¼ cup more of the liquid called for in recipe
Crème fraîche	sour cream in most recipes *or* ½ sour cream + ½ heavy cream in sauces. Note that crème fraîche can be boiled but sour cream cannot.
Cumin	1 part anise + 2 parts caraway or fennel seed (grind if necessary)
Dill seed	caraway *or* celery seed
Egg (1)	1 tablespoon cornstarch + 3 tablespoons water *or* 3 tablespoons mayonnaise *or* ½ mashed banana + ¼ teaspoon baking powder
Evaporated milk	half-and-half or cream
Flour	cornstarch *or* instant potato flakes *or* pancake mix
Garlic (1 medium clove)	¼ teaspoon minced dried garlic *or* ⅛ teaspoon garlic powder *or* ½ teaspoon garlic salt (omitting ½ teaspoon salt from recipe)
Ghee	clarified butter
Herbs, fresh (1 tablespoon)	1 teaspoon dried herbs

Honey (1 cup, in baked goods)	1¼ cups granulated sugar + ¼ cup more of the liquid called for in the recipe
Lemongrass	lemon juice *or* lemon zest *or* finely chopped lemon verbena *or* lime zest
Lovage	celery leaves
Marjoram	oregano (use small amount) *or* thyme *or* savory
Masa harina	cornmeal
Mascarpone	8 ounces cream cheese whipped with 3 tablespoons sour cream and 2 tablespoons milk
Milk (in baked goods)	fruit juice + ½ teaspoon baking soda mixed in with the flour
Milk (1 cup)	½ cup evaporated milk + ½ cup water *or* ¼ cup powdered milk + ⅞ cup of water
Milk, whole	same as above + 2½ teaspoons melted and cooled butter
Milk, evaporated	half-and-half OR cream
Molasses	honey
Nutmeg	allspice *or* cloves *or* mace

Oregano	marjoram *or* thyme
Pancetta	lean bacon (cooked) *or* very thinly sliced ham
Polenta	cornmeal *or* corn grits
Poultry seasoning	sage + a blend of any of these: thyme, marjoram, savory, black pepper, rosemary
Rosemary	thyme
Saffron (⅛ teaspoon)	1 teaspoon dried yellow marigold petals *or* 1 teaspoon safflower petals
Sage	poultry seasoning *or* savory *or* marjoram
Self-rising flour (1 cup)	1 cup all-purpose flour + 1½ teaspoons baking powder + ⅛ teaspoon salt
Shallots	scallions *or* leeks *or* yellow onions
Shortening (baked goods only)	butter *or* margarine
Sour cream	1 tablespoon white vinegar + milk (let stand 5 minutes before using) *or* 1 tablespoon lemon juice + evaporated milk *or* plain yogurt
Tahini	peanut or almond butter

Tarragon	anise (use small amount) *or* chervil (use larger amount) *or* a pinch of fennel seed
Tomato paste (1 tablespoon)	1 tablespoon ketchup *or* ½ cup tomato sauce (reduce some of the liquid in recipe)
Turmeric	mustard powder
Vanilla extract (baked goods only)	almond extract *or* any other extract
Vinegar	lemon juice for cooking and salads or wine in marinades
Yogurt	sour cream *or* buttermilk *or* mayonnaise (in small amounts)

Who Knew? Readers' Favorite

Casseroles and baked goods should always be cooked at the temperature specified in the recipe, with one notable exception: If you are using a glass baking dish, reduce the oven temperature by 25°F. Glass heats more slowly than metal, but it retains heat well. Failing to lower the temperature can result in burned bottoms.

Greasing the Pan

When you need to grease a baking pan, choose vegetable shortening. Butter has a low smoke point and burns easily, and salted butter can cause food to stick to the pan.

Wax Paper Prescription

When braising or stewing meat or poultry, always place a piece of waxed paper under the lid. It will collect the moisture that would otherwise dilute your dish.

Defrosting in the Microwave

If you've ever defrosted meat or fish in the microwave, you probably know that the "defrost" or low-power settings are your best bet for ensuring that the outer edges of the food don't cook before the middle can defrost. But here's something you might not know: Arranging loose pieces of meat in a single layer with thickest parts or largest pieces toward the outside will also ensure more even defrosting.

Meat Market Primer

Wish you could always pick the most tender cuts of meat? These hints will help. When purchasing a chuck roast, look for white cartilage near the top of the roast. If you can spot a roast with cartilage showing, you've found the first cut, which will be the most tender. When purchasing an eye of round roast, try to find the one that is the same size on both ends. For round steak, look for uneven cuts, which are the ones closest to the sirloin.

Look for Lines

As you probably know, white streaks running through meat are fat. But even if you're diet-conscious, you should always choose well-marbled meat, which will be the most tender, since the animal didn't exercise those muscles very much. Fat is a storage depot for energy, and for meat to be well-marbled, an animal must be fed a diet high in rich grains such as corn (which is where we get the old saying that corn-fed beef is best). The fat imparts flavor and provides moisture that helps tenderize the meat.

The Wrapping Is Everything

When choosing meat or poultry in the supermarket, look out for liquid on the bottom of the package. If it's there, it means the food has been frozen and thawed; the cells have ruptured, releasing some of their fluids. To store meat in the refrigerator, wrap it in clean plastic wrap or waxed paper. The supermarket wrapping often contains residue.

Green Ham and Eggs?

Have you ever purchased a ham that has a greenish, glistening sheen? This effect occasionally occurs when a ham is sliced and the surface is exposed to the effects of oxidation. It isn't a sign of spoilage, but is caused by the nitrite modification of the meat's iron content, which tends to produce a biochemical change in the pigmentation.

Who Knew? Readers' Favorite

To easily slice meat or poultry, partially freeze it beforehand and your knife will glide right through.

Meat Miracle

All meat (except organ meats and ground beef) should stand at room temperature for a few minutes before cooking. This allows it to brown more evenly, cook faster, retain more juices, and stick less when frying.

Fish Safety

Seafood is responsible for a lot of food poisoning, but it's perfectly safe and very healthy if treated correctly. If you can't use a fish immediately, remove it from its original wrapping and rinse in cold water. Wrap it loosely in plastic wrap, store in the coldest part of the refrigerator, and use within two days.

Egg Safety

Because eggs can contain bacteria before they're even cracked, when preparing a hollandaise or béarnaise sauce, it might be best to microwave the eggs briefly before adding them to the sauce. To do so, first separate the egg yolks completely from the whites (do only two eggs at a time). Then place the two yolks in a glass bowl and beat them until they are well combined. Add 2 teaspoons lemon juice and mix thoroughly again. Now cover the bowl and microwave it on high until you see the surface of the mixture beginning to move. Cook for 10 seconds past this point, remove the bowl, and beat the mixture with a clean whisk or fork until it's smooth. Return the bowl to the microwave and repeat the previous step: Cook 10 seconds past when the surface starts to move, remove, and whisk till smooth. Let the mixture stand (covered) for 1 minute. Your yolks are now free of salmonella and will still be usable in your sauce!

A Good Temper

When adding raw eggs or yolks to a hot mixture, be sure to mix part of the hot mixture into the eggs, and then gradually add this new mixture to the hot mixture. Called "tempering," it may be extra work, but it makes the eggs less likely to curdle and separate.

Cracks Are Whack

Bacteria love eggs, so if you find a cracked egg in the carton, throw it out; it is probably contaminated. The refrigerator shelf life of eggs is about five weeks from the "sell by" date.

Egg White Wisdom

When beating egg whites for a recipe, remove all traces of yolk from the bowl with a Q-tip or the edge of a paper towel before trying to beat the whites. The slightest trace of yolk will prevent the whites from beating properly, as will any trace of fat on the beaters or bowl.

Who Knew? Readers' Favorite

For perfectly peeled hard-boiled eggs, crack the eggs slightly on your counter, then place them in a bowl of cool water. The water will seep in and loosen the egg from its shell, making sure you don't accidentally take off half the white when you're trying to peel it.

Washing Winner

When washing vegetables, place a small amount of salt in a sink full of cold water to draw out any sand and insects.

Bag the Baking Soda

You may have heard the old household tip that baking soda added to the cooking water will help vegetables retain their color, but it will also cause them to lose texture and vitamins. To help veggies keep their color, forget the baking soda and simply cook them for no more than 5–7 minutes.

Make It Hot

If you need to add more water to vegetables as they are cooking, make sure the added water is as hot as possible. Adding cold water to already-cooking veggies may affect their cell walls and cause them to toughen.

Carrot Can-Do

If you only have a few carrots to peel, a standard vegetable peeler will get the skins off. But what if you have a whole bunch? To slip the skin off carrots in one giant batch, drop them in boiling water, let them blanch for 5 minutes, then place them in cold water for a few seconds. The skins will slide off easily.

Peeling Potatoes

The easy way to peel a potato is to boil it first, then drop it into a bowl of ice water for a few seconds to loosen the skin.

Potato How-To

A new (red) potato has more moisture than other potatoes. Use new potatoes in dishes such as potato salad; they absorb less water when boiled and less mayonnaise when prepared, allowing your salad to have better flavor and less fat. They'll also break apart less easily when you mix the salad. Russet and Yukon gold potatoes are better for baking and making french fries. They are drier, meatier, and starchier, so they have a lighter texture when baked. Their lower water content means the oil will spatter less when you fry them. When baking a potato, make sure you pierce it so steam can escape; otherwise, it may become soggy.

Who Knew? Readers' Favorite

Hot potato or cold, it's hard to keep them from slipping out of your hands as you peel them. Screw a corkscrew partway in to keep a raw potato steady—one hand on the corkscrew handle, one on the peeler. For a cooked potato a fork easily does the job.

Cruciferous Cooking

When you cook cruciferous vegetables like broccoli, cabbage, and cauliflower, never use an aluminum or iron pot. The sulfur compounds in the vegetables will react with the metal. For instance, cauliflower will turn yellow if cooked in aluminum, and brown if cooked in iron.

Onions Go First

When sautéing onions and garlic together, sauté the onions first for at least half of their cooking time. If you start the garlic at the same time as the onions, it will overcook and possibly burn, releasing a chemical that will make the dish bitter.

Creating Caramelized Vegetables

Caramelized vegetables have nothing to do with caramel candy, but they taste almost as good. Caramelizing is the process of oxidizing the sugar content of a vegetable, which produces a sweet, nutty flavor and a brown color. To easily caramelize an onion or other vegetable, toss the slices in olive oil and roast them in a 400°F oven for 10–30 minutes, or until golden brown. You'll love the flavor for stir-fries and on top of pizza.

Pitting Practice

This trick is for adults only: To easily remove an avocado pit, thrust the blade of a sharp knife into the pit, twist slightly, and the pit will come right out.

When It's Good to Add Sugar

Cooking fruit? To make sure it doesn't get mushy, always add sugar to the cooking syrup. The sugar will draw some of the fluid back into the cells to maintain equilibrium in the sugar concentration, and the fruit will retain a more appealing texture.

Frozen Berry Delight

Frozen berries are filled with just as many healthy antioxidants as fresh ones, and in winter they are an excellent source of vitamin C and small amounts of vitamin A and calcium. If you're not going to enjoy the berries while they're still frozen, thaw them in the refrigerator. The fruit will have time to reabsorb its sugars as it thaws.

Mango Mission

If you slice open a mango and it tastes too acidic, place it in warm (not hot) water for ten minutes. This will speed up the process of its starches turning into sugars, and it will be sweet in no time! Just make sure not to leave it in the water for more than ten minutes, as it might begin to shrivel.

Who Needs a Juicer?

Instead of purchasing a handheld juicer (also known as a reamer) for fruit, simply use one blade from a hand mixer instead. Halve the fruit and twist the blade into it for easy juicing.

Shelling Secret

The easiest way to shell pecans, walnuts, and other nuts? Freeze them first. It shrinks the nut away from the shell and makes the job a breeze. Another easy way to shell nuts is to soak them in boiling water for 15 minutes.

The easiest way to clean a cheese grater is to spray it with vegetable oil before grating any cheese, which will make it less sticky. Afterward, rub the crusty heel from a stale loaf of French bread over the dirty end, and your cleanup is finished!

Grating Soft Cheese?

It's easier to grate Cheddar and other softer cheeses if you place them in the freezer for 10–15 minutes before grating. If the cheese is really soft, don't even bother with the grater. An easier method is to just push it through a colander with a potato masher.

Grater Priorities

Here's a chef's secret for keeping a grater clean so you can use it repeatedly without washing: Simply grate the softest items first, then grate the firmer ones.

CHAPTER 2

Breakfast and Lunch

Fresh-Tasting, Reheated Coffee

When you keep coffee warm in a coffeepot, it will only stay fresh for about 30 minutes after brewing. If your morning pick-me-up needs tastes stale, add a pinch of salt to your cup before reheating it. You won't taste the salt, but your coffee will taste like it's just been brewed.

Who Knew? Readers' Favorite

Who doesn't enjoy an iced coffee on a sultry summer day? To make sure melting ice doesn't dilute your drink, make ice cubes using the small amount of coffee left at the bottom of your coffee pot each morning. Use them in your iced coffee, and it will never taste watered down. This is also a great tip for iced tea!

Easy, Sweet Coffee

If you love sweetened, flavored coffee, simply mix ¼ fresh vanilla bean or 1 teaspoon cinnamon with 1 cup sugar in a food processor until well-blended, then add a little scoop to your next cup. It's usually much cheaper than buying flavored coffees or creamers, and it tastes better, too.

Coffee Combos

If you're like us, you know it's worth it to spend the extra money on high-quality coffee. The great thing about buying coffee in bulk is that you can easily mix the premium stuff with the not-so-premium stuff. We use 3 parts gourmet coffee with 1 part of the cheap stuff, and even we can't tell the difference!

Incredible Iced Coffee in an Instant

If you love iced coffee in the summer, make it even better with the help of a martini shaker or capped thermos. Pour in the coffee, milk, ice, and any flavoring, then cover and shake. The shaking will add lots of air to the mixture, making it light, frothy, and delicious.

How to Save Your Cream

If your cream or half-and-half has begun to develop an "off" odor, but you desperately need it for your coffee, try mixing in $1/8$ teaspoon baking soda; it will neutralize the lactic acid that is causing the cream to sour. Before you use the cream, however, taste it to be sure the flavor is still acceptable.

The Most Important Meal of the Day

For a quick and healthy breakfast, make waffles and pancakes ahead of time, then freeze them. When you and your family are ready to eat, pop them in the toaster to reheat. This tip saves both time and money.

Don't Pucker Up

It's surprising, but true: A small amount of salt will make a grapefruit taste sweeter.

Breakfast Bar Saver

Don't have time to eat anything but a breakfast bar in the morning? Store it in a glasses case to make sure it doesn't get smushed in your purse or bag on the way to work.

If you're hooked on instant oatmeal packets, try this trick instead for big savings. Buy instant oats in bulk, then combine ¼ cup of them with a ½ teaspoon each of sugar and cinnamon, and a pinch of salt in a sandwich bag. Pre-pack several and you're set for the week.

Toasty Treat

For a different type of toast, lightly butter a slice of bread on both sides and cook it in a waffle iron. Your kids will love it!

With Eggs, Your Bowl Matters

Aluminum bowls and cookware tend to darken eggs. The reason? Aluminum reacts chemically with the egg protein. A copper bowl, if you happen to have one, is best for beating eggs. The copper will release ions during the beating process that cause the protein in the whites to become more stable. The next best material to use is stainless steel; however, we recommend adding a pinch of cream of tartar to stabilize the whites.

Save Your Yolks

Believe it or not, you can save egg yolks for later use. If you have leftover yolks from a recipe that uses egg whites, slide them into a bowl of water, cover with plastic wrap, and store them in the refrigerator for a day or two. It beats throwing them out!

Poaching Eggs

The fresher the egg, the better it is for poaching. The white will be firmer and will help to keep the yolk from breaking. In addition, salt, lemon juice, and vinegar will make egg whites coagulate faster. Add a dash of one of these ingredients to the poaching liquid to help eggs keep their shape.

Sunny Side Secrets

When frying eggs, make sure the butter or margarine is very hot—a drop of water should sizzle. However, the heat should be reduced just before the eggs are added to the pan. Cook them over low heat until the whites are completely set. Add a couple drops of water and cover the pan just before the eggs are done to get a perfect white film over the yolks.

A Surprising Use for That Old Cappuccino Maker

Use your cappuccino maker for a speedy breakfast treat. Place the foamer (not the milk-uptake valve!) into a mug with a beaten egg inside. The steam will cook it into a scrambled egg in seconds!

For the Best-Ever Omelet

To make a great omelet, be sure the eggs are at room temperature (take them out of the fridge 30 minutes beforehand). Cold eggs are too stiff. For a super fluffy omelet, add ½ teaspoon baking soda for every three eggs. Also, try adding a drop or two of water instead of milk. The water increases the volume of the eggs at least three times more than the milk does.

Who Knew Readers' Favorite

Cleaning up after a yummy scrambled egg breakfast? Use cold water. It cleans dried egg off pans and utensils better than hot water, which causes the protein to bind to surfaces and harden.

Pancake Secrets

Short-order cooks and chefs have a host of tricks to make the lightest pancakes. Here are a few we've learned:

+ Don't overmix the batter—you don't want the gluten in the flour to overdevelop and allow the carbon dioxide that creates the little air pockets to escape. It's better to leave a couple of lumps in the batter.

+ Refrigerate the batter for up to 30 minutes. This further slows the development of the gluten and the leavening action.

✦ Always stir the batter before you ladle it onto the griddle. The ingredients can settle; stirring recombines them and aerates the mixture.

✦ Make sure you flip pancakes as soon as air bubbles appear on the top, then flip them back over if necessary to finish cooking them. If you wait until the bubbles break, gas escapes, and your pancakes won't be as light and fluffy.

✦ If you like brown-on-the-outside pancakes, add a little extra sugar. The sugar caramelizes, giving a browner color to the pancakes. Also, some people swear by the addition of a tablespoon of pure maple syrup (the real stuff—no imitations!) to your pancake batter.

✦ For perfectly formed pancakes, use a meat baster to squeeze the batter onto the griddle. It gives you so much control you'll finally be able to make those animal-shaped pancakes your kids have been begging you for!

Key to a Clean Griddle

When cooking on the griddle, you'll get better results if you clean it between each batch of pancakes or whatever you happen to be making. Do this easily with coarse salt wrapped in a piece of cheesecloth. The salt will provide a light abrasive cleaning and won't harm the surface if you're gentle.

Gauge Your Griddle

Pancakes and other griddle treats often require a precise temperature to cook to their best. But how do you know when the surface has reached the right temperature? Flick a few drops of water on the heated griddle. If the surface is 325°F (the perfect temperature for pancakes), the droplets will skitter and dance— steam causes the drops to rise, but gravity brings them back down. If the griddle is 425°F or hotter, the water drops will be propelled right off the griddle.

Who Knew? Readers' Favorite

Here's a trick to keep waffles from sticking to the waffle iron: Beat a teaspoon of white wine into the batter. You'll never taste the wine, but it will keep the batter from adhering to the hot surface.

Syrup Substitute

Out of maple syrup and still want waffles this morning? Make this delicious substitute. Combine ⅓ cup butter, ⅓ cup sugar, and ½ cup frozen orange juice concentrate in a saucepan. Cook over medium heat, stirring constantly, until the sugar has dissolved and the mixture is syrupy.

Wax Your Waffle Iron?

Waffle day is so much less fun when we have to beg and plead with the waffles to come out of the iron. Here's a quick fix if the "nonstick" material on your waffle maker has worn out: Place a sheet of wax paper in the iron, close, and heat up. Remove and now give it a try: thanks to the transferred wax, the waffles should pop out.

Another Chopstick Trick

Seems like the most-fun kitchen gadgets are the most annoying to clean. Here's a trick for the waffle maker—put a paper towel over a chopstick and go to work on the grid. Idiot reminder: Wait 'til it cools first!

Splattering Solution

To keep bacon from splattering, soak it in ice-cold water for 2–4 minutes, and then dry it well with paper towels before frying it. Or try sprinkling the bacon with a bit of flour before cooking.

Bacon Wrapper

If you're cooking less than a full package of bacon, how do you store the extra slices? Just roll each slice into a tight cylinder, place in an airtight plastic bag, and freeze. Simply thaw and unroll when you're ready to cook!

Stop Sausage Splitting

Keep sausages from splitting by piercing the skin in one or two places while they are cooking. A quick dredging in flour before cooking will reduce shrinkage.

Soggy Lunch?

If your kids complain that the sandwiches you make in the morning are mushy by lunchtime, put the mayonnaise (or any condiment) in a Ziploc bag, and stick it in the lunch box. This way, the kids can season their own sandwiches at lunchtime by turning the bag inside out and rubbing it on the bread.

Who Knew? Readers' Favorite

Kid's lunchbox starting to smell funky? Freshen it up with bread and vinegar! Just moisten a slice of bread with white vinegar and let it sit in the closed lunchbox overnight. In the morning, any bad odors should be gone.

Lunchbox Lesson

Freezing juice boxes is an excellent way to make sure your child's drink will still be cold at lunchtime. Plus, it keeps everything else in the lunchbox cool!

Be Prepared

Make school-day mornings a little less crazy by preparing a few days' worth of the kids' sandwiches at the same time (without condiments), then freezing them. Each morning, just toss the pre-made sandwich in their lunchboxes, add a small container or plastic bag with the condiments, and by lunchtime, the bread will be soft and fresh-tasting.

Forget About Refreezing

When any type of meat or lunchmeat is refrozen, the fat content may cause the food to go rancid. And this is only one reason why meats should not be frozen again after they've been thawed— the texture of the meat can suffer, and improper thawing can promote bacterial growth. Instead, refrigerate leftover meats; they can be stored safely for four days.

Mixed Nuts

If you buy all-natural peanut or almond butter, you know that it doesn't take long for the oil to separate from the rest of the spread. Solve this problem by storing your nut butter upside-down when you first buy it. When you flip it over, the oil will be evenly distributed throughout.

Stab That Potato!

When baking potatoes, pierce the skin with a fork to allow the steam to escape. Your reward will be a wonderfully fluffy texture.

Oil, Not Foil, for Baked Potatoes

Did you know that wrapping a potato in foil won't actually make it bake faster? Rubbing it lightly with vegetable oil, however, will.

Quick Quiche Tip

Quiches, especially those made with onions and mushrooms, should not be allowed to cool. Both of these vegetables have a high water content, which will be released into the quiche as it cools. The result: a soggy crust and runny filling. If buying a pre-made quiche, look for ones that don't have onions or mushrooms, and when making your own, make sure to serve after letting it sit for 10 minutes (which will prevent oozing).

Tomato Soup Tip

Cream-of-tomato soup can be tricky to make from scratch. To keep it from curdling, add the ingredients in the right order: Pour the tomato base into the milk instead of the milk into the tomato. Stirring a small amount of flour into the milk also helps.

A Smoother Finish for Soups

When serving creamed soups from the can, beat or whisk the soup 10–15 seconds before heating for a silky smooth texture.

Warm Sandwiches

Who doesn't love a warm sandwich? Luckily, you don't need an expensive sandwich press to make delicious heated sandwiches—just use your microwave! When heating a sandwich in the microwave, you'll get the best results using firm, textured bread such as French or sourdough. The filling should be heated separately. If the filling is heated in the sandwich, be sure to spread it evenly over the bread and very close to the edges. Wait a few minutes before eating the sandwich, as the filling may remain very hot even if the bread is cool to the touch.

Ring Around the Onion Ring

Cooking onion rings? Make sure you fry only a few at a time to prevent them from sticking together and to ensure even cooking.

Fantastic Fries

For the best french fries, soak cut potatoes in ice-cold water in the refrigerator for an hour; this will harden them so that they absorb less fat. Dry them thoroughly, then fry them twice. First cook for 6–7 minutes, drain well, and sprinkle them lightly with flour (this step makes them extra crispy and crunchy). Then fry them again for 1–2 minutes, until golden brown.

Who Knew? Readers' Favorite

Salt homemade potato chips by putting them in a paper bag with salt and shaking. This way, the salt is evenly distributed—and the paper absorbs the excess grease. Save calories wherever you can!

Salad Starter

Who doesn't love perfect carrot peels on top of salads? Getting this great look is easy. Just peel off slices of carrot with a vegetable peeler, then drop them into a bowl of ice water.

Quickie Salad Dressing

If you want to make a quick and unique salad dressing, just place a small amount of olive oil and wine vinegar inside an almost-empty ketchup bottle. Shake it up and drizzle over your salad. Voilà!

Salad Saver

For the crispiest salad, prepare it in a metal bowl and then place it in the freezer for one minute before serving.

Stop Soggy Salad!

Avoid wet, limp salads by placing an inverted saucer in the bottom of the salad bowl before you throw in all your veggies. The excess water that is left after washing the vegetables and greens will drain under the saucer and leave the greens high and dry.

Hard-Boiled How-To

Who doesn't love a hard-boiled egg? Great for snacks or a light lunch, these tasty treats are easy to prepare—especially with our hard-boiled-egg tips and tricks.

✦ You can prevent boiled eggs from cracking by using lemon. Just cut a lemon in half, then rub the cut side on the shells before cooking them. You can also add a pinch of salt to the water before to prevent cracks.

✦ If an egg does crack during boiling, remove it from the water and, while it is still wet, pour a generous amount of salt over the crack. Let the egg stand for 20 seconds, then put it back into the boiling water.

✦ Boiled eggs should be cooled at room temperature before refrigerating.

✦ To easily remove the shell from a hard-boiled egg in one piece, exert gentle pressure while rolling it around on the counter, then insert a teaspoon between the shell and the egg white and rotate it.

✦ Always cool a hard-boiled egg before you try to slice it; it will slice more easily and won't fall apart. Your best implement if you don't have an egg-slicer? Unwaxed dental floss makes slicing hard-cooked eggs easy.

✦ Using your hard-boiled eggs for egg salad? The fastest way to chop eggs is to peel them, place them in a bowl, and run a pizza cutter through them several times.

CHAPTER 3

Dinner

For the Best Roasted Chicken and Turkey

Who doesn't love chicken and turkey? Poultry is not only a popular choice for dinner, it's also inexpensive! Make cooking easier with these tips.

✦ Chicken and turkey must be thoroughly cleaned inside and out before cooking, in order to remove any residue that may be left from the slaughtering process. If you detect a slight "off" odor when you open the package, rinse the bird under cool water, then submerge it in a solution of water plus 1 tablespoon lemon juice or vinegar and 1 teaspoon salt per cup of water. Refrigerate 1–4 hours before cooking.

✦ Try basting your bird with a small amount of white zinfandel or vermouth—it will help crisp the skin, and the sugar in the alcohol will impart a brown color and glaze to the outside of the meat. Or brush the skin with reduced-sodium soy sauce during the last 30 minutes of cooking to produce a beautiful burnished color.

✦ A chicken or turkey cooked at a constant 375°F will be juicier than one cooked a higher temperature because more fat and moisture will be retained.

✦ Have a V-rack? Try cooking your next bird breast-side down on the V-rack for the first hour. The juices will flow to the breast and make the meat moist and tender. Then remove the V-rack. After trying this method, you will never buy another commercially prepared self-basting bird!

✦ If your roasted chicken or turkey tends to be too dry, try stuffing a whole apple inside the bird before roasting. (Just toss the apple afterward.) You can also line the bottom of the pan with lemon and onion slices. They'll give the bird a lovely flavor and ensure it stays moist.

✦ For the most tender bird you've ever eaten, try submerging the chicken or turkey in buttermilk and refrigerating for two to three hours before cooking.

✦ Once poultry has finished cooking, it should be allowed to rest for about 20 minutes before carving. As with other roasts, this standing time allows the proteins in the meat to reabsorb the juices, so they stay in the meat rather than spilling onto the cutting board.

Rack It Up

A V-rack is one of the best ways to roast a chicken or turkey, but if you don't have one, here's a free and easy substitution. Remove the grates from your gas stove burners and wrap them in foil. Poke a few holes to let juices through, then rest them against the sides of the roasting pan. Voilà: impromptu V-rack!

Dark Versus Light

Chicken breasts cooked with the ribs intact stay moister than the boneless variety. But if you're cooking chicken parts separately, remember that dark meat takes longer to cook than white meat does because of its higher fat content. Start the dark meat a few minutes before the white, so that the white meat doesn't dry out.

Skinning a Bird?

The easiest way to skin poultry is to partially freeze it first. The skin will come right off the bird with almost no effort.

Stock-Making Secrets

One mistake people frequently make when preparing stock is to place soup bones in the water after it has come to a boil. This tends to seal the bones and prevent all the flavor and nutrients from being released into the stock! The bones should be added to the cold water when the pot is first placed on the stove to allow the maximum release of flavors, nutrients, and especially the gelatinous thickening agents that add body to the stock.

Who Knew? Readers' Favorite

Make your own bouillon cubes by freezing leftover chicken broth in ice-cube trays. Once frozen, the cubes can be kept in resealable plastic bags until needed. They are easily defrosted in the microwave—or just toss them directly into a soup or sauce, and they'll melt quickly.

The Best Breaded Breasts

Always refrigerate chicken breasts after flouring, but before cooking. The coating will adhere better that way. Also, for a delicate coating, try adding a teaspoon of baking powder to your batter and club soda instead of water.

Common-Sense Breading

When breading chicken cutlets, make sure you don't bread your fingers, too! Always use one hand for wet ingredients and the other for the breadcrumbs.

For Super-Tender Pork

When roasting a pork loin, cook it with the fat-side down for the first 20 minutes, so that the fat begins to liquefy. Then turn the roast over for the balance of the cooking time, and the fat will baste the meat.

Ham Purchasing Secrets

If you're going to buy a canned ham, purchase the largest one you can afford. Most smaller canned hams are made from bits and pieces glued together with gelatin. Cured hams are injected with a solution of brine salts, sugar, and nitrites. The weight of the ham will increase with the injection, and if the total weight goes up by 8 percent, the label will usually say "ham with natural juices." If the weight of the ham increases by more than 10 percent, the label must read "water added."

Perfectly Sliced Ham

If ham is on the menu, ask your butcher to slice it when you buy it. When it's time to cook, just secure the ham slices together with unwaxed dental floss, and bake as usual. When it's done, you won't have to slice it, and the slices will look perfect. Slicing it ahead of time will also allow the glaze to penetrate the meat a little more deeply.

For Less Salty Ham

To make your ham less salty, pour a can of ginger ale over it, then rub the meaty side with salt at least an hour before baking it. This will cause the salt water in the meat to come to the surface, which will reduce the saltiness of the ham. Discard the mixture, but tdon't rinse the ham before cooking.

Ham Bone Help

To easily remove a ham bone, slit the uncooked ham lengthwise down to the bone before placing it in the pan—but leave the bone in place. While the ham is baking, the meat will pull away and the bone will come out easily after the ham is cooked. Leaving the bone in will also lead to moister meat.

"Shanks" for the Tip

When purchasing a lamb shank, be sure it weighs at least 3 pounds. If the shank is any smaller, the percentage of bone will be too high in relation to the amount of meat.

When you are preparing meatloaf, try rubbing the top and sides with a small amount of water instead of tomato sauce. This will stop the meatloaf from cracking and drying out as it cooks—and who wants a dry meatloaf? If you like a tomato flavor, add tomato sauce 15 minutes before the meat is fully cooked.

Hamburger Helpers

If you are preparing hamburger (or meatloaf) with very low-fat meat, mix in one well-beaten egg white for every pound of meat. This egg white will give the meatload a richer flavor without adding a lot of fat. Add a package of instant onion-soup mix to a pound of meat for tons of flavor, and mix in some cottage cheese or instant potatoes to keep it moist and make less meat feed more people!

Easy-Greasy

If you wet your hands with cold water before shaping sausage or hamburger patties, the grease won't stick to your fingers.

No More Meat Funk

When you refrigerate cooked beef, its fat oxidizes quickly, which will often give day-old burgers an "off" taste. If you know you'll be eating tonight's meal tomorrow as well, discourage fat oxidization by not cooking the beef in iron or aluminum pans, and by not salting the meat until you are ready to eat it.

Beef Up the Dark

The best-tasting beef should be a dark red color with slightly yellowish fat. If the fat is too white or the meat is bright red, the beef hasn't been hanging long enough and will be tough and not as tasty. It's better if there's some fat marbled throughout, as this makes it tender.

Meatballs for Health

When eating pasta, try to balance the meal with some protein to allow for balanced blood-sugar levels. Maybe that's why Grandma always made spaghetti with meatballs!

Who Knew? Readers' Favorite

Want the fastest way to make meatballs? Well, here it is! Shape the meat mixture into a log and then cut off slices, which then roll easily into balls.

Moister Meatballs

If you insert a small piece of cracked ice into the center of your meatballs before browning them, they will be moister. But be careful—you'll need to experiment to make sure the centers don't remain raw. Cut open a meatball and check the doneness to determine the proper browning time.

When Should You Season A Steak?

The jury's still out on which stage in the cooking process you should season a steak. One authority says to salt before cooking, another equally respected one says to salt after cooking. If you salt before, you get the benefit of a nice salty flavor through-and-through, but the salt tends to draw liquid from the meat, so make sure you're replenishing its juices. Whether you decide to salt before or after, you should never use ground pepper on any meat that is to be cooked in a pan with dry heat. Pepper tends to become bitter when scorched in a dry pan.

Press for Doneness

When cooking steak, it's good to know that the internal temperature of a rare steak is 135°F, medium-rare is 145°F, medium is 160°F, and well done is 170°F. However, an experienced chef rarely whips out a meat thermometer. Meat has a certain resiliency at different temperatures, and a chef can just press the steak with a finger to tell whether the meat is rare, medium-rare, medium, medium-well, or well done. As meat cooks it loses water, and the more it cooks, the firmer it becomes. Try pressing on your steaks to get a sense for how they feel at different stages of doneness, and you'll never need to cut them open to find out again.

Against the Grain

Here's a simple tip to make your meat more tender. When it's ready to slice, make sure to cut it against the grain (look for slight lines on the surface).

A Great Use for Stale Bread

If you're broiling steaks or chops, save a few slices of stale bread and set them in the bottom of the broiler pan to absorb fat drippings. This will eliminate smoking fat, and it should also reduce any danger of a grease fire.

Who Knew? Readers' Favorite

To tenderize tough meat without tenderizer, use baking soda. Just rub baking soda all over the meat, refrigerate for a few hours, and rinse well before cooking. For extra tenderizing, cover the meat with slices of kiwi.

Let the Air Flow for Roasts

Always use a shallow pot for cooking roasts. This will allow air to circulate more efficiently. Elevating the meat by cooking it atop celery ribs, carrot sticks, and thick onion slices also helps get the air underneath the meat (and gives it a great flavor!).

Timing Roasts

Don't have a roasting chart nearby? Then follow this rule of thumb: Beef roasts will take about 20 minutes for the first pound and about 15 minutes for every pound thereafter. The USDA recommends cooking beef to an internal temperature of at least 145°F.

To Cover or Not to Cover: That Is the Question

The two methods normally used for cooking a roast are dry heat (without liquid) or moist heat (with liquid). When the meat is covered, steam is trapped in the pan. Many cooks use this method to prevent roasts from drying out. Dry heat (with the lid off) will brown the outside of the roast, and, if you wish, you can baste it every 15 minutes to provide the desired moisture. If you go the moist heat route, lower the temperature by 25°F, and make sure to turn the roast or cook it on a rack so its underside won't get mushy.

Let the Roast Rest

Let a roast stand at room temperature for about 15 minutes before you carve it. This gives the juices time to be reabsorbed and distributed evenly. When you cook a roast, the juices tend to be forced to the center as those near the surface are evaporated by the heat. Resting the roast also allows the meat to firm up a bit, making it easier to carve into thinner slices.Meat gets tougher as it cools on your plate, because the collagen, which has turned to a tender gelatin, thickens. The best way to eliminate this problem is to be sure you serve steak on a warmed or metal plate. After carving a roast, keep it in a warmer or put it back in the oven and leave the door ajar.

Perfect Leftovers

When storing a cooked roast in the fridge, place it back into its own juices whenever possible. When reheating sliced meat, place it in a casserole dish with lettuce leaves between each of the slices. The lettuce provides just the right amount of moisture to keep the slices from drying out.

Break It Down

To tenderize a tough steak, salt it generously for an hour before cooking to break up tough proteins. Then just wipe off the salt before cooking.

Sugar and Salt for Meat

Before sautéing meats, sprinkle a tiny amount of sugar on the surface. The sugar will react with the juices and then caramelize, causing a deeper browning as well as an improved flavor.

Who Knew? Readers' Favorite

Wine corks (the natural kind, not plastic) contain a chemical that, when heated, will help tenderize beef stew. Just throw in three or four corks while cooking your stew, and don't tell anyone your secret!

You Can't Spell "Tender" without "T"

The tannic acid in strong black tea can tenderize meat in a stew, as well as reduce the cooking time. Just add ½ cup strong tea to the stew when you add the other liquid. It will also give your stew a great brown color.

Let Stews Sit

The perfect "leftover" meal, stews are usually best prepared a day in advance to allow the flavors to blend—or, as the romantic French say, marry.

Stew's Secret Ingredient

Cooking a lamb or beef stew? Try this secret ingredient: Add a few tablespoons of black coffee and your stew will have a nice dark color and a rich taste. This tip also works well for gravies.

Quick Thickeners

An easy method of thickening stews, soups, or creamed vegetables is to add a small amount of quick-cooking oats, a grated potato, or some instant mashed potatoes. Never add flour directly, as it will clump. However, you can mix flour with melted butter and add that mixture to your dish.

For Tender, Tasty Chili

Marinate the meat for your chili in beer. It's a great tenderizer for tough, inexpensive cuts of beef, and it will add great flavor. All you need to do is soak the meat for an hour before cooking, or marinate it overnight in the refrigerator.

Seasoning Removal Remedies

Here's a great tip when cooking with whole garlic cloves that you plan to remove before the dish is served: Stick a toothpick firmly in the garlic so it will be easy to take out. Put herbs that fall apart during cooking in a tea infuser to make them easy to remove.

The Goods on Gravy

If you're like most people, you probably use flour or cornstarch to thicken gravy. Because flour thickens somewhat slowly, make sure you don't use too much! Gravy thickens as it cools, so if you use too much flour, the gravy can become unappealingly congealed by the time you're ready for seconds. It can also taste "floury" rather than having the flavor of the meat juices it's made with. To dispense with the flour entirely, deglaze your roasting pan with water, then add a small amount of butter before reducing the mixture over high heat while stirring frequently until it is the right consistency.

It's in the (Fish) Eyes

If you're buying whole fish, check out the eyes, which should be clear, and the gills, which should be transparent and bright red in color. Don't be afraid to ask the fishmonger to show you the fish close up—they might give you a fresher fish if they think you know what you're looking for!

Tipping the Scales

If you're gutsy enough to scale your own fish, rub white vinegar on the scales, let the fish sit for about 10 minutes, and they'll rub right off. Put the fish in a large plastic bag first (hold it by the tail) to keep the scales from flying all over your kitchen.

Get Rid of Fishy Smells

Before handling fish, rub your hands with lemon juice, and you won't smell of fish for the rest of the day! After frying fish, put a little white vinegar into the pan to help get rid of the odor on the surface.

Testing Fish for Doneness

To test fish for doneness, insert a thin-bladed knife into the thickest part of flesh. If it's done, it will be just barely translucent in the center. Even though it might not look quite ready, the fish will continue to cook after you remove it from the heat.

Who Knew? Readers' Favorite

If you're grilling or broiling thick fish steaks, marinate them for 15 minutes in lemon or lime juice before cooking. The acid from the juice "cooks" the flesh a bit, cutting down on the time it needs to stay on the heat—so your fish is less likely to dry out.

Cornflake Your Fish

For added crunch with fewer calories, use cornflakes instead of breadcrumbs to coat fish fillets. Not only do cornflakes contain fewer calories than breadcrumbs, they are less absorbent and give a lighter covering, so the fish will absorb less oil.

Dry Fish Fries Better

When frying fish, be sure the surface of the fish is dry before putting it in the oil. Moisture can cool the oil down and make the fish cook unevenly.

Quick and Easy Fish

Our favorite way to prepare fish is also super quick and tasty. Wrap your fillets individually in foil, adding a bit of chopped onion, salt and pepper, a sprig of dill, and a drizzle of olive oil. Bake for 30 minutes in a 350°F oven, then unwrap for a tender, flavorful dinner.

Frozen Fish Fix

Pining for fresh fish but stuck with frozen? Try this: Cover the frozen fish in milk until it thaws, then cook. It will taste fresher, and your family will never know it was frozen.

Serving Fish

Fish tends to cool very quickly, so it's best served on warm plates or a warmed platter. Garnish your fish with a wedge of lemon or other citrus.

To steam fish fillets in the microwave, place them in a shallow microwavable dish (a glass pie plate is ideal) with the thinner parts overlapping at the center of the dish. Sprinkle with lemon juice or herbs if you like, season with salt and pepper, then cover the dish with plastic wrap (making sure it doesn't touch the fish) and cook for 3 minutes per pound. If your microwave doesn't have a turntable, rotate the dish about halfway through the cooking time.

All About Anchovies

You can reduce the saltiness of anchovies by soaking them in ice water for about 15 minutes. Because of their high salt content, anchovies will keep about two months under refrigeration after the jar is opened, and up to a year without refrigeration in a sealed can. Once opened, they should be kept covered with olive oil in the fridge.

The Skinny on Shrimp

Shrimp are low in fat, delicious, and one of the most inexpensive kinds of shellfish you can buy. For the most tender shrimp, cool them down before cooking by either place them in the freezer for 10–15 minutes, or setting them in a bowl of ice water for five minutes. If you're boiling them, drop them into boiling broth or court bouillon for one minute, and then turn off the heat and let stand for 10 minutes. Sautéed shrimp are done when they are firm and pink, in just 3–5 minutes. Grilled shrimp cook in about seven minutes. No matter how you're cooking them, shrimp cook fast! So make sure to keep a close eye on them. As soon as they turn pink, they're done. (If they are already pink when you purchase them, they've been cooked, and all you have to do is heat them up.) To make sure you don't overheat shrimp, plunge them in cold water once they've turned pink to immediately stop the cooking process.

Full and Frozen

Frozen shrimp can make for a quick and easy meal, but try to avoid shrimp that have been peeled and deveined before freezing, which usually causes a loss of texture and flavor.

For Lobster You'll Love

It might sound crazy, but the taste, texture, and color of microwaved lobster is far superior to boiled or steamed, and microwaving produces an evenly cooked, tender lobster. Unfortunately, you can only cook one lobster at a time, so put your oven on the lowest heat and use it to keep already-cooked lobsters warm until your entire meal is done. To cook a lobster, place it in a large, microwavable plastic bag with ¼ cup water, and knot the bag loosely. A 1½ pound lobster should take five to six minutes on high, providing you have a 600–700 watt microwave. If you have a lower wattage oven, allow about eight minutes. To be sure the lobster is fully cooked, separate the tail from the body. The tail meat should be creamy white, not translucent. Even when microwaved, the lobster must still be cooked live because of the enzymatic breakdown that occurs immediately upon its death. To stop the lobster's movements, put it in the freezer for 10 minutes before cooking to dull its senses.

Eating a Lobster

If you're eating a whole lobster and bibs aren't really your thing, cover the lobster with a napkin or towel before twisting off the legs and claws. This will keep the juices from squirting out.

Crayfish Know-How

Like lobsters and crabs, crayfish (also known as crawfish or crawdads) are always cooked live. However, all the meat is found in the tail. To remove the meat easily, gently twist the tail away from the body, then unwrap the first three sections of the shell to expose the meat. Next, pinch the end of the meat in one hand while holding the tail in the other, and pull the meat out in one piece.

Who Knew? Readers' Favorite

The most effective way to get rid of sand and grit from clams is to soak them in water with a bit of cornmeal stirred in. It irritates the clams, and they expel the sand while trying to eliminate the cornmeal.

Opening Shellfish

Cooking shellfish at home can be a lot of fun (not to mention, delicious), so don't be intimidated by the task of opening the shells! First, wash the shells thoroughly. Hold the clam or oyster in your palm and slip the tip of an oyster or butter knife between the upper and lower shells. Run the knife around the edge of the shell and pry until you hear a pop at the hinge. Loosen the clam or oyster and remove any shell fragments.

Oyster Answers

Store live oysters for up to two days in the refrigerator in a single layer with the larger shell down, covered with a damp towel. Oysters are easy to overcook, so cook them carefully. If you are poaching them, take them out as soon as their edges start to curl.

Mussel Madness

Mussels are a succulent seafood treat, and they're not hard to make. Here are some tips to make delicious mussels.

✦ When purchasing, make sure they're alive by tapping their shells, which will snap closed. Any mussels that don't close are probably dead and shouldn't be eaten.

✦ Live mussels will keep in the refrigerator for two to three days if placed on a tray and covered with a damp towel. Spread them out; never pile the mussels on top of one another.

✦ Clean them with a brush under cold running water, and discard any that have a non-clear liquid coming out of them. If they have a visible "beard," brush it off just before cooking, as removing it will kill the mussel.

✦ To cook them, all you have to do is boil them in a pot. Mussels are ready when their shells open, and any mussels that aren't open should be discarded. Serve over pasta or with french fries, and enjoy!

Clam-Cooking Know-How

The shells of healthy clams should be closed when you buy them. They will gradually open as the clams cook. (If you keep the clams on ice, they will also probably relax and open their shells.) Like mussels, if a clam's shell doesn't open by itself when the clam is cooked, it should be discarded.

Prevent a Clam Calamity

Once clams are dug up, they must be cleansed of sand and debris. To accomplish this, the clams should be allowed to soak in the refrigerator in a solution of one part salt to 10 parts water for several hours or overnight. If you're pressed for time, rinse them in a bowl of fresh water, changing it frequently, until no sand remains.

The Truth About Clam Chowder

Chefs always add clams to their chowder during the last 15–20 minutes of cooking. If added too early, clams can become either tough or too soft.

Who Knew? Readers' Favorite

If you like dry, fluffy rice, try this trick as soon as the rice is done cooking: Wrap the lid with a cotton dishtowel and set it on the pot for about 15 minutes. The cloth will absorb the steam.

Secrets for Perfect Mashed Potatoes

No matter how long we spend cooking a delicious cut of meat, we find that the mashed potatoes are always more popular at our dinner table. Here are some of favorite tips for perfect mashed potatoes.

- ✦ Never pour cold milk into cooked potatoes. It will change the taste of the starch, giving it an unpleasant flavor, not unlike cardboard. The milk should be warmed in a pan (preferably with a small amount of garlic or chives for flavor) before being added.

- ✦ Buttermilk will give the potatoes a great flavor.

- ✦ If you're watching your weight, save some of the cooking water from the potatoes and use that instead of butter or cream.

- ✦ A pinch or two of baking powder will give mashed potatoes extra fluff. Never put baking soda in potatoes; it will turn them black.

- ✦ Don't overmix or overcook potatoes. The cell walls will rupture, releasing an excess of starch and resulting in gluey potatoes. Potatoes should be mashed with a vertical motion, not stirred in a circular motion, to minimize the damage that occurs by crushing the cells on the wall of the bowl.

✦ Try adding powdered milk or instant potato flakes for extra-fluffy mashed potatoes.

✦ Squeeze some fresh lemon juice into your mashed potatoes instead of butter or oil. Season with freshly ground black pepper for a no-added-fat mash that is flavorful and goes fantastically well with roast chicken.

Pasta Perfection

Cook pasta only until it is slightly chewy (what the Italians call al dente, or "to the tooth"). Always use plenty of water, and keep the water at a rapid boil—the pasta needs to move around as it cooks, to keep it from sticking together. Some cooks like to salt the water, but we find it tends to toughen pasta. Use a pinch of sugar instead, and salt just before serving. After it's cooked, don't rinse it. The sauce will cling better to the residual starch, and the noodles will retain more nutrients.

Stuffing Secrets

✦ Never stuff a turkey or other fowl and leave it overnight, even in the refrigerator. Cooking the bird may not kill all the bacteria, and hundreds of cases of food poisoning occur every year because birds are stuffed and then left for too long before roasting.

✦ If you plan to cook your stuffing in the turkey, consider this tip: Pack it into a piece of cheesecloth before placing it in the bird. When you're ready to remove the stuffing, simply pull the cheesecloth out, and none of the stuffing will be stuck inside the turkey. You can also seal the opening of the bird with a slice of raw potato.

✦ If the stuffing inside the bird is never enough (or if your family picks at the turkey and trimmings before the meal is served), try this. Fill some buttered muffin pans with additional stuffing and bake in a very hot oven. You'll have a stuffing treat that's crunchy on the outside and moist on the inside. Yum!

Lentils Done Easily

Lentils are delicious—and great for you! When cooking them, make sure to add a few teaspoons of oil. It will prevent the pot from spilling over, and actually helps in the cooking process.

A Bean Bonanza

Beans are as delicious as they are nutritious. Here are a few tips for preparing them.

✦ To tell whether a bean is fully cooked, squeeze it. There should be no hard core at the center. Be aware that cooking the beans with an acidic ingredient, such as tomatoes, will slow down the cooking time.

✦ If you're making beans as a side dish, add a small amount of brown sugar or molasses at the end of cooking for a delicious flavor.

✦ You can make dry beans less gassy by soaking them overnight with fennel seeds. Use a teaspoon of fennel per pound of beans.

Vegetarian Protein Powerhouses

It's important to make sure your family gets the appropriate amount of protein each day. However, the protein doesn't need to come in complex forms like meat, fish, and poultry, which are the biggest contributors to a costly grocery bill. Try substituting combinations of simple proteins like beans, tofu, mushrooms, and even nuts in your meals at least once a week to save money and boost nutrition.

Who Knew? Readers' Favorite

You don't have to avoid baked beans because you fear they'll make you gassy. Instead, just add a dash or two of baking soda to the beans when they're cooking, and their gas-producing properties will be dramatically reduced.

Cooking Corn

Never add salt to the water when boiling corn; table salt contains traces of calcium, which will toughen the kernels. Instead, add a little milk, which will bring out the sweetness of the corn.

Easy Eggplant

Fried or roasted eggplant is delicious, but if you try preparing it as-is it will normally come out quite bitter. Luckily, it's easy to remove this bitter taste. Before cooking eggplant, cut it into thick slices. Salt the slices, and let them drain on a wire rack or in a colander for 30 minutes. Then rinse them well and pat dry. This procedure will also reduce the amount of oil they absorb during frying.

Mushroom Maker

Mushrooms can be kept white and firm during sautéing if you add ¼ teaspoon lemon juice for every 2 tablespoons butter or olive oil.

Getting Rid of Celery Strings

For the most part, celery is easy to cook—the pectin in its cells breaks down easily in water. However, celery strings, which are made of cellulose, are virtually indestructible and won't break down under normal cooking conditions. Even the body has a difficult time breaking the strings down, and many people can't digest them at all. Remove the strings before preparing celery with this simple trick: Once you remove a stalk from the bunch, place it curved-side up on the counter or a cutting board, then grab hold of the very bottom (white part) of the stalk and quickly bend it up. It will crack off the bottom of the celery, but the strings will still be attached.

Better Brussels Sprouts

Brussels sprouts are an excellent source of vitamins A and C, and although they get a bad rap, our kids adore them. Store them in the fridge to prevent their leaves from turning yellow. Cut an X on the stalk end of each sprout to ensure even and quick cooking.

Get Choppin'!

Trust us, no one hates the tedium of chopping vegetables more than we do. However, it's absolutely essential when you're trying to save money on groceries. No more baby carrots and pre-minced garlic! Invest in a good knife, and the job will go much more quickly. If you've got teenagers, teach them how to safely cut up fruits and veggies and put them to work. If you can manage to chop up all the vegetables you need for a whole week and put them in containers in the fridge, cooking dinner every night will be unbelievably more manageable.

Perfect Peas

Here's a quick tip for one of our favorite vegetables: When cooking shelled fresh peas, add a few washed pods to the water. They will improve the flavor and give the peas a richer green color.

Who Knew? Readers' Favorite

Baking stuffed apples, tomatoes, or bell peppers in a well-greased muffin tin will help them to hold their shape—and make sure they don't tip over when you take them out of the oven.

Sprightly Spinach

Always cook spinach in an uncovered pot. The steam that builds up when a pot is covered causes the plant's volatile acids to condense on the lid and fall back into the water. Keeping the lid off will make sure your spinach keeps its lovely green color.

Cauliflower Cooking

Cauliflower cooks in 10–15 minutes, and overcooking will cause it to turn dark and tough, so make sure to keep an eye on the pot. Add a small amount of lemon juice to the cooking water to keep it white, and to reduce the odor replace the hot water when it's halfway done. Never cook cauliflower in an aluminum or iron pot, because contact with these metals will turn the vegetable yellow, brown, or even blue-green!

Beet Red

To make sure beets keep their red color through the entire cooking process, cook them whole with at least two inches of stem still attached, and add a few tablespoons of white vinegar to the water.

Rescuing Lost Veggies

Cooking Thanksgiving dinner and your vegetables turned to mush? Simply add some herbs along with tomato sauce or cream. Then top with cheese and/or bread crumbs and stick in the oven for 30 minutes. Your family is sure to be impressed with your new recipe for "vegetables gratin"!

Simple Garlic Trick

Chopping your own garlic instead of buying it pre-minced can be a real pain but a huge money saver. Use this simple trick to make it a little easier on yourself: microwave the garlic for about eight seconds to make it easy to peel. Once the cloves are peeled, drizzle a tiny amount of oil over them to make them less sticky when you're trying to chop them.

Fixing a Hot Mess

Ow! If you or your child bites into a piece of pizza that's too hot to eat, reach for a glass of milk. Milk will soothe the roof of your mouth better than cold water because the protein in milk will create a protective film over any burns. Now let the pizza cool a bit before you take another bite!

The Knife Test

You've had a hectic day, but luckily you had a frozen casserole in the freezer! Unfortunately, you were in such a rush you have no idea how long ago you popped it in the oven. To tell if your casserole is heated through, insert a butter knife into the center, lift it out, then slowly and carefully press it to your wrist. If the knife is hot, you'll know the casserole is too.

CHAPTER 4

Desserts

Make a Great Cake

For the best-tasting cakes ever, always bring the eggs, milk, and butter to room temperature before you make your batter.

For the Sake of the Cake

If a cake recipe calls for flouring the baking pan, use some of the dry cake mix instead. The cake will absorb the mix, and you won't have a floury mess on the outside when the cake is done.

Who Knew? Readers' Favorite

To keep the frosting from sticking to your knife as you cut the cake, dip your knife into a glass of cold water between each cut.

Egg Substitution

When baking a cake, try substituting two egg yolks for one whole egg. The cake will be very rich and dense, because the yolks won't hold as much air as the whites. This isn't exactly a healthy tip, but it sure tastes good!

Keeping Your Cake Light

For a light, moist cake, enhance your cake flour by adding 2 tablespoons cornstarch to every cup of flour, then sifting them together before you add to the mix. You may be surprised by the results!

Popping Your Cake's Bubbles

Make sure you get rid of any bubbles in your cake batter before baking it. This is easily accomplished by holding the pan an inch or two above the counter and tapping it two or three times to release any air pockets. Just be careful—the batter might spatter.

We Heart Cakes

A heart-shaped cake is easier to make than you might think. Simply divide your cake batter between one round pan and one square one. When the cakes are cool, cut the round cake in half. Turn the square cake so it looks like a diamond and set the half-rounds on the two top sides. Voilà!

Piece of Cake!

If you're about to show off your cake prowess by cutting up baked cakes and re-assembling them in an impressive configuration, try freezing the cake first. Fresh cakes, especially those made from a box mix, often crumble easily, but freezing will make your knife glide right through. Freezing detracts little from the taste of your cake, as long as you don't frost it first.

Cake Magic

If you find icing too sweet or too rich, try this cake topping: Set a paper lace doily on the cake, and then dust lightly with confectioners' sugar. Carefully lift the doily off the cake, and admire the beautiful design. Try colored confectioners' sugar or a mixture of confectioners' sugar and cocoa powder.

Here's a new twist on transporting frosted cakes. Don't just insert toothpicks and cover in plastic, because the sharp ends can puncture the plastic and result in a gooey mess. Instead, attach miniature marshmallows to the toothpicks before covering. Strands of spaghetti can also be used instead of toothpicks.

Keep a Cake from Sticking

Does your cake stick to the plate? Sprinkle a thin layer of sugar on a plate before you put a cake on it. Not only does it prevent the cake from sticking, it also makes the bottom delightfully crunchy.

Stale Cake Cure

If you need to store a cake more than a day or two, put half an apple in the container. The apple will provide just enough moisture to keep the cake from drying out too soon.

Frost in Translation

Want to freeze a cake, but don't want the frosting to stick to the plastic wrap? Here's a handy tip for doing just that. First, put it in the freezer without any wrapping. Once the frosting is frozen, cover the cake with plastic wrap. The cold frosting won't stick to the wrap.

Awesome Icing Hints

Even if you've just made the most delicious cake ever, it still won't be a hit unless your finishing touch—the icing—holds its own. Here are a few of our favorite tips for perfect icing.

✦ If you sprinkle a very thin layer of cornstarch on top of a cake before you ice it, the icing won't run down the sides.

✦ To keep icing from hardening, just add a very small amount of white vinegar after it is whipped. You can also add a pinch of baking soda to the confectioners' sugar. This will help the icing retain some moisture and it will not dry out as fast.

✦ If you're making your own chocolate icing, add a teaspoon of unsalted butter to the chocolate while it is melting to improve the consistency.

✦ Here's a great bakers' trick to make it easier to decorate the top of a cake: With a toothpick, trace the pattern, picture, or lettering before you pipe the icing on. This will give you a guide, so you'll make fewer mistakes.

✦ If you're having a problem keeping a layer cake together when you're icing it, stick a few bamboo skewers into the cake through both layers; remove them as you're frosting the top.

✦ To keep the cake from sliding around on the plate as you're icing it, place a dab of frosting in the middle of the plate before you place the cake on top. The icing will keep the cake in place, and by the time you've served all the slices, no one will notice the little bit of extra frosting on the bottom.

Who Knew? Readers' Favorite

To give the icing that silky look that professionally made cakes always seem to have, ice it as usual and then blow air from a hairdryer over the top of it for a minute. It will melt the icing slightly, giving it the shiny appearance you're looking for.

Keep Leftover Cake Moist

If you have leftover cake, you have more self-control than we do! To keep the inside of the cake (where you made the last slice) moist, place a piece of white bread next to the exposed surface. The bread can be affixed with a toothpick or a short piece of spaghetti.

Three Cures for Domed Cakes

Unfortunately, part of baking is always trial and error. If your cakes "dome" when baked, the problem may be caused by one of these common errors: the oven temperature was too high, your pan was too small, or the balance of liquid, egg, flour, and fat was off. Time for a new trial!

The Big Fat Truth

The texture of a cake depends on the type of sweetener and fat used. These ingredients affect how tender the cake will be, so be sure you use the right ones. Never substitute granulated sugar for confectioners' sugar and vice versa. Cakes made with oil are very tender and moist—oil doesn't hold air as well as butter or shortening, so eggs and other thick ingredients must trap the air.

Angel Food Aid

Never bake an angel food cake on the top or middle rack of the oven. It will retain moisture better if baked in the lower third of the oven, and always at the temperature specified in the recipe.

Angel Food Fact

An angel food cake can be left in the pan and covered tightly with foil for up to 24 hours or until you are ready to frost it.

Say Cheesecake!

When preparing a cheesecake, go exactly by the recipe and don't make any substitutions. You'll have a much better chance at success. Here are some other pointers for perfect cheesecake.

- ✦ Be sure that the cream cheese is at room temperature before using it.

- ✦ When you bake a cheesecake at a low temperature, there's less chance of it shrinking from the sides of the pan.

- ✦ Don't open the oven for the first 30 minutes when baking cheesecake! The cheesecake may develop cracks or partially collapse.

- ✦ Cheesecakes will develop cracks when they are overcooked. They're done when the center of the cake is still wobbly and shaky—which may look underdone to you.

- ✦ Flourless cheesecakes need to be baked in a pan of water (called a bain-marie, or water bath) to keep the eggs from coagulating.

- ✦ Cheesecake cracks can be repaired with whipped cream cheese or sweetened sour cream, but you'll be able to see the repair. It's better to top the cake with berries if it has too many cracks.

Who Knew? Readers' Favorite

It's always disappointing when you remember you have one last bit of ice cream in the freezer, only to open it and find it's covered in ice crystals. To keep this from happening, store your ice cream container in a sealed plastic bag in the freezer. It will stop ice crystals from forming. You can also cover the top of your ice cream with aluminum foil before you put the lid on top.

Perfect for a Summer Day

You'll never buy a box of popsicles again after you learn this easy recipe for the homemade variety. Simply pour juice into waxy paper cups, then add a small plastic spoon or tongue depressor to the middle once they are half-frozen. When they're completely solid, peel away the cup for an icy treat.

Cool Sundae Station

Repurpose a plastic ice cube tray by making it into a sundae station to talk about. Use the various compartments for nuts, crushed cookies, candy, and other toppings, then serve with ice cream and let the kids make their own sundaes. (Don't be surprised if they dump everything on top.)

Banana Fun

A great and healthy summer treat for kids is to cut a banana in half (horizontally, not vertically), put a popsicle stick in the flat end, dip it in some melted chocolate or sundae topping, and freeze it for a few hours on waxed paper. Your kids will love you for these banana treats! (At least for a little while.)

Who Knew? Readers' Favorite

Keep your ice cream cones leak-free with this simple tip: Place a miniature marshmallow or chocolate kiss in the bottom of the cone before adding the ice cream. Either of them can help prevent the cone from leaking—and they're a delicious treat at the end!

Shimmering Pies

Do you want your pies to glisten like those in the bakery? It's easy with this trick: Just beat an egg white and brush it over the crust before baking. This works especially well for a pie that has a top crust, like apple pie.

When It's Good to Be Flaky

Even if your pie's filling is near perfect, you won't win any accolades for your creation unless its crust is up to par. Here are a few tips for making perfectly flaky piecrusts.

✦ Be sure the liquid used in your piecrust dough is ice cold. In fact, anything hot going into a piecrust will affect it.

✦ Add a teaspoon of vinegar to the water for an even flakier crust, or substitute sour cream or whipping cream for the entirety of the water.

✦ Low-gluten flour such as pastry flour is your best bet. Cake flour is too soft and won't give the crust the body it needs, and bread flour has too high a gluten content and would make a tough crust. As a substitute for pastry flour, combine two parts all-purpose flour and one part cake flour or instant flour.

✦ Replace the shortening or butter with lard. Lard has larger fat crystals and three times the polyunsaturates as butter, making the crust flakier.

Pie Dough Know-How

Never stretch pie dough when you are placing it in the pan. Stretched dough usually shrinks from the sides.

Pie Serving Secret

Pies with graham cracker crusts can be difficult to remove from the pan. However, if you dip the bottom of the pan in warm water for 10 seconds, the pie will come right out without any damage.

Pumpkin Pie Loves Marshmallows

For a unique pumpkin pie, put small marshmallows on the bottom of the pie, just above the crust. As the pie bakes, the air in the marshmallows expands and the marshmallows rise to the top.

Who Knew? Readers' Favorite

Making graham cracker crust can turn into quite a mess—particularly when pressing the crumbs into the pie plate with greasy, buttered hands. Stop the crumbs from sticking by putting your hands into a plastic bag before the pressing begins!

Get Rid of Soggy Bottoms

It's always disappointing when you slice into your carefully prepared pie only to find that the bottom is soggy. If you have a problem with fruit or fruit juices soaking the bottom of your piecrust, brush the bottom crust with egg white before adding the filling. This will seal the crust and solve the problem. If your fruit filling is simply too wet, thicken it up. The best thickener is 3–4 tablespoons of minute tapioca. Just mix it with the sugar before adding to the fruit. Other solutions for soggy pie bottoms include prebaking the piecrust, partially cooking the filling, or brushing the crust with jelly before you fill it. When using a cream filling in a pie, sprinkle the crust with granulated sugar before adding the filling to keep the crust flaky.

Cutting a Creamy Pie

Spray a small amount of vegetable oil on your knife before cutting a pie with a cream filling. This will stop the filling from sticking to the knife.

For Extra Tasty Tarts

Here's a pastry chef's trick to add flavor to a lemon tart or pie: Rub a few sugar cubes over an orange or lemon, then include the cubes in the recipe as part of the total sugar. The sugar tends to extract just enough of the natural oils from the peels of the fruits to add some flavor.

Tender Pastries

Add some sugar to your pastry recipe to help tenderize the dough. Pastry dough should look like coarse crumbs after you cut in the fat (butter, shortening, etc.).

Store your rolling pin in the freezer. It's much easier to roll out pastry dough and piecrusts with a frozen rolling pin.

Fire up Your Flambé

If you're making a flambéed dish, you have more guts than we do! Just be warned that you may have trouble igniting brandy when it's not hot enough. Some chefs warm the brandy gently before adding it to food to ensure that it will light. If it's too hot before being adding it to the dish, however, it may ignite too soon. Serving a dessert that's flambéed? Try soaking sugar cubes briefly in a lemon or orange extract that contains alcohol, then set them on the dessert and carefully ignite.

A Lower-Cal Cookie

If you're making cookies, choose the soft drop, more-cakey versions rather than the rolled variety—they generally contain more air per serving and therefore, fewer calories.

Dough To-Do

When you mix cookie dough, only stir as much as you must to fully combine the ingredients—over-stirring can cause the cookies to become tough. Unbaked cookie dough may be frozen and thawed when you're ready to bake. Wrap the dough tightly in a freezer bag, try to resist eating any, and stick in the freezer for up to one month.

Chilly Dough

Cold cookie dough will not stick to the rolling pin. Refrigerate the dough for 20 minutes for the best results.

I Want Cookies!

If you give your kids cookies as treats, you can save a lot by making a batch of cookies every week or two rather than buying them at the store. This is a great activity for the parent who doesn't do most of the cooking. Have him or her (OK, it's probably a him) spend twenty minutes making cookies with the kids on the weekend, and you'll have enough to last you until next time.

Avoid Heavy Baked Goods

To keep cookies or butter cakes from becoming too heavy, be sure the butter is at room temperature before you cream it with the sugar. Try to avoid softening butter in the microwave, as it's likely to melt.

Margarine Mayhem

When making cookies with margarine, be aware that the firmness of the dough will depend on the type of margarine used. Be sure to use stick margarine, not margarine from a tub. Note that margarine made from 100 percent corn oil will make the dough softer. When using margarine to make cookies, you may need lengthen the chilling time or place the dough in the freezer instead of the refrigerator. If you're making cutout cookies, the chilling time should be at least one hour in the refrigerator. Dough for drop and bar cookies doesn't have to be chilled.

Maintain the Moisture

Keep soft cookies, cakes, and pancakes deliciously moist by adding a teaspoon of jelly to the batter.

Who Knew? Readers' Favorite

Our favorite part of oatmeal cookies, is—naturally—the oatmeal! Boost the oatmeal's flavor by toasting it lightly before adding it to the batter. Simply sprinkle the oatmeal on a baking sheet and heat it in a 300°F oven for about 10 minutes. The oats should turn a golden-brown.

Burned Bottoms?

If you've ever burned the bottoms of your cookies when baking a number of batches, the baking sheets may be to blame. Let the baking sheets cool between batches—when you start with too hot a surface the cookies may burn. Two to three minutes cooling time is usually long enough. Another alternative is to line the baking sheets with parchment paper—simply lift the cookies, still on the parchment paper, right onto the cooling rack.

Cookie Cooling

Cookies can go from beautiful to burned in no time. To lessen the chance of this happening, take the cookies out of the oven when they are not quite done, but don't transfer them to the cooling rack right away—let them sit on the hot pan for a minute or two to finish baking. Then transfer to the rack to cool fully.

An Improvised Cooling Rack

If you're baking cookies or pies and don't have a cooling rack, simply line up a bunch of butter knives in alternating directions (first with the blade towards you, then with the blade away from you), and put the baking sheet down on top of them. You can also use old egg cartons.

Browning Cookies

If your cookies typically don't brown enough, bake them on a higher rack in the oven. Other techniques to boost browning include substituting a tablespoon or two of corn syrup for the sugar, using egg for the liquid, and using unbleached or bread flour in the recipe.

Who Knew? Readers' Favorite

Dye your cookie dough, not your hands, by dropping food coloring into a bag with the dough. Knead a bit and roll around to even out the color. You can use right away or keep in the freezer. Either way, you'll have fun, colorful cookies, and save lots of time on hand cleaning.

Cookie Dough Spoon Saver

Is your cookie dough sticking to everything? It's easy to get a spoonful of cookie dough to drop to your baking pan if you first dip the spoon in milk.

Nonstick Mixing

Making cookies? Spray the beaters with a little vegetable oil or nonstick cooking spray and you won't have to stop every few seconds to scrape the batter off the beaters and back into the bowl.

Cookie Cutter Tip

To get a sharp edge on your cookies when using cutters, dip the cutter in flour or warm oil occasionally during the cutting process.

Crisper Cookies

If crisp cookies are what you're after, be sure your cookie jar has a loose-fitting lid. This allows air to circulate and evaporates any moisture.

Storing Cookies

Rinse out coffee cans and store cookies in them. Use the original lids, or stretch plastic wrap across the top and seal with a rubber band.

Who Knew? Readers' Favorite

To keep your cookies chewy, add half an apple or a slice of white bread to the cookie jar. This will provide just enough moisture to keep the cookies from becoming hard.

Getting Your Brownies Out of a Sticky Situation

If your baked goods are stuck to the pan, wrap the bottom of the pan in a cold, wet towel for a few minutes. Once the pan is cooler, your brownies or bar cookies may come out more easily.

Whip It Good

Whipping up some cream? Heavy cream will set up faster if you add seven drops of lemon juice for each pint of cream. But you don't necessarily need heavy cream to make whipped cream. Light cream can be whipped to a firm, mousse-like consistency if you add a tablespoon unflavored gelatin dissolved in 1 tablespoon hot water for every 2 cups of cream. After whipping, refrigerate it for two hours.

How to Get the Creamiest Custard

Making perfect custard takes time and patience, but these tips should help. For a super-rich custard, add 2–3 egg yolks in addition to your usual amount of eggs. For a custard that is creamy rather than solid, stir the mixture continuously over low heat to keep the protein from setting too quickly. The milk helps separate the egg proteins from one another, which allows the custard to coagulate at a higher temperature and reduces the possibility of curdling. Never replace the milk with water, because your custard will not set. You should also never try to speed up the cooking process by increasing the heat.

Meringue Magic

Not only is homemade meringue delicious, but it will also impress your friends—especially if you use these tips for getting the best meringue and the highest peaks.

- ✦ Make sure that your egg whites are at room temperature. As you beat, add 2–3 tablespoons of superfine or granulated sugar for each egg used. Keep beating until the peaks stand up without drooping.

- ✦ For the fluffiest egg whites, add a pinch of salt before whipping, and use a copper bowl if you happen to have one.

- ✦ To keep the peaks firmer for a longer period of time, add 1/8 teaspoon of white vinegar per egg white while beating. To get more meringue per egg white, add 2 teaspoons cold water for each egg white before beating.

- ✦ How do you know if beaten egg whites are stiff enough? Just run a knife through the middle of the bowl—if they whites stay separated, they're ready.

- ✦ Remember, if it's rainy (or even damp) outside, the meringue peaks will not remain upright! It might be better to save your baking for a drier day.

✦ Occasionally, meringue will develop small droplets of water on its surface shortly after being removed from the oven. This beading is caused by overcooking, so to prevent this, bake meringue at a high temperature (between 400°–425°F) for a short time—four to five minutes.

When boiling syrup, one of the more frequent and annoying problems is that it crystallizes. The easiest way to avoid this is to put a pinch of cream of tartar in the syrup while it's cooking. This adds a small amount of acidity—just enough to prevent crystals from forming but not enough that you should taste it.

The Candyman Can

Cooking up your own candy is as delicious as it is fun. Experienced candy makers know that it's tricky to keep the sugar from crystallizing during cooking. A simple solution? Heat the sugar over low heat, without stirring, until it's completely dissolved. To eliminate the sugar crystals that inevitably cling to the sides of the pan, cover with a tight-fitting lid and continue cooking the syrup for three to four minutes. The steam that's generated will melt these pesky crystals.

Can-Do Candy

Making candy? Not only do we recommend using a larger pot than specified in the recipe to keep the hot, bubbling syrup safely away from your hands, we also recommend using your heaviest pot. Pots made out of thinner material tend to heat unevenly, which will make it harder to properly heat the syrup.

Egg Secret

When making a soufflé, it's best if you use egg whites from eggs that are at least a week old (but not yet expired). Why? Very fresh eggs contain more water, which can make your soufflé taste grainy.

The Collapsible Soufflé

Be careful when you're making a soufflé. Air bubbles are trapped when you beat the egg whites, and when a soufflé is placed in the oven, the air expands, causing the soufflé to rise. If the soufflé is punctured or shaken, however, the air will be released too early and the soufflé will collapse. It's also true that a soufflé must be served as soon as it is removed from the oven. Soufflés begin to collapse as soon as they start to cool down. So it's best to serve them right in the baking dish.

CHAPTER 5

Parties, Entertaining, and Special Occasions

Hot Cross Buns

Having a dinner party? Here's a great tip for keeping dinner rolls warm long after they've come out of the oven. When you put the rolls in the oven to bake, put a ceramic tile in, too. By the time the rolls are done, the tile will be (very!) hot. Place it in the basket and put your rolls on top. The tile will keep them warm. You can also use aluminum foil instead of the tile, but it won't retain the heat as long.

For Cheese Plate Praises

Always bring cheese to room temperature one hour before serving it. Even if the cheese becomes a little melty, the flavor will be much better.

Who Knew? Readers' Favorite

To keep meat or cheese hors d'oeuvres moist, cover them with a damp paper towel, then cover loosely with plastic wrap. Many fillings (as well as bread) dry out very quickly, but with this tip, you can make these simple appetizers first and have them on the table when guests arrive.

Creative Fruit Display

For a fun display on your buffet table, hollow out a melon, orange, or grapefruit and fill it with cut-up fruits (and maybe even some miniature marshmallows). For an even more attractive holder, you can scallop the melon edges or cut it in the shape of a basket.

Booze Clues

Having a party? Instead of buying "wine rings," which go around the base of wine glasses to mark whose drink is whose, simply keep a dry-erase marker on hand and have guests write their names (or a funny message) right on their glass.

Rubber Bubbly

Having a New Year's party? Put your child's inexplicable Silly Bandz obsession to good use! These rubber bands in fun shapes are perfect for putting around the stems of champagne glasses so your guests can tell whose bubbly is whose.

For a Sweet Sparkle

For a snazzy New Year's treat, color some granulated sugar by adding a few drops of food coloring to it. Then wet the rim of each champagne glass and press into the sugar to give it a sweet, colorful rim—perfect for guests who find champagne a little too dry.

Don't Stick a Cork in It!

Nothing kills a party like a stuck cork. Old method: Shove the cork all the way into the bottle and apologize to guests for the tiny pieces floating in their Cabernet. New method: Soak a washcloth in hot water and fold around the bottle's neck. When the glass expands, it will release its death grip on the trapped cork.

Fast Filter

The next time you attempt to open a bottle of wine only to have cork end up in the bottle, reach for a (clean) comb! Just hold the comb over the spout and pour, and it will catch any bits of cork.

Leprechaun-Worthy Lager

Even wondered how bars turn their beer green on St. Patrick's Day? It's as easy as adding 3–4 drops of green food coloring to a pint glass of beer. This trick will work best with light-colored beer.

Shaken, Not Stirred

Who needs a martini shaker? Instead of buying this expensive bar tool, simply use a stainless steel thermos with a screw-in lid. If there's no way to close the sipping hole on the top, make sure to cover it with your thumb while you shake!

A "Cool" Idea

To keep ice cubes from melting at a party, put them in a bowl, and then set that bowl in a larger one filled with dry ice.

Keep Your Punch Cold

Drinking punch that's half water is never fun, but ice cubes can melt so quickly when left out in a bowl. One of the easiest ways to keep a large punch bowl cold is to make larger ice cubes, as it will take one giant ice cube much longer to melt than many little ones. To make a long-lasting, large cube, fill a rinsed-out milk or juice carton half-full with water. Then peel off the cardboard when it's time to use.

Ice Cube Math

If you run out of ice at a party, you're in trouble! But how do you know how much to buy? Use this simple metric. If you're serving mostly cocktails, the average person at a party will go through 10–15 cubes. When you buy ice cubes in the bag, you will get about 10 cubes per pound.

Who Knew? Readers' Favorite

Champagne lost its fizz? Place a raisin in the glass and the last bits of carbon dioxide that remain will cling to the raisin, then be released again as bubbles. You can also try throwing a few raisins into the bottle before you make the final pour.

Better Than the Bathtub

If you're having a party and have run out of space to cool beverages, don't go buy a Styrofoam cooler. Instead, fill your washing machine with ice and store bottles and cans inside. The lid will keep everything cool, and once the ice melts you can simply run the rinse cycle to get rid of the all the water.

Back On the Wagon

For the spring and summer picnic seasons, use your kids' wagon or wheelbarrow as a drink cooler: Just fill it up with ice, add your cold beverages, and enjoy your days in the sun.

Party Time!

Here's a cute way of sending out unique party invitations. Write the invite on a blown-up balloon with a permanent marker, then deflate it and put it in the mail. Your guests will have to blow up the balloon to read the invitation.

Harvest Party Lights

We love this festive-for-fall decoration: Cut a slice off the side of an apple so it lays flat on a saucer or candleholder. Then cut a hole out of the top and you have an instant votive or tea light holder! Coat the hole with some lemon juice to keep the apple from turning brown.

Eliminate the Drip

Don't spend extra for dripless candles—you can make "regular" candles dripless with this simple procedure. Place the candles in a shallow pan and add enough water to cover them. Then add 2 tablespoons salt per candle, and mix or agitate until the salt dissolves (you might want to take the candles out while mixing, then put them back in). Let the candles soak in the saltwater for two to three hours, then rinse them and let them dry. Wait at least 24 hours before using them and they'll be virtually dripless. The salt water hardens the wax, which makes it burn more slowly and cleanly, reducing the chance of messy drips onto linens or furniture.

A Must for Candles

Bringing out the candles for your party? Put them in the freezer the night before, and they'll burn more slowly and drip less when you take them out.

Who Knew? Readers' Favorite

You just had a great dinner party, except now your candlesticks left wax drippings all over the place. To remove candle wax from just about anything, simply put the item in the freezer. Leave for a couple of hours and the wax will peel off easily.

Tin Can Candle

Having an outdoor party? Washed-out tin cans make great holders for votive candles around your garden. They'll give off a shimmering, silvery glow, and you won't mind if they get dirty!

Marshmallow Candleholders

To add a little color and whimsy to a birthday cake, make natural candleholders from small marshmallows, thus protecting your cake from melting wax. Keep them refrigerated for best results. The best part is that you can give them to guests to eat after the candles are burned out, as long as they don't have any wax on them.

A Thoughtful and Thrifty Gift for a Bride-to-Be

Here's a wonderful, one-of-a-kind gift for a bridal shower: Buy a blank hardcover book, add dividers, and create a family cookbook. Just ask the bride and groom's families to provide their favorite treasured recipes.

Two-for-One Bridal Gift

Turn your gift packaging into part of the gift itself. For a bridal shower, wrap your gift with a pretty bath, kitchen, or tea towel. Write a recipe on the gift tag, or use a recipe card for the tag, and tie a bow with a beautiful ribbon and a kitchen utensil, such as salad tongs, inserted inside.

Cupcakes for Kids' Parties

Having a birthday party for your child? Consider serving cupcakes instead of one large cake, which will eliminate the need for forks and paper plates—and save you money. (Just serve on napkins.)

Put a College Student to Work

If you're hosting a party that requires you to hire someone like a clown, face painter, or bartender, head to your local college first. There you'll find hundreds of young people who will do the job for a lot less than a pro. Put up at ad near the cafeteria, and stop by the career office to see if they have an online "bulletin board."

Who Knew? Readers' Favorite

Little kids usually end up eating cake with their hands anyway, so try this fun dessert treat: Place flat-bottomed ice cream cones in a high-sided baking pan and fill them two-thirds full with cake batter. Bake at 325°F for 30 minutes, and once they cool you can hold your cake and eat it, too!

So the Wind Won't Blow It All Away

If your picnic is windier than you expected, keep your tablecloth in place with the help of some nonskid shelf liners. Lay them out in strips at the corners of the table and the tablecloth will stay put!

Impromptu Trash Can

Having a party and need an extra trash bin for your guests? Just repurpose your hamper. (Your dirty clothes will be fine in a garbage bag in the closet until tomorrow.)

CHAPTER 6

The Perfect Barbecue

Get Your Grill In Shape for BBQ Season

When Memorial Day rolls around, make sure your outdoor grill is prepped for the first barbecue of the season. Clean the grates by placing them in the tub and covering them with very hot water and one cup each ammonia and dishwasher detergent. Cover with old fabric softener sheets and soak overnight. The next day, don your rubber gloves, scrub away, and watch the grease dissolve.

Who Knew? Readers' Favorite

A great way to clean your barbecue grill is with wet newspaper. After cooking, just place it on a warm grill for one hour with the lid closed. You'll be amazed how easily the grime comes off!

A Grill-Cleaning Trick

Save on expensive grill cleaners by simply using WD-40 instead. Get rid of charred food by removing the grates from the barbecue and spraying them with the oil. Let sit for five to ten minutes, then wipe off and clean with soap and water.

Onions to the Rescue!

Your BBQ chicken was a hit, but your grill is a mess. What to do? Dip half an onion in vegetable oil, put it on your grill fork, and scrub it over the hot grates. There are enzymes in onions that break down grime, and the oil will help softer the grilled-on gunk.

Just Say No to More Lighter Fluid

When the coals start to die down on your grill, don't squirt them with more lighter fluid, which not only costs money, but can also leave your food tasting bad (not to mention, burn the hair off your arm). Instead, blow a hair dryer on the base of the coals. The hairdryer acts as a pair of bellows, and your fire will be going again in no time.

Great Grilling

Spraying your grill with a bit of vegetable oil before you start grilling will make cleaning even easier, and your grill even hotter (which will put those cool "grill marks" on your meat and veggies). For the easiest clean-up, coat the grill with vegetable (or canola) oil before starting the fire, then wipe it with a wet rag shortly after you are through. Never spray the oil on the grill after the fire has started—it may cause a flare-up.

A Tasty Grill

To help reduce smoke and improve the flavor of food on your grill, use an onion! Cut a red onion in half, pierce it with a fork, and dip in water. Then use the onion half to wipe down the grill rack.

Tongs Are Terrific

Always use tongs when turning meat on the grill. When a fork pierces the meat, it releases some of its juices, making it dry out more quickly.

Keep Chicken from Stickin'

When grilling chicken, always grease the rack well. Why? Because as the bird cooks, the collagen in the skin turns into a sticky gelatin, which will in turn stick to the grate. Another way to solve the problem is to sear the chicken on the grill, and then finish it in a preheated oven for 15–20 minutes, breast-side up.

Who Knew? Readers' Favorite

If you're grilling a steak on a closed barbecue, here's a neat trick to impress your friends. Open a can of beer and place it on the hottest part of the grill. It will boil and keep the meat moist, while adding flavor, too.

Prevent a Barbecue Blunder

Remember that barbecue sauces contain sugar, and high heat can burn the sugar as well as some of the spices in the sauce. Wait to apply the sauce until about five minutes before your meat is fully cooked. Another secret is to use low heat and leave the meat on the grill for a longer period.

The Hubbub About Rubs

Applying a rub is a common method of seasoning the surface of meats and poultry. A dry rub is simply a blend of various herbs and spices that doesn't penetrate the meat. The rub provides a tasty coating, which usually forms a brown crust of concentrated flavor. (Yum!) Rub on the seasoning before you begin to grill the meat, and let it sit awhile for the coating to take hold.

Burger Buzzkill

While undercooked burgers may pose a risk of E. coli poisoning, well-done burgers may contain a potentially harmful carcinogen called heterocyclic aromatic amine (HAA). This compound is formed when meat is cooked at too high a temperature. To avoid HAA, try these tips:

✦ Choose lean cuts of beef. Sizzling fat creates smoke, which creates HAA.

✦ Place the ground beef in a microwave oven on high power for 1–3 minutes just before you cook it. HAAs form when browning occurs, but precooking meat before it goes onto the grill reduces the amount of time HAAs have to form.

✦ Reduce the amount of meat in your burgers by adding mashed black beans, cottage cheese, or cooked rice and you will have a safer—not to mention delicious—medium-well burger.

For a Juicy Steak

You may think that searing a steak at a high temperature will keep the juices in. Nonsense! Searing does cause the browning that creates a good flavor, but it doesn't seal in the juices. A steak cooked slowly and at a lower temperature is more tender and juicier than one cooked at an extremely high heat. If you want to sear a steak, only do it for a minute or two on each side, then lower the temperature and let it cook more slowly.

Speedier Grilling

When you are grilling for a crowd, and your grill isn't big enough, you can save time by utilizing your oven, too. Place a few layers of hamburgers between sheets of foil on a cookie sheet and bake them in a 350°F oven for 15 minutes. Then throw them on the grill for 5–10 minutes more, and they'll be fully cooked but still have that grilled taste. Hot dogs may be done the same way, but only bake them for 10 minutes.

Thick Is the Trick for Grilling Fish

If you plan on grilling fish, be sure to purchase steaks that are at least one-inch thick. Fish dries out very quickly on the grill, so the thicker it is the better. The skin should be left on fillets while grilling and removed after they are cooked.

Lemon Aid

Grilling fish is always a drag because the skin inevitably gets stuck to the grate—particularly when cooking salmon. Avoid this by placing a few thin slices of lemon or lime on the grill, and then the fish on top. Not only will your cleanup be easier, but the citrus flavor will also taste great with the seafood.

Who Knew? Readers' Favorite

When grilling shrimp, always thread them onto the skewers lengthwise, so they won't curl on the grill. They'll also be less likely to fall into the fire.

Perfect Grilled Corn

Doing some grilling? Impress your guests by barbecuing fresh corn to perfection this way: Before grilling, peel all but the innermost layer of husk from the corn, and trim the excess silks as well. Place on the grill and as soon as the husk darkens enough that the outline of the kernels is visible through it, remove the corn. It will be perfectly cooked and have a wonderful, smoky flavor.

Veggies on the Grill

When grilling vegetables in aluminum foil on the grill, try placing a sprig of fresh herbs within each foil wrap. Marjoram is the most popular choice, but almost any herb will do: try tarragon, Italian parsley, sage, chives, dill, chervil, oregano, and thyme. It will give your veggies a fresh, wonderful taste.

Potato Salad Trick

If you would like a richer color to your potato salad (and who doesn't?), try adding a small amount of mustard when you are mixing it.

For Divine Deviled Eggs

To keep yolks centered when boiling eggs for deviled eggs, stir the water while they are cooking. And to keep them from wobbling on the platter when they're done, cut a thin slice off two sides of the egg before you halve it lengthwise. This will give each egg half a flat base.

The Coal Truth

Though they may be more work than a gas grill, charcoal grills impart an amazing smoky flavor to meats and veggies. Here are a few tips to get the most out of your charcoal grill.

✦ To add flavor to barbecued foods, place dried herbs on the hot coals. Some of our favorites are savory, rosemary, and basil.

✦ If the coals become too hot or flare up, squirt them with water from a mister or a bulb baster.

✦ Store charcoal briquettes in airtight plastic bags— they absorb moisture very easily and won't be as easy to light if exposed to air.

Who Knew? Readers' Favorite

To keep your cooler fresh and odor free, throw in 10–15 charcoal briquettes, close the top, and leave it overnight. In the morning, clean the cooler with soapy water, and it will smell like new.

Plain Vanilla

Before you put your cooler away, wipe the inside down with a paper towel or rag that has been dampened with water and a few drops of vanilla extract. The alcohol in the vanilla works as a disinfectant and your cooler will smell great!

For the Fastest Cold Beer

The best way to chill beer or soda rapidly is to fill a cooler with layers of water, ice, and salt, then plunge the beers inside. In about 20 minutes or less, the beer will be ice cold! Even if the ice water is warmer than your freezer, it will still absorb the warmth from the bottles or cans more rapidly and efficiently than the cold air of the freezer does. Just remember that premium lagers should be served between 42°F and 48°F and ales between 44°F and 52°F, so don't let them get too cold.

Frozen Grapes

If you want to keep your wine (or other beverage) cool on hot summer days, use frozen grapes instead of ice cubes. They'll keep the drink cold and they won't dilute it or change the taste as they thaw. Just make sure you wash them before freezing!

Perk Up Your Tabletops

Linoleum or vinyl floor tiles are excellent for covering picnic tabletops. You can also use linoleum on kitchen shelves, instead of contact paper. It will last a long time and is easy to keep clean.

How to Save S'More Marshmallows

Rock-hard marshmallows don't have to be thrown out. You can soften them up in a resealable plastic bag placed on top of warm water. Now go get that grill fired up again.

Ultimate Frisbee Plates

Having a barbecue? Super-power your paper plates by placing them on top of Frisbees. Or cover your Frisbee with foil and it's perfect for serving food right off the grill.

'Cue Tool Holder

It might not be a great Father's Day present, but an old oven mitt makes an ideal holder for barbecue utensils. Use its hanging loop to attach it to your grill and insert tongs or anything else you need.

Who Knew? Readers' Favorite

Before you light up your Weber grill, put a little bit of cat litter in the grease tray. It not only will prevent any flare-ups, it will keep the tray from overheating and warping.

Keep It Clean

Make sure to remove the ashes from the bottom of your grill after each use, because the ashes can retain moisture and cause your grill to rust. Before you remove the ashes, try sprinkling them with used coffee grounds. The grounds will keep the ash from blowing up into your face.

CHAPTER 7

Baking Tips

Your Level Best

The next time you get chopsticks with your Chinese take-out, keep a few for your kitchen. Even if you haven't mastered the art of eating with them, they're perfect for leveling off cups of flour and other dry goods.

Warm for Cakes, Cold for Pastries

When baking cakes and cookies, the ingredients should always be at room temperature. For pastry, it is just the opposite—the ingredients should be cold.

Who Knew? Readers' Favorite

Electric stand mixers are a boon for bakers, because the dough hook attachment reduces or eliminates the need to knead. To keep the dough from climbing up the hook, spray it with nonstick cooking spray or vegetable oil before turning the mixer on. This is also a great tip for when you're using a hand mixer.

Don't Skip the Salt

Although it may be tempting for health reasons, never omit the salt from your bread recipe. Salt strengthens and tightens the gluten, keeping bread from becoming crumbly.

Moldy Bread?

You may know that you can usually just cut mold off of cheese, but the same does not hold true for bread. If you see the slightest sign of mold on baked goods, throw the item out. Mold sends out "feelers" that often can't be seen.

Yeast Saver

Where should you store yeast, you ask? Always keep it in the refrigerator, because the cold will slow down deterioration. Bring the yeast back up to room temperature to help it dissolve at the normal rate.

Weak Flour?

Adding a bit of ascorbic acid (vitamin C) to flour when baking bread can help to strengthen weak flour. For every 6 cups flour, add a pinch of powdered ascorbic acid to the yeast. Ascorbic acid is easiest to find in the form of vitamin C tablets in the vitamin or cold remedy section of your drugstore.

Who Knew? Readers' Favorite

Consider keeping a clean powder puff in your flour container. It's a great way to dust flour onto rolling pins or pastry boards. And remember, always store your flour in the freezer to prevent any sort of bug infestation.

Perfectly Greased and Floured Pans

Recipes for baked goods often call for greased and floured pans, a process that involves oiling a pan down, then sprinkling flour inside and shaking the pan until it's equally distributed. However, professional bakers don't often use this method because it can leave flour on your baked goods or make them cook unevenly. Instead, they mix up a batch of "baker's magic," and now you can, too. Mix ½ cup room temperature vegetable shortening, ½ cup vegetable oil, and ½ cup all-purpose flour. Blend the mixture well and use it to grease pans. It can be stored in an airtight container in the refrigerator for up to six months.

Bread Pan Pandering

It's never good to be dull...unless you're a bread pan. For the best results when baking, avoid a shiny bread pan. A shiny pan reflects heat to such a degree that the bread may not bake evenly. However, a dark pan may cook the bread too quickly, resulting in burned bottoms. Your best bet? A dull aluminum pan.

Who Knew? Readers' Favorite

Making cupcakes or muffins and don't have enough batter to fill the tin? Before sticking them in the oven, fill the empty holes in the tin halfway with water. It will extend the life of the tin and make sure the other muffins bake evenly.

Blending Basics

When baking, it is important that all the ingredients be blended well, without being mixed too much. If you need to sift flour, add the other dry ingredients (such as leavening and salt) to the flour before you sift.

Kneading Know-How

Don't skimp when kneading bread—it's what distributes the yeast and other ingredients evenly throughout the dough. If dough isn't kneaded properly, it won't rise evenly. Electric bread machines, stand mixers, and food processors make short work of this important task, but if you're kneading dough by hand, rub a small amount of vegetable oil onto your hands before you begin, which will make kneading thick dough easier. A wooden cutting board is your best bet for kneading bread, but other surfaces will work. Just be sure to flour the board adequately.

A Proper Cool-Down

After you've removed bread from the oven, cool it on a wire rack. This will allow air to circulate around the bread and should prevent any soggy areas from developing in the loaf.

Dough Won't Rise?

One of the most frequent problems bread bakers encounter is yeast dough that doesn't rise adequately. If your dough won't rise, check out the following tips to see if you can pinpoint the cause.

✦ Your dough may be too cool, which reduces the level of yeast activity. Dough can rise at lower temperatures—even in the refrigerator—but it takes several hours or overnight to attain the same volume that it can in an hour or two at 80–90° F.

✦ The yeast may have been prepared with water that was too hot, which can kill it. The water must be under 120°F for optimum results.

✦ The yeast may have been too old. Proof your yeast before using it to be sure it's not ready for retirement. Dissolve a little sugar in some warm water, then sprinkle in the yeast. The mixture should begin bubbling within 5–7 minutes. If it doesn't, the yeast is too inactive to provide proper leavening and should be thrown away.

Who Knew? Readers' Favorite

We love this secret for a perfect loaf of bread, given to us by a baker friend: Put some ice cubes in a shallow pan and put it in the oven with your loaf of bread. This ice cubes will produce a dense steam, and as the water evaporates, the crust becomes hard and crispy. The steam also will allow the bread to rise more evenly, giving you a crumb that's firm and chewy.

(Not Too Much) Garlic Bread

Want a hint of garlic without a too-garlicky taste? You can make a lightly scented garlic bread by adding 1 teaspoon of garlic powder to the flour when you're making white bread.

Flavored Crusts

The next time you make a pie, add a little flavor to the crust by tossing a pinch of ground spice or a few minced herbs into the flour. Use cinnamon or ginger with an apple or other dessert pie, and try finely chopped parsley with a quiche or meat pie.

Buttermilk: Not Always Bad for You

Buttermilk can be substituted for 2 percent or whole milk in most pastry or bread recipes. Buttermilk is less than 1 percent fat, almost equal to skim milk, but it has a thicker consistency.

Creamy Cream Cheese

When baking a recipe that calls for cream cheese, be sure it's at room temperature before you start, and make sure you beat it so it's light and fluffy before adding any other ingredients, especially eggs.

Flour the Fruit

Bread, muffins, and other baked goods are fun (and delicious) to make with dried fruit, but the fruit often sinks to the bottom because it doesn't have a lot of moisture and becomes more even solid during baking. If you coat it with a little flour, though, it'll stay put.

Go Gently

If you make bread with 100 percent whole-wheat flour, it will be moister if you add the flour to the water slowly and mix gently. Whole-wheat flour absorbs water at a slower rate than do other types of flour. Reserve ¼ cup flour and knead in a tablespoon or so at a time as needed.

When bread dries out, it hardens. But to make hard bread as good as knew, wrap the loaf tightly in a damp paper towel for 2–3 minutes, then remove the towel and heat the bread in a 350°F oven for 15–20 minutes. When French or Italian bread hardens, sprinkle the crust with cold water and heat at 350°F for 8–10 minutes.

What Kind of Crust Do You Want?

Different liquids will impart different characteristics to the crust of your bread. Water, a common choice, will cause the top of the bread to be crisp, and will significantly intensify the flavor of the wheat. Save some of the water you've used to boil potatoes and it will add a unique flavor, make the crust smooth, and cause the dough to rise faster due to the high starch content. Milk gives bread a rich, creamy color and leaves the bread with a fine texture and a soft, brown crust. Eggs will provide a moister crust. A liquid sweetener such as molasses, maple syrup, or honey will cause the crust to be dark brown and will also keep it moist.

Vegetable or meat broth will give the bread a special flavor and provide you with a light, crisp crust. Alcohol of any type will give the bread a smooth crust with a flavor that may be similar to the alcohol used, especially beer; just don't use too much or you'll kill the yeast. Coffee and tea are commonly used to provide a dark, rich color and a crisp crust. But our favorite tip may also be the easiest not to mess up: A couple of minutes before you bread is done, just brush some apple cider vinegar onto the crusty. It will be a lovely brown color, and nice and shiny!

For Perfect Popovers

If you want the lightest popovers every time, puncture them with a fork when you remove them from the oven to release the air inside.

Puff Pastry Perfection

Puff pastry dough is made from flour, butter, and water. A small amount of butter is layered between dough that is folded several times to form as many as 700 layers. When you cut puff pastry dough, be sure to use a very sharp knife and cut straight down; never pull the knife through the dough or cut the dough at an angle. Doing so will cause the ends to puff up unevenly as the pastry bakes.

Removing Muffins

To easily remove muffins or rolls from a pan, set the pan on a damp towel for about 30 seconds. Use an old towel, because the pan might stick.

Stale Muffin Trick

If the delicious muffins you slaved over have gone stale, here's an easy trick to make them fresh again: Place them in a brown paper bag and squirt them with water two or three times from a spray bottle. Then place the bag in your oven with just the pilot light on overnight. By morning, they'll be ready for breakfast!

Beautiful Biscuits

Who doesn't love a tasty biscuit? Not only are they delicious, but homemade biscuits are also a great way to spruce up a leftover or frozen meal. Here are some tips and tricks for making the best-tasting biscuits.

- ✦ Handle the dough gently. Overworking the dough and re-rolling the scraps makes for tough biscuits.

- ✦ If your biscuits are heavy and dense, check your baking powder for freshness and make sure that you are properly sifting all the dry ingredients together. Even blending of the ingredients is key, so if you don't have a sifter, put the dry ingredients into a large sieve and shake them into the mixing bowl, or whisk them together.

- ✦ If you like your biscuits to be a rich golden color, add a teaspoon of sugar to the dry ingredients. It helps the crust to caramelize (and only adds 16 calories to the whole batch!).

- ✦ If you're using a cutter to cut your biscuits, dip it in flour first so the dough won't stick to it. Be sure to press the cutter straight down—don't twist it even slightly. Doing so seals the edges of the biscuits and they won't rise as high.

- ✦ Shortening is the preferred fat for biscuits. Butter makes for more solid biscuits, and oil makes them greasy.

- ✦ For super-soft biscuits, brush them with milk or melted unsalted butter before baking, then arrange them in a cake pan so the sides touch one another.

Glazing Over

Before you put rolls in the oven, make a delicious glaze for their tops that your guests are sure to appreciate. Lightly beat an egg white with a tablespoon of milk and brush on each roll. You'll love it!

Who Knew? Readers' Favorite

When you're done with an afternoon of baking, sprinkle your messy countertop with salt, and the doughy, floury mess that you've left behind can be easily wiped away with a damp sponge.

Reheating Rolls

The quickest way to reheat biscuits or rolls? Sprinkle them lightly with water and wrap them in foil. It should take about five minutes in a preheated 350°F oven.

Best Croutons Ever

If you really want to impress your dinner guests, make some homemade croutons for your salad. Here's how: After cutting your leftover bread into cubes, fry the pieces in olive oil and a little garlic powder (not garlic salt), a pinch of parmesan cheese, and parsley until golden brown, then let cool on paper towels. They freeze well, too!

Save Those Bread Bags

Don't forget to save your store-bought bread bags for the times when you bake bread. They are perfectly sized for homemade breads.

For the Best Baked Sale Item

For your next bake sale, write out the recipe for your baked good on an index card and tape it to the serving plate or box. That way, if buyers find your goody to their liking, they'll know they can make it themselves in the future. They may also be more likely to buy your item if it comes with a free recipe!

CHAPTER 8

Making Your Food Last Longer

Know Your Terminology

When shopping, only the term "use by" means that you shouldn't eat the food after the date indicated. "Sell by" dates are only an indication for the store, and foods will usually keep one to two weeks after. "Best before" is only an indication of food quality, not of food safety, so again, your perishables may still be good to eat.

The Best Ways to Freeze Food

Freezing food is vital for being able to save money, because it allows you to buy food when it's on sale, make it when you have time, then save it for later. It seems like it should be as easy as just shoving food in the freezer, but there are a number of tips that will make your food taste better after defrosting.

✦ Never use quick-cooking rice in a dish that will be frozen, as it becomes mushy when reheated. Use regular or long-grain rice instead.

✦ Don't add toppings to dishes to be frozen; add when serving.

✦ When preparing most vegetables for freezing, they should be blanched, not fully cooked. This will lessen the enzymatic activity in the vegetable, and reheating will complete the cooking process. To blanch, simply steam or boil vegetables for about half the time you normally would cook them, then plunge them into ice water and drain. Potatoes and squashes are the exception to this rule—they should be fully cooked.

✦ Freezing causes russet or Idaho potatoes to fall apart; if you need them to stay whole or in chunks, use potatoes with red skin or waxy flesh.

✦ Freezing tends to intensify the flavors of certain foods, such as garlic, peppers, and cloves. Use less in a dish that you will freeze, and when reheating, taste and add more as needed.

✦ On the other hand, use more onion than you would otherwise, because freezing tends to cause onion to lose its flavor. Herbs and salt also tend to diminish in flavor, so it's best to add them after freezing, when you're reheating the dish.

✦ Avoid freezing sauces. Egg-based sauces and those high in fat tend to separate when reheated, and cheese- or milk-based sauces are prone to curdling. Don't try to freeze mayonnaise, salad dressing, or jam. Most gravies will thicken considerably when frozen, but they can be thinned when reheated.

✦ Artificial sweeteners do not freeze well, so don't substitute them for sugar.

✦ Don't freeze any bakery item with a cream filling because it will become soggy. Custard and

meringue pies, for example, don't freeze well.
The custard tends to separate and the meringue
becomes tough.

✦ Cool already-cooked foods in the refrigerator
before freezing. Cooling them quickly prevents
bacterial growth.

Prepare to be Frozen!

When you freeze foods, evaporation continues and fluids are
lost. The entire surface of meat must be protected from this
process with a moisture-resistant wrap. The best way to wrap
meats for freezing is in plastic wrap covered by a protective
freezer paper or aluminum foil. This will not eliminate evaporation
entirely, but it will reduce the risk of oxidation and rancidity.

Consume It or Freeze It!

Small cuts of meat will spoil more quickly than larger cuts and
should not be kept in the refrigerator for more than a day or two.
Liver, sweetbreads, and cubed meats should be cooked within
one day or be kept frozen.

Meatless Mondays

Never buy meat from the supermarket on Monday morning.
It's likely that those packages for sale were not sold over the
weekend, and most shipments of fresh meat arrive on Monday
afternoon or on Tuesday.

How Long Does Raw Meat Keep in the Freezer?

Buying meat when it's on sale and keeping it in your freezer is a great way to save on groceries. Unfortunately, you can't keep it in there forever! Here is a helpful guide to how long different kinds (and cuts) of raw meat will keep at 0°F, the optimal temperature for your freezer.

MEAT	MONTHS	MEAT	MONTHS
Bacon	1	Ground pork	2–3
Beef	9	Ham	3
Chicken (in parts)	9	Pork (chops or ribs)	6–9
Chicken (whole)	12	Pork roast	9
Cold cuts	1	Rabbit	6–9
Duck	4–6	Sausage	2
Fish (fatty)	3	Shellfish	4–6
Fish (lean)	6	Turkey (in parts)	6
Goose	4–6	Turkey (whole)	12
Ground beef	2–3	Venison	6–12

You'll find it's well worth your time to cook an entire turkey every now and then, especially after Thanksgiving and Christmas when the prices drop dramatically. Stuffing is one of our favorite foods, so we love having "fake Thanksgiving" every once in the while. Then we chop up what we don't eat, throw it in the freezer, and use in soups, stir-fries, casseroles, and tons of other meals.

A Meat Freezing Secret

When slicing up beef or pork into bite-sized pieces to save for later, first partially freeze the meat by placing it in the freezer for 1–2 hours. You'll find it's much quicker and easier to slice.

Score One for Easy Thawing

Use this trick to make unfreezing a portion of ground meat easier. Place the meat in a resealable plastic bag, flatten, then score into sections (like a tic-tac-toe board) by pressing a butter knife into the bag. Seal the bag and stick it in the freezer, and when you need just a little ground meat you'll easily be able to break off a chunk.

Lemons at the Ready

If you have a bunch of lemons that are about to go bad—you guessed it, freeze them! First cut in slices, then freeze on a baking sheet or in between pieces of wax paper. They're perfect for adding to glasses of water.

Fruity Freezes

Blueberries and cranberries are two more foods that are easy to buy when in abundance and freeze for later. Place them in a single layer on a cookie sheet and place the sheet in the freezer. Once they're frozen, you can transfer them to a resealable plastic bag. Frozen berries are great in smoothies, pies, and even eating cold!

Getting Rid of Tomato Paste Waste

When we used to clean out our fridge, the thing we'd end up throwing away every time was half-empty cans of tomato paste. Even though tomato paste doesn't cost that much, we still felt like we were throwing away money. So now, when we've used a couple of tablespoons of tomato paste, instead of putting the rest of the can in the fridge, we separate out the unused portion into plastic bags—usually about 2 tablespoons per bag—and freeze. When our next recipe calls for tomato paste, we simply turn the bag inside out and plop the frozen paste right into the pot. If you don't want to use the plastic bags, you can also accomplish this using an ice cube tray!

Who Knew? Readers' Favorite

Keep raw ginger in a sealed plastic bag in the freezer, and it will last pretty much forever. Best of all, you don't need to defrost it before you grate it into stir-fries, sauces, or whatever else you're making.

Deep Freeze

The freezing process can decrease the flavor of some foods, which is why all the foods in the freezer section of your grocery store have been flash frozen in seconds (usually with the help of some liquid nitrogen). It's important that frozen foods don't thaw and refreeze before you eat them, so on hot days make sure to visit your store's freezer section last. That way, your purchases have less time to thaw.

Stock Up

When carving a chicken or turkey, it's easy to make a stock at the same time. Place all unused parts in a pot with celery and onion (using the skins of the onion will give the stock a nice, rich color), then heat up to boiling. Reduce the heat and simmer while you make dinner. Then turn off and skim the fat when cooled. Stock can be used for gravies, soup (naturally), and to add flavor to rice, potatoes, and tomato sauce. This free and easy seasoning would have cost you up to $5 for a quart at the grocery store!

Freezing Stock

To easily freeze the delicious stock you've just made into smaller portions, line a drinking glass with a resealable plastic bag. Pour the stock into the glass until it's about three-quarters full, then seal the bag and lay flat on a baking pan. Repeat until you've used up all your stock, laying the bags on top of one another. Once they're frozen, you can move them anywhere in the freezer that there's room.

To make your soda last longer, decrease the amount of air that the carbon dioxide (which causes the fizz) has to escape into. This is easily accomplished by squeezing in the sides of the bottle after you pour a glass.

Making Condiments Last

It's frustrating to have to throw out condiments like sour cream, mayo, yogurt, and mustard because you didn't use the entire container before it went bad. However, you can easily combat this by changing containers as you use up the item. Using a smaller container exposes the condiment to less air— and fewer bacteria. The trick, of course, is making sure you successfully transfer every bit of mayo possible from the jar to the tiny Tupperware. We usually do our container downsizing right before we're about to use the condiment on something. That way, we can scrape out what we don't transfer onto our sandwiches.

Say Cheese

Believe it or not, you can successfully freeze many varieties of cheese without sacrificing taste or texture. Cut it into small blocks, place in sealed plastic bags, and then keep it in the freezer for when you need it. Cheese varieties that can be frozen successfully include Brick, Cheddar, Camembert, Edam, Gouda, Mozzarella, Muenster, Parmesan, Port du Salut, Swiss, Provolone, Mozzarella, and Romano. Small cheeses, such as Camembert, can even be frozen in their original packages. When removed from the freezer, cheese should be put in the refrigerator and used as soon as possible after thawing.

A Great Tip for Noodle Soups

If you can't already tell, we freeze practically everything. Two frozen items that sometimes take our friends by surprise are cooked rice and cooked noodles. If you accidentally make too much, simply put them in an airtight container in the freezer. Though they won't hold up well enough to eat plain, they'll be perfect for soups!

Spice Saving Secret

Make dried herbs and spices last last longer by putting half of the amount into a sealed, airtight container when you purchase them. Label the container and keep it in your freezer. When the spice on-hand loses its aroma, replace it with your stash in the freezer, and you'll never have to be irritated about throwing away that unusable mustard seed or marjoram again.

The Life of Spice

If you're using McCormick brand spices, and you're not sure if they're past their prime, just go to McCormick.com/Spices101.aspx. There you can type in the code on the bottom of the container and find out if the spice is still good. And don't forget to transfer your spices to smaller, airtight containers as you use them. Air makes them stale!

What You Never Knew About Milk

When you know your milk is going to go bad before you can use up the rest of it, separate it out into a few sealable containers and put them in your freezer. That's right, milk can be frozen! If you use skim milk, it can be thawed and drunk later and you'll never be able to tell the difference. For other varieties of milk, use for sauces or baking after thawing. This is a great strategy when you find milk at a deep discount. Buy as much as you can and freeze for later!

Don't Always Ditch the Fat

It might sound counterintuitive, but buying fattier meat can actually help your food go further—and keep your waistline intact. You're likely to eat less, assuming you cut off the fat when it's on your plate. And fattier meat generally has a better taste, so a little bit goes a long way.

Who Knew? Readers' Favorite

To avoid the absorption of refrigerator odors, always store eggs in their original carton on an inside shelf of the refrigerator. Before you put away the carton, though, turn each egg upside down. Storing eggs with the tapered end down maximizes the distance between the yolk and the air pocket, which may contain bacteria. The yolk is more perishable than the white, and even though it is more or less centered in the egg, the yolk can shift slightly and will move away from possible contamination.

Egg-cellent!

For eggs that last practically forever, separate them into whites and yolks, then freeze them separately in a lightly oiled ice-cube tray. When frozen, pop them out and store in separate Ziploc bags in the freezer. These frozen eggs are perfect for baking, and will last longer since they're separated.

Leftover Rice

Rice can be stored in the fridge for a longer amount of time if you store a slice of toast on top of it. The toast will absorb excess moisture and keep the rice fluffy and fresh.

Should Produce Be Refrigerated?

Refrigerating your produce can help it keep longer, but not all produce does well in the cooler temperatures. The majority of fruits and vegetables handle cold fairly well, but naturally enough, the exceptions are tropical fruits, whose cells are just not used to the cold. Bananas will suffer cell damage and release a skin-browning chemical, avocados don't ripen when stored below 45°F, and citrus fruit will develop brown-spotted skin. These fruits, as well as squash, tomatoes, cucumbers, bell peppers, melons, and pineapples, are best stored at 50°F—so keep them out of the fridge unless you've already cut them and need to keep them fresh. Most other vegetables, including lettuce, carrots, and cabbage, will do better in your refrigerator, as will fruits like apples and pears. Garlic, onions, shallots, and potatoes should never be refrigerated because the cold will cause sprouting, loss of flavor, or conversion of their starch to sugar. Keep these foods out of the refrigerator (at a little cooler than room temperature, if possible) and in a dark cabinet. Humidity is also an important factor, so fruits and vegetables should always be stored in the refrigerator crisper bins, which will prevent them from drying out.

For Happy Peppers

If you're only using half of a bell pepper for a recipe, make the other half last longer with this simple trick. When you're slicing the pepper, make sure to leave the seeds and membrane intact on one side. Then store this side in a sealed plastic bag or container in the fridge. Leaving the seeds intact will make the pepper last longer.

Let Your Produce Breathe

Wrap all produce loosely; air circulation around fruits and vegetables reduces spoilage. A sealed perforated plastic bag is ideal—make your own by simply poking several holes in an ordinary sandwich or freezer bag.

Why There's a Sponge in Our Fridge

The next time you buy a pack of kitchen sponges, throw one in the fruit and vegetable drawer of your fridge. The sponge will absorb moisture before it can work its way into your produce, meaning it will last longer. Most kitchen sponges are also treated with anti-bacteria agents, giving your fruits and veggies even extra protection. Replace the sponge when you replace the baking soda in your fridge, a couple of times a year.

A Home for Your Potatoes

Never refrigerate potatoes, because that tends to turn potato starch to sugar. Potatoes will last longer and remain solid longer if they are stored away from light in a cool, dry spot, preferably at 45–50°F. If white potatoes are stored below 40°F, they tend to release more sugar and turn sweet. Air must circulate around potatoes; otherwise, moisture will cause them to decay.

Keep Potatoes for Longer

It is best to purchase potatoes in bulk bins—not in bags, which make it hard to determine which are bruised. If you store fresh ginger with potatoes it will help keep them fresh longer. Half an apple stored with potatoes will stop the sprouting by absorbing moisture before the potato does.

Don't Toss Those Potato Peels!

If your family loves mashed potatoes as much as ours does, here's a great way to use the nutritious skins in their own dish the next night. In a bowl, sprinkle the potato peelings with salt and pepper, mix with a bit of Italian dressing, and then stick them in the oven at 400°F until crispy (about 20 minutes).

Who Knew? Readers' Favorite

It is always a good idea to line the crisper bins of your refrigerator with a few paper towels or sheets of newspaper to absorb excess moisture. Mold spores love moisture, but the towels will keep it away.

Separate Your Onions and Potatoes

Potatoes hate onions...at least until they're cooked together. Onions should never be stored with potatoes because moisture from the onions can cause potatoes to sprout. Onions also release gases that will alter the flavor of a potato.

Onion Color Counts

Yellow and white onions can be kept for a longer amount of time than red ones, as they have a lower sugar content. Store in an open space that's cool and dry, and away from bright light, which can make them bitter. Don't store them anywhere that may become damp.

Keep Onions Fresh

The sugar content in yellow onions makes them spoil quickly if they are stored closely together—who knew? The solution is to store your onions in an old (clean) pair of pantyhose, making knots in the legs so the onions can't touch. It might look a little weird, but it works!

An Onion's Better Half

If you need only half an onion, use the top half first, because the root half will store longer in the refrigerator (it won't sprout).

A Second Life for Your Onion

If you have an onion that starts to sprout, place it in some soil in a pot on a windowsill and, as it continues to sprout, snip off pieces of the sprouts to use in salads. These tiny greens are flavorful and mild.

Water Your Asparagus!

To make asparagus last longer in the refrigerator, place the stem ends in a container of water, or wrap them in a wet paper towel and put in a plastic bag. Like flowers, the asparagus will continue "drinking" the water and stay fresh until it's ready to use.

Spinach Saving Solutions

Spinach will keep in the refrigerator for 2–3 days, as long as it's stored in a sealed plastic bag. To preserve its shelf life, don't wash it or cut it before you are ready to prepare it. Want to freeze fresh spinach? Remove the stems, blanch the leaves in boiling water for two minutes, then run under cold water and dry before you freeze. Removing their stems will allow the leaves retain more of their moisture. Spinach will keep in the freezer for 10–12 months.

Who Knew? Readers' Favorite

The best way to store celery is to wrap it in aluminum foil and keep it in the fridge. It will last for weeks and weeks.

Save Your Celery Leaves

Don't throw away celery leaves—while they don't work well with dips, they still have a wonderful flavor. When chopping celery, set the leaves aside on a paper plate, let them dry, and throw them in stuffing, salads, and soups for great extra flavor.

Cucumber Rules

When storing a cucumber, keep it away from apples and tomatoes, which will shorten its life. Cucumbers stay fresh for up to a week, when the water content starts to drop.

Avoid Frosted Vegetables

When shopping in the freezer aisle, avoid packages of frozen vegetables that have frost on them. It's a sign that the food has thawed and been refrozen, and a percentage of moisture has already been lost.

Lettuce Abuse?

To make sure iceberg lasts as long as possible, you should remove the innermost core before you store it. An easy (and admittedly fun) way to do this is to hit the lettuce against a hard surface and then twist the core out.

Revive Wilted Greens

To crisp cut-up greens like lettuce, cilantro, or anything else that wilts, soak them in ice water for 15–20 minutes. This also works for limp asparagus and carrots!

Lasting Lettuce

Iceberg lettuce remains fresher longer than any other type of lettuce because of its high water content. Iceberg will keep for 7–14 days, whereas romaine lasts for 6–10 days, and butter (or Boston lettuce) for only 3–4 days.

Don't throw away the outer leaves from a head of lettuce! They come in handy when you need to cover foods in the microwave. You won't have to use a paper towel, and the leaves will keep your food moist.

Overcooked Overtures

If you've overcooked broccoli, asparagus, or any other vegetable, don't throw it away. Save it for later, when you can cut it up into small pieces and add to a soup, sauce, or stew. It'll cook down even further, so you won't notice anything but the taste.

Give Your Veggies a Haircut

If you've purchased a vegetable with a leafy top, such as beet greens or carrots, remove the green top before you store it in the fridge. The leafy tops will leach moisture from the root or bulb and shorten the vegetable's shelf life.

Storing Corn

Always store corn in a cool, dry location, and keep the ears separated in order to prevent them from becoming moldy. Remember that as it warms up, the sugar in corn converts to starch very quickly. (In fact, when corn is piled high in supermarket bins, the ears on the bottom will be less sweet because of the heat generated by the weight of the ones on top.) To freeze corn, blanch the ears for a minute or two in boiling water, drain, and immediately flush with cold water to stop the cooking. Freeze the ears on a tray, leaving room between them so the kernels aren't crushed and will hold their shape. Once the corn is frozen, place the ears in a sealed plastic bag. Frozen corn will keep for one year.

A Sweet Tip for a Sweet Pepper

If you eat pimientos, make sure to cover them in vinegar before storing them in the fridge. They'll last much longer!

Mushroom Musts

Ever wonder why mushrooms are usually sold in Styrofoam or cardboard containers? Plastic containers tend to keep the mushrooms too wet, and they go bad quickly. Fresh mushrooms have a shelf life of only 2–3 days and must be stored in the refrigerator in an open container. The original container or another paper product will work best. Never wash mushrooms before storing them—they'll retain the water and become soggy. If you must keep them for a few days, place a single layer of cheesecloth on top of the container. (If they do become shriveled, they can still be sliced or chopped and used in cooking.) To freeze mushrooms, wipe them off with a damp paper towel, slice them, sauté them in a small amount of butter until they are almost done, allow them to cool, and place them in an airtight plastic bag and freeze. They should keep for 10–12 months.

Separate Drawers

Store fruits and vegetables in separate drawers in your fridge. Even when chilled, fruits give off ethylene gas that shortens the shelf life of other fruit and vegetables by causing them to ripen more quickly.

Who Knew? Readers' Favorite

Broccoli will keep longer in the fridge if you store it like a bouquet of flowers. Cut about an inch off the stems, then submerge the stems in a bowl of water. This tip also works for asparagus, chives, and other stemmed vegetables.

Kill Two Birds with One Stone

If you have kids who don't like vegetables, you'll love this clever way to get more nutrients into them. If you have too many fruits and vegetables to use before they go bad, puree them in a blender with a little bit of lemon juice, then freeze. Defrost and add to sauces, soups, stews, enchiladas, and more—your kid won't be able to taste the difference! The key is making sure you don't dramatically alter the color of the dish you're serving. So if you're making a white sauce, for instance, try a puree of cauliflower and summer squash. Tomato-based sauces can usually handle one part "green puree" for every four parts tomato sauce. Pureed fruit works great in muffin recipes or mixed into ice cream. So grind up that broccoli and spinach and get going!

Tomatoes at the Ready

It's easy to make your own version of whole, peeled tomatoes that you would normally buy in a can. Buy a bunch of tomatoes when they're cheap, then core them and freeze them in an airtight container. When you're ready to use them in soups, sauces, or stews, hold each frozen tomato under warm running water and the skin will peel right off.

Making Tomatoes Last

For the best storage, keep tomatoes stem-side down in a cool place. If they're still attached to the stem, try to space them so that they're not touching.

High and Dry

The moisture content of fresh berries is high, so make sure to thoroughly dry them before you stick them in the fridge, or wait until you're ready to eat them before you wash them. Otherwise, they can easily rot. Also make sure to store berries, especially strawberries, loosely covered in the refrigerator.

Who Knew? Readers' Favorite

Never throw out overripe bananas! Stick them in the freezer once they get completely brown, and you can still use them later for banana bread and other baking projects.

"Orange" You Glad?

We hate throwing anything away, so you can imagine how delighted we were when we heard this great use for orange rinds. After you've peeled an orange, stick a small piece of the rind in a sealed container with brown sugar, fresh herbs, or anything else that easily dries out. The moisture in the orange is just enough to keep it fresh.

Keeping Grapes

Grapes will stay fresh only for three to five days, even if refrigerated. They keep best in a plastic bag in the coldest part of the refrigerator, but they must be washed very well before eating. If you do wash them before storing, make sure to dry them thoroughly, as they'll easily absorb the water. Grapes can be eaten frozen (they're especially tasty treats), and frozen grapes can be used in cooking; however, they become mushy when they're thawed because of the high water content. They'll keep in the freezer for about one year.

Long-Lived Lemons

Lemons will stay fresh for up to three months if you store them in a bowl of water in the fridge. Just change the water every week. Who knew?

Long-Lasting Raisins

Raisins will last for several months if they are wrapped tightly in plastic wrap or a plastic bag and kept at room temperature. They will last even longer (up to a year) if you place the plastic bag in the refrigerator.

Some of That "Can Do" Spirit

A wonderful and—dare we say it?—fun way to make your fruits and veggies last longer is to try home canning. You may think canning is just for country folk, but it's becoming more and more popular as a way to save money and make sure you're eating foods with the least amount of preservatives possible. Buy foods when they are in season, or better yet, grow your own and can to save for later. The biggest trick in canning is to make sure that no air (which contains bacteria) gets into your jars; this is achieved with a pressure canner or a boiling-water canner. Find out what these contraptions are and how to safely can fruit, vegetables, pickles, meat, poultry, seafood, salsas, pie filling, jams, and more from the USDA's extensive free Guide to Home Canning, available at Uga.edu/nchfp/publications/publications_usda.html.

Who Knew? Readers' Favorite

Don't spend money on store-bought bread crumbs. Set aside a special jar and pour in the crumbs from the bottom of cracker or low-sugar cereal boxes. Also add crumbs from leftover garlic bread and a few dried herbs, and soon you'll have seasoned bread crumbs! The great thing is that homemade bread crumbs are even better than store-bought, since their uneven texture helps make them stick.

Keeping Bread

Bread stays fresh for a longer time if you place it in an airtight bag with a stalk of celery. If you are going to freeze a loaf of bread, make sure you include a paper towel in the package to absorb moisture and prevent it from becoming mushy when thawed.

What to Do with Stale Bread

There are many uses for stale bread other than feeding the ducks at the pond! Spread with butter, minced garlic, and whatever dried herbs you have, then toast in the toaster oven and cube to make croutons. You can also cut the bread into smaller pieces, then chop in a blender or food processor to make bread crumbs (you may have to cut off the bottom crust first). If you find that your bread often goes stale before you use it, slice it and store in the freezer. Separate out slices and let sit for about five minutes at room temperature to defrost, or stick directly in the toaster. Frozen bread is also great to use for grilled cheese sandwiches—it's much easier to butter and it will defrost as it cooks in the pan.

Who Knew? Readers' Favorite

Never pay for aerosol cooking sprays. Instead, buy a giant jug of vegetable oil and add it to a clean spray bottle as needed. It's the same thing and will cost you a fraction of the price.

Herbal Remedies

Fresh herbs are a wonderful addition to any dinner, but they go bad quickly and are hard to freeze. To keep herbs fresh longer, loosely wrap them in a damp paper towel, store in a plastic bag, and keep in the vegetable crisper of the refrigerator. If you have more fresh herbs than you can use, hang them upside down to dry. (Tie them together and hang them from a peg.) In about a week, you'll be able to crumble off the leaves. The flavor won't be quite as wonderful as that of fresh herbs, but it will still be much better than commercial dried herbs. Another simple solution is placing chopped, fresh herbs in ice-cube trays. Fill the trays with water and then freeze. When it's time to add herbs to soups and sauces, simply pop as many cubes as you want out of the tray and throw them in the pot.

Tea Saver

Want to get more for your money when it comes to tea? Always buy the loose variety, and then use one-third of what's recommended. Just let the tea steep a little longer, and it will taste exactly the same.

Storing Dairy Products

It's better to store milk on an inside shelf—not on the door—toward the back of the refrigerator. Why? All dairy products are very perishable. The optimal refrigeration is actually just over 32°F; however, few refrigerators are ever set that low or hold that low a temperature. Most home refrigerators remain around 40°F, and the temperature rises every time the door is opened. Store cheese near the bottom of the refrigerator, where temperature fluctuations are minimal.

Adding a teaspoon of baking soda or a pinch of salt to a carton of milk will keep it fresh for a week or so past its expiration date. Just remember that leaving milk at room temperature for more than 30 minutes can reduce its life span.

Better Butter

Where you store butter will affect how long it lasts. It will keep for around six months in the freezer, but if you're storing it in the fridge, it will start to lose its flavor after three weeks. Butter tends to absorb odors and flavors more rapidly than other foods, so make sure to wrap it in a few layers of plastic wrap or foil before storing, especially in the freezer.

Save Those Butter Wrappers

After finishing a stick of unsalted butter, hold on to the wrapper. It'll come in handy when you need to grease a pan: Simply wipe the pan with it. But don't use wrappers from salted butter, since they may cause foods to stick.

For the Last Bit of Shortening

Here's a great tip for the really thrifty. If you want to get all the shortening or lard out of a can, pour 2 cups boiling water into the container and swirl it gently until the fat melts. Refrigerate the container until the shortening solidifies on the water's surface, then just lift or skim it off with a knife blade or a sharp-edged spoon.

Extend the Life of Your Cheese

To keep cheese mold-free longer, place a piece of paper towel that has been dampened with white vinegar in the bottom of a plastic container with a tight-fitting lid. Add three or four sugar cubes, which will attract the mold if some does form. Make sure to use a clean knife whenever you cut the cheese.

Keep Your Cheeses Longer

Before you store semi-hard cheeses like Cheddar, Swiss, or Gruyère, rub the cut edges with a little bit of butter. You'll never notice the taste difference, and the cheese will be less likely to dry out or become moldy.

How to Soften Cheese

To soften a piece of hardened (but not moldy) cheese, submerge it in a bowl of buttermilk for one minute. If it's still not soft, cover the dish and refrigerate it overnight.

Revive Moldy Cheese

Believe it or not, cheese with a little mold on it is still perfectly safe to eat once you remove the offending areas. The easiest way to do this is to take a knife or cheese grater, dip it in vinegar, and slice the mold off. Dip the knife in vinegar after each slice—it kills the mold and prevents it from coming back.

Cheese, Please!

A little bit of delayed gratification will pay off on pizza (or pasta) night. Grate a wedge of Parmesan or Romano cheese all at once, then store it in a Ziploc bag (one inside the other, if you need it to stay fresh for longer). Two benefits: you only have to wash the grater one time and you won't be tempted to buy that expensive pre-grated cheese.

The rinds of hard cheeses like Parmesan are great flavor enhancers for soups. Add a three-inch square to your next pot of soup, and when you're serving the soup, break up the delicious, melty rind and include a little piece in each bowl. It's completely edible.

Cottage Cheese Care

Because of its high water content, cottage cheese doesn't last as long as other food products in the refrigerator. To extend its life, store it in the container upside down. This will also work for other dairy products like mayonnaise and sour cream.

A Cottage Cheese Shortcut

When making meatballs, meatloaf, or hamburger patties, try adding ½ cup cottage cheese for every pound of ground meat. Not only does it add flavor and protein, but it will stretch your recipe to serve a few more people. You can also use cottage cheese as a substitute for sour cream. If your dip recipe calls for sour cream but you're out, cream some cottage cheese in your blender instead. The low-fat variety works best.

For Long-Lasting Marshmallows

In case you've always wondered where to store marshmallows, the answer is the freezer! To separate the frozen marshmallows later, just cut them with scissors dipped in very hot water.

Sweet Savings

To save money, purchase solid chocolate candy (usually in bunny or Santa form) after major holidays when it's gone on super sale. Store the chocolate in the freezer, then shave off bits with a vegetable peeler to use on top of desserts.

Keep Christmas Going Until Valentine's Day

After Christmas is over, snag a bag of tiny candy canes that are on sale and use them for these heart-shaped cupcake toppers. Flip one cane over and place against another one ("hooks" and bottom edges touching). Bake on a nonstick baking sheet at 325°F for 3–5 minutes. Pinch together to seal, then remove with a spatula.

Cake Keeper

This one you won't believe until you try it. Cubes of sugar can keep cake nice and moist for those rare occasions when you don't finish it all the first night. Make sure the container is airtight.

CHAPTER 9

Kitchen Problems Solved!

For Clean Knives Every Time

When trying to remove stubborn food debris from a knife, don't use a scrubber, which can ruin its finish. Instead, rub a cork over the knife, then wash it in warm water.

For a Clean Cookbook

To keep a cookbook clean, open, and still easy to read while preparing your meal, just place it under a glass pie plate—unless you're making pie, of course!

A "Cookmark"

Making dinner and need something to mark your page in the cookbook? Try using a single strand of raw spaghetti!

Keep Your Remote Clean While Cooking

If you like to channel surf while cooking, place your remote control in a plastic bag or plastic wrap. The buttons will still be visible, and the control will stay clean.

Kill a Kitchen Fire in Two Seconds Flat

If there's a grease fire in a pan, cover the pan immediately with a lid. You'll cut off the oxygen supply and the fire will go out. Baking soda is one of the best fire extinguishers. Always keep an open box next to the stove to dump onto grease fires—and never use water!

If you lost the knob to a pot lid, don't throw out the pot! Place a screw into the hole, with the thread side up, then attach a cork to it.

Stubborn Lid?

Have you ever left a covered pot on the stove only to find that the lid is stuck on? If this happens to you, just try setting the pot over moderate heat for a minute or two. Why? When you cook a food in a covered pot, the air inside the pot increases in pressure, raising the lid ever so slightly so heated air can escape. When you turn off the heat, the air pressure decreases (along with the temperature) and may become lower than the air pressure outside the pot. This decrease in pressure, combined with the water from the steam, creates a vacuum around the lid and seals it tight. The longer the lid is left on, the tighter the seal. Turning the heat back on will increase the air pressure, loosening the lid's seal.

Open a Stubborn Stuck Jar

An easy way to open a tight jar lid is to cover the top in plastic wrap to create a firm grip. Rubber kitchen gloves or rubber bands work well too. If the jar lid still won't budge, set it in a bowl with a little hot tap water for a few minutes, and then try again. Still stuck? Try this trick with a puncture-type can opener: Carefully work the pointed tip under the lid and gently loosen the cap. This should release enough pressure to allow you to open the jar.

Fixing Low-Flow Ketchup

Can't get the ketchup out of a stubborn bottle? Just stick a straw inside. Now when you turn it upside-down, the airflow through the straw will make the ketchup flow right out.

Get Rid of Food Smells

If your plastic storage containers smell of garlic, onions, or another potent food, wash them thoroughly, then stuff crumpled newspaper inside before snapping on the lids. In a few days, the smell will be gone.

Tame Tupperware Odor

Washing a plastic container with a stale smell over and over won't get rid of the sour odor, but this will. Wipe inside with tomato juice, wash as usual, dry completely and place in freezer (top and bottom separately). In a few days it will be as good as new.

Keep Wrap in Line

Plastic wrap loves to hug itself. Avoid this by keeping the box in the refrigerator. The cold keeps the wrap from sticking to itself.

Who Knew? Readers' Favorite

To lessen your cleanup time when using a food processor, protect the lid by first covering the bowl of food with a piece of plastic wrap. The lid will stay clean and you can toss the plastic wrap in the trash when you're finished.

Make Your Own Ziploc

If your plastic bags are not resealable, you can seal them yourself with this quick trick: Fold a small piece of aluminum foil over the end you'd like to seal, and iron it so both ends of the foil close over the plastic. This will ensure that the plastic doesn't melt.

Fuss-Free Blender Cleaning

Wash your blender in less than a minute with this simple trick! Just fill it halfway with hot water, then add a drop of dishwashing liquid, cover with its lid, and hit blend for 30 seconds. Suds will fill your blender and clean it without you having to disassemble the whole contraption.

Stop Syrup from Running

Frustrated with syrup running down the sides of the bottle, making a disgusting mess? Try this trick: Rub the threads at the neck of the bottle with a small amount of vegetable oil. The oil will prevent the syrup from running and the cap from sticking next time you open it. This also works for molasses and honey containers.

Making Coffee More Drinkable

If you're sensitive to acidity in coffee, but love the pick-me-up in the morning, here's a tip to reduce the acid level: Just add a pinch of baking soda to the drink! You can also use this tip to decrease the acid in other high-acid drinks and foods.

For Mugs That Look As Good As New

To remove coffee or tea stains from a ceramic mug or pot, gently wipe them with a lemon sprinkled with salt. The salt will act as an abrasive, while the acid will get rid of the tannins.

Cure Cloudiness in Iced Tea

Cloudiness is common in brewed iced tea, but it can be easily prevented. Simply let the tea cool to room temperature before refrigerating it. If the tea is still cloudy, try adding a small amount of boiling water to it until it clears up.

Easier Iced Tea

Is there anything more refreshing than iced tea in the summer? When making a big pot of tea, here's a tip to easily add and remove your tea bags. Just wrap the strings around a chopstick, then place the chopstick over the top of the pot.

A Fizzy Fix

Have you ever had the problem of soda fizzing over the top of an ice-filled glass? Here's a quick trick that will make the cubes fizz less. Put them in the glass first, then rinse them for a few seconds. Pour out the water and add the soda. Since the surface tension of the ice will have changed, the soda won't fizz over.

Make Flat Soda a Thing of the Past

When you pour a warm soft drink over ice cubes, the gas escapes from the beverage at a fast rate because the ice cubes contain more surface area for the gas bubbles to collect on, thus releasing more of the carbon dioxide. This is the reason that warm beverages go flat rapidly, and warm drinks poured over ice go flat even faster. To slow down the process, add ice after you've poured the drink and the bubbles have dissipated.

Slow Down Soda Bubbles on the Go

Yes, there is a way to keep open soda from going flat. Not for a month, but for an hour or so. Leave an open can or bottle inside a sealed Ziploc bag while you run out to do your errands, and it will still be bubbly when you get back.

Who Knew? Readers' Favorite

Wine sediment is harmless, but it doesn't always look too nice. Get rid of sediment, and any bits of cork, by pouring your wine through a coffee filter and into a decanter before you serve it.

Add Flavor and Fun

Here's a neat trick to save the last bit of wine at the end of the bottle. Freeze it in ice cube trays, then store the cubes in a freezer bag. Use them in wine coolers and any dish that calls for wine.

Salt Shaker Shakeup

When your salt gets sticky in high humidity, keep it flowing freely by adding some raw rice to the shaker to absorb the moisture. Rice absorbs moisture very slowly under these conditions and lasts for a long time.

Two Glasses Stuck Together?

The next time you find two drinking glasses stuck together, try this: Fill the top glass with ice water and then place the bottom one in a few inches of hot tap water in the sink. It should only take a few seconds for them to come unstuck.

Loosen Up

Our little guys are great about emptying the dishwasher, but here's what we often have to do when reaching for a glass afterward—unstick them, by putting ice in the top one and setting the bottom one in a bowl of warm water. Remember high school chemistry? Heat expands. Cold contracts.

An Amicable Parting

End the tug-of-war over glasses that are stuck one inside the other. Instead, use vegetable oil as a lubricant around the attached part. Works for glass bowls as well.

Who Knew? Readers' Favorite

Make your own version of sippy cups using real glassware you already have. If your glasses are slippery, put a wide rubber band around them so children can get a better grip.

Unstick Stuck Ice Cube Trays

If your ice cube trays stick to the bottom of the shelf, try placing a piece of waxed paper underneath the tray. Freezing temperatures do not affect waxed paper.

Freezer Freeze Up

A common problem with icemakers is that they freeze up. Next time this happens, just use a blow-dryer to defrost it. (For safety's sake, keep the dryer away from any pooling water.) To prevent this problem in the first place, release a few ice cubes every few days.

Microwave Mishap

If someone accidentally turns on the microwave when it's empty, it can damage the oven. To avoid any problems, just keep a cup of water in the microwave when it is not in use.

Make Cooking with Olive Oil Easier

Olive oil is healthful as oils go, but it has a low smoke point, which means that it will break down rapidly when exposed to heat. You can increase the smoke point of olive oil by adding a small amount of canola oil, which has a very high smoke point. If your recipe calls for tablespoon of olive oil, use 2½ teaspoons olive and ½ teaspoon canola oil and sautéing will be easier.

How to Save a Burned Meal

If you accidentally scorch dinner, set the pot or dish into cold water immediately. This will stop the cooking action and minimize the damage. Carefully remove any unharmed food—don't scrape it—then discard whatever is unsalvageable. When you reheat the edible leftovers, set a fresh piece of white bread on top to remove the burnt odor. Alternatively, there's always pizza delivery!

Burned a Roast?

There are few kitchen disasters more disheartening than burning a roast. But there's help! First, remove the roast from the pan and cover it with a towel dampened with hot water for about five minutes, which will stop the cooking. Then remove or scrape off any burnt areas with a sharp knife, and put the roast back in the oven to reheat if necessary.

Ham Too Salty?

A little salt in ham is a good thing, but if your ham slices are too salty, place them in a dish of low-fat milk for 20 minutes before heating, then rinse them off in cold water and dry them with paper towels. The ham won't pick up the taste of the milk, but it will taste much less salty.

Defrost in a Flash

The best way to thaw turkey is on a shallow baking sheet in the refrigerator, in its original packaging, allowing 24 hours for every five pounds of bird. But if it's Thanksgiving morning and you've forgotten to stick the bird in the fridge, the fastest, safest method of thawing frozen poultry fast is to place it—still wrapped in plastic—in a bowl (or bucket) of cold water. Check the water regularly and change it as the water warms up—you should never use hot water, as it will promote bacterial growth.

Zap Microwave Odors

Fresh fish is a summertime treat, but fresh fish smell in your microwave is not. Get rid of fish or other microwave odors by putting a quartered lemon or a small bowl of vanilla in your microwave for a minute or two on high.

Get Rid of That Fish Smell

If you've been preparing fish and want to remove the smell from your hands, try washing them with water and a bit of toothpaste. Lemon juice and a little salt will also work well.

Stop Separation Anxiety in Gravies

Does your gravy separate? If so, simply add a pinch or two of baking soda to emulsify the fat globules in a matter of seconds.

Gravy Savers

Gravy is so delicious, yet so easy to mess up. To help prevent lumpy gravy, add a pinch of salt to the flour before using any liquid. If lumps persist, use your blender to smooth it out. If your gravy burns, just stir in a teaspoon of peanut butter to cover up the burnt flavor without altering the meaty taste.

Skimming the Fat without the Refrigerator

You can de-fat soup or gravy easily even if you don't have time to refrigerate it. Remove it from the heat for 5–10 minutes. Put four or five ice cubes in a piece of cheesecloth and swirl it around the soup or gravy. Fat is attracted to the cold, and should stick to the cheesecloth. It will also be attracted to lettuce leaves—stir a few leaves into the soup for a few minutes, and then discard them. Another method is to add a slice of fresh white bread on top of the fat for a few seconds. After the bread absorbs the fat, it should be disposed of—if you leave the bread on the soup too long, it will fall apart.

Too-Salty Solutions

If your soup or stew is too salty, use one of these methods to make it less so. If it won't affect the taste, add a can of peeled tomatoes or a small amount of brown sugar. Alternatively, stir in a slice or two of raw apple or potato, let simmer a few minutes, then discard the apple or potato.

Spicy Salves

Overspiced your dinner? Just add a bit of sugar, honey, or maple syrup. The sweet flavor allows your tastebuds to handle more hot, saving your meal.

Egg Separation Made Easy

If you don't have an egg separator, the easiest way to separate yolks from the whites is to crack them into a funnel. The whites slide out, leaving the yolk behind.

It's easy to tell whether an egg has been hard-boiled: Spin it. If it wobbles, it's raw—the yolk sloshes from one end of the egg to the other. Hard-cooked eggs spin evenly, because the yolk is held in place by the cooked egg white. Reduce your risk of spinning an egg right off the counter by adding a drop or two of food coloring to the water when you boil them. It will dye the shells so you can tell the difference between the two kinds.

Fishing Out Eggshells

If you've ever gotten eggshell in a bowl of cracked eggs and tried to fish it out with your finger, you know how hard it can be. A better tool than your finger—and even a spoon? An eggshell half that you were able to break cleanly. The edge cuts through the egg whites easier than other implements.

Don't OD on Mayo

Too much mayonnaise or salad dressing can ruin a dish. To fix the problem, try adding breadcrumbs to absorb the excess.

Unstick Your Rice

If your rice tends to stick together when you cook it, add a teaspoon of lemon juice to the water when boiling. Your sticky problem will be gone!

Rice Repair

If you burned the rice, fear not! It's white bread to the rescue. Get rid of the scorched taste by placing a slice of fresh white bread on top of the rice while it's still hot, and covering it for a few minutes.

Pizza Cutting Prescription

Pizza cutters are great—until they start to get dull. One of easiest ways to cut a pizza is to use clean scissors with long blades—you can cut from top and bottom, and then you can cut the pizza into slices quickly. Make sure the scissors are sharp and used only for food.

A Plan for Pizza-Making

Making pizzas at home is a great way to save money and get the kids involved in making dinner. But homemade pizzas often lack the crispness of pizzeria pies. Here's one tip that should help: Add the cheese before the tomato sauce. Cheese has a lower water content than tomatoes do, so the crust won't get as soggy.

Insta-Peel for Tomatoes

Need to quickly peel tomatoes for a recipe? The easiest way is to place them in a pot of boiling water for a minute. The skins will practically fall off.

Keep Tomatoes from Staining Your Plastic

Plastic containers are perfect for keeping leftovers and sauces, but tomato sauce will often stain clear plastic. To keep this from happening, simply spray the container with nonstick cooking spray before pouring in tomato-based sauces. To remove a plastic stain, cover the area with mustard and leave overnight.

Easing the Acidity of Tomatoes

Some people are unable to eat spaghetti sauces and other tomato-based foods because of their high acid content. Adding chopped carrots and cooking them with tomato dishes will reduce the acidity without affecting the taste.

No-Sugar Sweetener

Carrots are a natural sweetener. To sweeten a soup, stew, or sauce without adding sugar, stir in a small amount of pureed carrots. Use one of the sweeter carrot varieties.

For a Guacamole Emergency!

If you bought a whole bunch of avocados for your guacamole and one or two are still not ripe enough to use, try this tip—which isn't ideal, but will do the trick. Prick the skin of the unripe avocado in several places, then microwave it on high for 40–70 seconds, flipping it over halfway through. This won't ripen the avocado, but it will soften it enough that you'll be able to mash it with ripe avocados and your guests won't notice the difference.

Keep Guacamole Looking Fresh

You may look good with a tan, but your guacamole sure doesn't! To keep the avocados from oxidizing (which causes the brown color), cut them with a silver or stainless steel knife, and leave the pit in the dip (until serving). Sprinkle lemon or lime juice on the surface of the dip, and cover tightly with plastic wrap until you're ready to eat.

Sippy Cup Redux

It's a beautiful, fresh, colorful salad until—no! Stop the floodgates! Someone over-dressed it and now it's barely edible. Titrate your vinaigrette with a baby sippy cup. Mix inside the cup, shake (covering the opening), and scatter over the salad with its perfectly sized spout.

Reduce Green Odors

Kale, cabbage, and collard greens are delicious to eat, but can sometimes smell stinky when they're being prepared. Make sure not to overcook them, which will make them release more odors. Also try placing a few unshelled pecans in the saucepan while cooking to help absorb any scents.

Who Knew? Readers' Favorite

Did you know potatoes can remove some stains from your hands? Just rub raw potato slices against the stain under water.

Peeled Potato Prescription

You've managed to talk your kids into helping you with tonight's scalloped potatoes, but now the potatoes are peeled long before you need them! To keep peeled potatoes from discoloring, place them in a bowl of cold water with a few drops of white vinegar, then refrigerate. Drain before cooking and add a small amount of sugar to the cooking water to revive some of the lost flavor.

Keep Fruit Looking Fresh

Even though the taste isn't affected, it's still disappointing to unveil your fruit salad only to discover a thin layer of brown oxidation all over the fruit. A common method for keeping cut fruit looking fresh is to add a bit of lemon juice. However, an even more effective method is to fill a spray bottle with water and a few dissolved vitamin C tablets (usually available in the vitamin and nutritional supplement section of your drugstore). Spray this mixture on the cut fruit and not only will you stop the oxidation, you'll also be getting added vitamins!

The Brown Bag Trick

Fruit normally gives off ethylene gas, which hastens ripening. Some fruits give off more gas than others and ripen faster. Other fruits are picked before they are ripe and need a bit of help. If an unripe fruit is placed in a brown paper bag, the ethylene gas it gives off does not dissipate into the air but is trapped and concentrated, causing the fruit to ripen faster. To get it to ripen even more quickly, add a ripe apple—one of those ethylene-rich fruits.

Perking Up Apples

If apples are dry or bland, slice them and put them in a dish, and then pour cold apple juice over them and refrigerate for 30 minutes. OK, so it's kind of a cheat, but it will make sure picky eaters get their nutrients!

Who Knew? Readers' Favorite

Making jam? If you add a small pat of butter when cooking fruits for preserves and jellies, there will be no foam to skim off the top. The fat acts as a sealant and prevents the air from rising and accumulating on top as foam.

Apple Botox

To prevent baked apples from wrinkling, peel the top third or cut a few slits in the skin to allow for expansion.

Juice for Juice

If you've been cooking with berries and your hands are stained, try removing the berry juice stains with a bit of lemon juice.

Raisin Rejuvenation

Sad-looking raisins? To plump them up to perfection, place them a small baking dish with a little water, cover, and bake in a preheated 325°F oven for 6–8 minutes. Or, pour boiling water over the raisins and let them stand for 10–15 minutes.

Chopping Dried Fruits

Raisins and other dried fruits won't stick to your knife (or anything) if you first soak them in cold water for 10 minutes.

Who Knew? Readers' Favorite

Chopping nuts in a blender? Try adding a small amount of sugar. It will keep the nut pieces from sticking together.

Quick-Rising Solutions

It's not always a good idea to artificially quicken the amount of time it takes your bread dough to rise (the flavor of the bread may not be as complex), but if you're in a time crunch, it's always nice to have a back-up plan. To speed whole-wheat bread dough's rising time, add one tablespoon of lemon juice to the dough as you are mixing it. When it comes to other breads, a little heat does wonders when it comes to cutting down on rising time. Set the dough (either in a bowl or a loaf pan) on a heating pad set on medium, or over the pilot light on a gas stove. You can also use the microwave to help speed up the rising process by as much as one-third. Set ½ cup hot water in the back corner of the microwave. Place the dough in a well-greased microwavable bowl and cover it with plastic wrap, and then cover the plastic wrap with a damp towel. With the power level set at 10 percent, cook the dough for six minutes, and then let it rest for 4–5 minutes. Repeat the procedure if the dough has not doubled its size.

Slow Down Browning Baked Goods

If you're having a problem with bread browning too fast, set a dish of water on the oven rack just above the bread. The added humidity in the oven will slow down the browning. This will work with cakes as well.

Double-Decker

If you don't have an insulated or a thick baking sheet, there's a simple solution: Try baking the cookies on two sheets, stacked one on top of the other. It will eliminate burned bottoms caused by a too-thin pan.

Rust Remover

To treat rust on metal baking dishes and cookware, sprinkle powdered laundry detergent on the spot, then scour with the cut side of half a raw potato.

Prevent a Pudding Problem

Lay a sheet of wax paper directly onto a custard or pudding while it is still hot to keep a skin from developing.

Is Your Brown Sugar Lumpy?

Brown sugar loses moisture rather quickly and develops lumps easily. To soften hardened sugar, place the sugar in a tightly covered dish with a slice of fresh white bread or half an apple, cover the dish tightly, and heat for 15–20 seconds in the microwave. Let it stand five minutes before using. The moisture from the bread or apple will produce enough steam to soften the sugar without melting it. Store brown sugar in the freezer to keep it from getting lumpy in the first place.

Who Knew? Readers' Favorite

Keep your brown sugar soft and lump-free with this simple trick: Just throw a couple of marshmallows into the bag with it.

More Tips for Lumpy Sugar

Granulated sugar clumps less than brown sugar, but it's still easy to get lumps. Keep this from happening by sticking a few salt-free crackers in the canister to absorb the moisture; replace the crackers every week.

Soften Hardened Marshmallows

If you find an old bag of marshmallows that have hardened, add a slice of very fresh white bread or half an apple to the bag to soften them. Unfortunately, it's not a quick fix: you might need to leave the bag for one or two days until the marshmallows absorb the moisture.

When Movie Night Goes Wrong

If you've ever burned popcorn in your microwave, you know that it stinks, and the smell likes to permeate the entire household. Make it smell fresh again by stuffing the microwave with crumpled newspaper for a few hours (but don't turn on the microwave!). Remove the paper, and boil water and baking soda in a glass bowl for five minutes, and the smell should be gone.

Who Knew? Readers' Favorite

Are your popcorn kernels too pooped to pop? It's probably because they have lost too much moisture, but they can be revived. Soak the kernels in water for five minutes, then dry them off and try again.

Perfectly Popped Popcorn

This simple trick will make sure almost every single kernel pops when you're making popcorn—and who doesn't want more popcorn? Just store your unpopped popcorn kenernels in the freezer, and pop them when they're still cold. (Unfortunately, this won't work for microwave popcorn.)

Perfectly Popped...Nuts?

Toasted nuts are often an essential (and delicious) part of recipes. Want to know how to make sure your nuts won't burn, even if you aren't looking at them? Toast them in a popcorn air popper! Just add ¼ cup nuts, plug it in for 60 seconds, and your nuts will be a perfect golden brown.

Simple Spout

It's silly to buy a spout for oil when you have one practically built in! When you first purchase a bottle of oil, poke a small hole in the protective seal with a chopstick or paring knife. Keep it stored with the cap on.

Cut Down on Paper Towels

When preparing a recipe that requires you to dry something you've just cooked on several layers of paper towels to absorb the grease, use this trick. Lay down several sheets of old newspaper, then place a single layer of paper towels on top.

Rolling Pin Replacement

If you don't have a rolling pin on hand, reach for a zucchini. The dough won't stick, and it's not as unseemly as using a shampoo bottle.

Keep Your Eye on the Recipe

In our house, recipe cards are always sliding under permission slips, falling into the sink, or just plain vanishing. A new trick we learned: Use a fork in a medium-sized glass as a recipe card stand. The card goes between the tines, and the recipe will be easy to see when you need it.

Thawing Cheesecakes

One of our kid's groups sells frozen cheesecakes as a fundraiser, so we always end up with several cheesecakes in our freezer each year! If you're eating a frozen cheesecake, thaw it in the refrigerator instead of at room temperature—we've found they end up much creamier this way, even though it might take a little longer.

Picture Perfect Pasta

If you still have old 35mm film canisters hanging around your house, use them in the kitchen! These canisters are ideal measuring tools for pasta: fill one with uncooked spaghetti to measure out the proper amount to make. One canister of spaghetti will feed two people.

The problem: You love store-bought butter spreads, but you know the trans fats inside aren't good for you. The solution? Make your own at home! Just combine a stick of butter and ¼ cup canola oil with a hand mixer. It will be soft and easy to spread!

Lightning Grease Remover

If you're cooking at the stove and grease splatters onto your clothes, think fast. Grab some baking soda from the cupboard and rub it into the spot to absorb as much grease as possible. This will make it more difficult for the stain to set, and it will soak up most of the grease before it works its way into the fibers of your clothes.

Just Cool It!

Make sure you let your pots and pans cool before you wash them. Drastic changes in temperature can cause them to warp, meaning they won't heat evenly and will be harder to cook with.

Supercharge Your Dishwasher

Keep a spray bottle filled with water and a bit of dishwashing detergent near your dishwasher. If a dish is heavily soiled, spray it down before you put it inside. The detergent gets working on the food immediately, so you won't have to rinse your dishes before putting them inside, or run a separate "rinse" cycle before you do your dishes.

Doing Dishes?

Sprinkle a little baby powder onto your hands before placing them inside rubber gloves. They'll come off more easily, and your hands won't get that clammy feeling from too much sweat while you're doing the dishes.

Cook Your Dishes Clean

Here's a terrific way to make your post-dinner clean up a breeze: Remove cooked-on food from pots and pans effortlessly by filling them with water, adding a tea bag, and simmering. The tea's acid will break up food.

Great Grater Cleaning Tip

What's the easiest way to clean a messy cheese grater? Reach for a lemon! Just rub the pulp-side of a cut lemon across a grater and it will clean off any stuck-on cheese.

Who Knew? Readers' Favorite

Where do you keep your scouring pads? Believe or not, we keep them in a plastic bag in our freezer. That way, we don't have to worry about them rusting, and they'll last a lot longer.

Make Your Own Bowl Scraper

Have you ever seen those bowl scrapers in kitchen stores that sell for $3 to $10? These circular, plastic tools are easy to make at home. Simply take the lid of a round take-out container, cut it in half, then remove the rim. Instant savings!

Cheap Clips

Instead of buying those clips for fastening cereal and chip bags, simply buy a box of large binder clips from an office supply store. They're the exact same thing at less than half the cost.

The Ice Trick

When you go away on vacation, fill a sealable plastic bag with a few ice cubes and put it in the freezer. If a power failure occurs while you are away, the ice will melt and refreeze in a solid block, alerting you that your frozen food has been defrosted.

For a No-Scratch Stack

Stacking fine china? Insert paper plates between the real plates before stacking to prevent scratches. You can use the same trick for stacking nonstick pans.

Who Knew? Readers' Favorite

When you're preparing a big meal and need more counter space, try this clever quick fix: Simply open a drawer in your kitchen and cover it with a heavy-duty cutting board. Voilà!

CHAPTER 10

Secrets of the Supermarket

The Gift of Groceries

Need a little help budgeting your trips to the supermarket? Many chains now offer prepaid gift cards. Buy one for yourself and think of it as a portable checking account that you "withdraw" from it every time you shop. With a dedicated grocery "account," you'll find it's easier to keep a tighter rein on your spending.

Work for It!

If you have a few spare hours each week, you can get huge savings on your groceries by joining a food co-op. Co-ops are run completely by neighborhood volunteers, and in turn offer gigantic discounts to their members. Most co-ops allow you to choose what job you do (stocking, cash register, billing, cleaning, etc.), and many allow you to work a different number of hours depending on what job you do (the person cleaning up for the butcher will work fewer hours than someone doing paperwork, for instance). To find out if there is a co-op in your area, visit CoopDirectory.org/directory.htm.

For the Freshest Food Around

Have you ever heard of community-supported agriculture? Known as CSAs, they connect local farmers with their communities by offering people a "share" in the farm. You sign up for shares, then each week during the farming season you receive a box of seasonal produce—and sometimes even staples like milk and eggs. The downside is that you usually don't have much choice in what you're getting. But if you like to buy locally grown foods, the prices can't be beat. To find out if there is a CSA program near you, visit LocalHarvest.org.

Meet You at the Meat Locker

If you live in the Midwest, you are lucky to have access to the best meat in the country. You are also lucky to be able to purchase meat from the farmers themselves, in the form of stores called meat lockers. At your local meat locker, you can buy large packages of meat cut into different portions—for instance, one package may include skirt steaks, rib eyes, half a dozen ground patties, pork chops, spare ribs, and more. Packages usually come out to $1.50–$2.00 per pound, which can be a substantial savings when you're getting choice cuts of meat. If you don't have the room to store so much meaty goodness, split it with a friend!

Go Native

Especially in cities, stores by and for immigrants abound. Whether it's a Mexican, Indian, Ethiopian, Chinese, or Korean grocery, you'll find cheap deals on foods that are native to that country. Bulk spices can be especially cheap, and you'll also find items such as inexpensive tortillas and avocados. We never buy rice unless it's from an ethnic market, as it's usually up to 80 percent cheaper than buying it at the grocery store.

Who Knew? Readers' Favorite

Many dollar stores have more than just easy decorations, cheap toys, and fake flowers—they have food! Make sure to check the prices for canned goods and other staples in your neighborhood dollar store. You may be surprised at the deals you find.

Come for the Cough Syrup, Stay for the Soup

You may not think of CVS, Walgreens, and other drugstores as good places to buy food, but many of them carry weekly specials on staples and snacks such as soup, spaghetti sauce, and soda. It's worth it to take a walk down their food aisle while you're in the store, and always check the circular to see if anything you use is on special.

New Stores Spell Savings

Whenever a new grocery store opens up in our area, we always stop by to take a look. It may be a pain to navigate differently laid-out aisles, but new supermarkets always offer big sales and the lowest prices possible in their first few weeks and months of business as an incentive to get customers to switch stores. Many stores also offer contests and giveaways to celebrate their grand opening, so plan a visit during that first week.

Leaner Isn't Always Better

Even if you want to prepare low-fat meals, you don't always have to buy the leanest (and most expensive) ground beef. If you're preparing hamburgers on a grill or on a broiler rack, most of the fat will be lost during the cooking process, so stick with the less-lean (and more affordable) varieties.

Memorize This Meat Chart

You're at the supermarket, and both boneless chicken breasts and whole chickens are on sale! The whole chicken seems cheaper, but it also has skin, bones, and other parts you don't want to eat...so how do you know which to buy? Use the list below to see how many servings are in each cut of meat, and then figure out your unit price from there. The column on the left indicates the type of meat and the cut, and the column on the right indicates the number of servings per pound.

MEAT	SERVINGS PER POUND	MEAT	SERVINGS PER POUND
Chuck roast	2.5	Chicken, Leg quarters	2
Cubed steak	4	Chicken, Whole	2
Ground beef	4	Fish, Dressed, (scales head, and tail removed)	2
Rump roast	3		
Strip steak	2	Fish, Fillets	2
T-bone steak	2	Steaks, Whole (bone-in)	2.5
Top loin steak	3	Bacon	6
Chicken, Boneless breasts	4	Pork, Boneless top loin	3
Chicken, Boneless thighs	3	Ham	5
Chicken, Bone-in breasts	2.5	Pork chops	3
Chicken, Bone-in thighs	2.5	Pork roast	2

MEAT	SERVINGS PER POUND	MEAT	SERVINGS PER POUND
Sausage	4	Turkey, Legs	2
Turkey, Bone-in breasts	3	Turkey, Whole	2.5
Turkey, Ground	4		

Freezer Patties

Never buy meat that's already been shaped into patties (unless it's on sale). Instead, buy your own, and shape it into patties yourself. Place a sheet of waxed paper between each, then place the entire stack in a resealable plastic bag in the freezer.

Market Watch

Supermarkets have started using their own wording on meat packages to make you think the meat you are buying is a better grade than it really is. Most of the major chains are buying more select-grade beef, but may call it by any number of fancy names such as "top premium beef," "prime quality cut," "select choice," "market choice," or "premium cut." Be aware that these titles don't actually mean anything!

More Meat Tips

Grocery stores make a lot of money on meat, so it's not surprising that they display the priciest cuts in the case! Get dramatic savings by asking the butcher to slice different cuts for you from the same primal (or section) of the cow or pig. These cuts can be as little as one-fifth the cost of the expensive, pre-packaged cuts, and they'll be just as tender and tasty. Here's what to ask for.

- ✦ If you're looking for rib eye steak, request chuck eye. You may need to ask the butcher to cut a 4-inch roast off the front of the boneless chuck, then to peel out the chuck eye and cut it into steaks.

- ✦ Instead of pork tenderloin, buy an entire loin roast and ask the butcher to cut it up for you.

- ✦ When cross rib roasts are on sale (which is usually quite often), ask your butcher to carve a flatiron roast for you from the cross rib, and ask him to cut it into boneless ribs. Don't be put off by this unattractive cut—that seam of what looks like gristle down the middle is actually a gelatin that will cook off. Meanwhile, these ribs will cut up just as well as short ribs, and they're boneless, so you'll get more for your money.

- ✦ Instead of buying ground beef, ask the butcher to grind up a bottom round roast for you.

- ✦ If you like Italian sausages, try asking for ground pork shoulder butt. It's also a great substitute for ground beef.

- ✦ Whenever you see cut-up beef for stir-fries or stroganoff, know that you're not getting the most for your money. Simply buy a rump roast and slice it (or ask the butcher to do it for you).

Get a Knife and Go For It!

Meat is expensive enough, but a big part of the cost is the price you're paying the butcher to cut it up for you. Buy the largest cuts of meat you can, then cut it up, wrap in foil, and put it in a plastic bag in your freezer. Here are some more tips for butchering meat.

✦ Many stores will butcher big cuts of meat for you for free, so ask before doing it yourself!

✦ Use the sharpest knife you have, and never use a serrated knife, which will shred the meat.

✦ If you're working with a cut of beef or pork with a bone in it, the first thing you will need to do is remove the bone. Using a filet knife, cut along the bone until the meat is loosened and you can pull it away.

✦ With a cut of beef like a sirloin tip, you can just cut it into portions that are the correct size for what you'd like to use them for. Start with the thickest portion and slice along the grain (muscle strands that all run in the same direction).

✦ Once you cook and eat a pork shoulder, you'll be so hooked you'll wonder why you never bought a huge slab of pig before. These may be hard to find at your local supermarket, but try requesting one at the butcher counter or checking at a local ethnic store. Marinate the pork shoulder overnight in your favorite seasonings, and cook on 400°F for a half hour, then on a very low temperature (around 250°F) for about five hours. The meat will come right off the bone, and it will be so juicy and tender everyone will want to know your secret.

✦ To cut up a chicken, turkey, or duck, first remove the legs, then separate the drumstick from the thigh by placing it skin-side-down on your cutting board and slicing right through the joint with a sharp knife (you should be able to feel where the knife will slide through). Place the bird on its back, then cut off the wings. Turn the remaining meat on its side and cut through the cavity of the bird starting from the tail end. Cut parallel to the backbone and slice the bones of the rib cage. Repeat on the opposite side of the backbone. Now all that's left is removing the breast from the backbone. Slice the breast in half if desired.

✦ To fillet a whole fish, make a vertical cut just behind the head and a horizontal cut on the top of the fish from the head to the tail. Use a metal spatula to lift out the fillet, running it over the bones from head to tail. Repeat on the other side of the fish.

✦ For illustrated instructions on how to cut any piece of meat, type the word "butchering" along with the type of meat into a search engine online. There are many tutorials (some including video) online.

Get It While It's Hot!

While perusing the cereal aisle, you'll quickly realize that hot cereals are cheaper than cold ones. Though they may not be as popular with your family, try saving money by making hot cereal at least once a week. It's often more nutritious, so it's worth it to make the switch.

Break Free From Brands

When you've been buying the same brand for as long as you can remember, it's hard to make the switch to generics. However, you'll be surprised when you find many generic and store-brand products taste exactly the same (or better!) for less than half the cost.

✦ Always buy generic baking ingredients such as flour, oil, and sugar. These generics are indistinguishable from their more-expensive counterparts. Frozen and canned vegetables are also usually exactly the same.

✦ As for products such as cereals, cookies, and crackers, basic is better—we've had good luck with plain granola, potato chips, and wheat crackers.

✦ No matter what the product, it never hurts to try. If you end up having to throw away one can of soup, you've wasted a dollar or two, but if you like it, you can save a lot over the course of a year.

✦ Save the boxes from name-brand products your kids are attached to, then empty the generic products into them. Your picky eaters won't know the difference if they can't see it on the outside.

Never Pay a Dollar For a Lemon Again

It may be a pain, but the best way to save on groceries is to shop at more than one market. You'll soon find that one store will have cheaper produce, one will have cheaper meat, and so forth. Explore grocery stores you've never shopped at— perhaps one that is closer to your workplace or gym rather than by your home—and you may find even lower prices. We've even found cheaper products at stores that are the same chain, just a different location. Write down the prices of your most frequently purchased items, or bring a receipt from an average grocery trip with you. That way you can be sure to remember where the prices are the most reasonable.

Shop Smart at the Grocery Store

Shop later in the day to take advantage of markdowns in your grocery store's bakery and meat departments. Also make sure to keep an eye on the prices at the salad bar. If you only need a few artichoke hearts or croutons, they may be cheaper to buy there by the pound than elsewhere in the store.

Know Your Store Brands

What is the name of the store brand at your local grocery store? What about at the store the next town over? Many stores have names for generic brands, like "White Rose, " "Equate," or "Kirkland," so make sure you're aware of what they are so you can keep an eye out for savings.

Buy Dry Beans

If you can help it, never buy beans, peas, or lentils in cans, unless they're significantly marked down. These items are much more cost-effective if you purchase them dry. You'll have to plan ahead in order to soak them overnight, but once you get used to this extra step, it will seem routine.

Who Knew? Readers' Favorite

Never, ever let us catch you buying sundae toppings in the ice cream aisle! These nuts and mini candies are up to 50 percent cheaper in the baking aisle, which often even has sprinkles, too. Melt some chocolate chips in a double boiler, then let them cool a bit, and add to the top of ice cream for your own "instant shell."

Mix It Yourself

Frozen, concentrated juice is almost always less expensive per glass than juice you buy in a bottle. Find a brand that says "100% juice" and mix with a pitcher of water for savings.

Weighing In

If you're buying produce that is priced by the item rather than by the pound (such as a head of lettuce, lemons, or avocados), take advantage of the store's scales and weigh the item to find the heaviest. This way, you'll be sure you're getting the most for your money.

Go for the Heavyweight

When considering prices of pre-packaged produce at the supermarket, weigh them first to make sure you're getting the best deal. I've found that bags of things like carrots, apples, and potatoes are often heavier than their package specifies.

—*Karen Hall, Lexington Park, MD*

Shake It Up

Supermarkets are continually misting their produce with water. That's because this keeps it fresher and makes it look more appealing to customers. Make sure you're not paying for all this moisture, however! When buying fruits and vegetables by the pound, give herbs, leafy greens, and other produce a good shake before you bag it.

The Lifespan of Your Produce

Tomatoes are on sale, and they'd be great to use in that fresh salsa you want to make for next week's picnic. But will they still be good? The handy list will give you a rough timeline of how long your ripe fruits and veggies will last once you get them home from the market.

UP TO THREE TO FOUR DAYS

Apricots

Artichokes

Asparagus

Avocados

Bananas

Cherries

Corn

Cucumbers

Eggplants

Grapes

Greens (lettuce, spinach, chard, etc.)

Mushrooms

Pineapples

Strawberries

String beans

Summer squash

Watercress

ONE WEEK OR LESS

Blueberries

Broccoli

Brussels sprouts

Cauliflower

Cranberries

Grapefruit

Leeks

Lemons

Limes

Oranges

Peaches

Pears

Peppers

Plums

Tomatoes

Watermelons

Apples   Garlic

Beets   Onions

Cabbage   Potatoes

Carrots   Winter squash

Celery

Snack Assembly

It's easy to turn bulk foods into convenience foods, ensuring that you don't get frustrated and start buying those always-expensive prepackaged snacks. Invest in a big box of sandwich bags and spend some time at the beginning of the week filling them with carrot sticks, strips of mozzarella cheese (which is the same thing as string cheese), or granola. It's also easy to make trail mix by purchasing nuts, seeds, and dried fruits and combining them.

Don't Fall for This Trick

Did you know that when an item is on sale, most customers are 14 times more likely to buy items that complement it at full price? Make sure you're not falling into this trap—the next time peanut butter is on sale, don't buy jelly; when laundry detergent is on sale, don't buy fabric softener; and when strawberries are on sale, don't buy those delicious sponge cakes! You get the picture.

Beware of Sneaky Supermarkets!

It's important to know that not all products are cheaper when you buy bigger sizes. Make sure to compare unit prices carefully at the store, because we have found that some items—like cereal and prepared frozen foods like french fries—are less expensive in smaller sizes. This is probably because the store knows these items are more likely to be purchased in bulk.

Who Knew? Readers' Favorite

If you love instant soups in single-serving sizes, it's easy to make your own at home rather than buying the more expensive versions in the store. First, purchase disposable, microwaveable cups made for hot beverages (if they have lids, all the better). After making your favorite soup, pour into the cups and cover with foil or plastic wrap if you don't have lids. Then when it's time for lunch, simply take out a cup and stick it in the microwave (of course, removing the foil first if you used it!).

Buy the Giant Juice

If you've been paying attention to prices at all, you know that buying a big jug of juice or soda is five or even ten times cheaper than buying one-serving bottles. When packing school lunches, use a thermos or reusable bottle instead of juice boxes or bottles. Make sure to have several, in case your child leaves one at school or you don't have time to wash it every evening. And if you simply can't work reusable bottles into your routine, consider buying empty bottles in bulk. The website Bottles.us sells plastic water bottles for about 50¢ per bottle, and while filling them and letting your child recycle them at school won't save as much as a thermos would, it's still much cheaper than buying Snapple from a vending machine.

Low-Cost Take-Out

If you're considering take-out for dinner, think first of your grocery store. Supermarkets often offer pre-made foods at a low cost to attract shoppers; you'll often find good prices on rotisserie chickens, french fries, coleslaw, pasta salad, and more. Just make sure you don't make any impulse purchases once you're in the store!

Can It

Save at the store by going canned—all recipes except for salads can be made with canned vegetables instead of the fresh ones. As long as you check the ingredients to make sure sugar hasn't been added, any vegetable in a can will taste nearly indistinguishable from a fresh one you cooked yourself, especially if it's going into sauces or casseroles.

Convenience Is Key

Remember the cardinal rule when it comes to saving money on food: If it's "convenient," it's probably costly. For example, pickles cut flat for sandwiches, juice in single-serving bottles, pre-shredded cheese, and "baby" carrots. Think carefully about what you're buying and if the convenience is worth it!

Sugar, Sugar

Don't buy colored sugar for your baking projects! Instead, buy a big bag of regular granulated sugar and add coloring at home. Just put the sugar in a resealable plastic bag and add a few drops of food coloring. Shake up the bag until the color is distributed, and add more food coloring if necessary. You'll get the exact same result at a small fraction of the cost.

Head to the Baking Aisle

Buying toppings for Sundae night? Stay away from the dessert aisle for your nuts, candy, and other toppings. These toppings can be found for much less in the baking aisle, and all you'll have to do is a little chopping. Also don't forget that a banana makes a cheap, delicious, and nutritious topping for ice cream!

Stick to the List

To make sure we don't impulse purchase things that aren't on our grocery list, we keep it right in front of us: taped to the cart! Slip a tape dispenser into your purse so you have tape handy. You'll not only make sure you stick to your list, you'll be much less likely to lose it midway down the aisle.

Deli Discount

Ask the folks at the deli counter if there's a discount for "bulk ends." These end bits are too small to slice in the machine, but can be sliced or cubed at home. They're often offered at half off!

Any Day's a Holiday

After major holidays, go to your grocery store and grab bargains on things like turkey, stuffing, canned pumpkin, and baking supplies. Then freeze the turkey and store the rest. When you're craving holiday food, you'll have a bunch already in your cabinet, all bought at a bargain price.

Who Knew? Readers' Favorite

Does your coffeemaker require cone-shaped filters? Save some cash by purchasing the less expensive round filters in bulk. You can buy a 500-pack for cheap, then shape the filters into cones so they fit your machine. With a few simple folds, they work just as well as the pricier alternatives.

Traveling with Food

When transporting perishable food from the supermarket, don't put it in the trunk. Always put it in an ice-filled cooler inside the air-conditioned car. If possible, you shouldn't leave food in a cooler for longer than an hour.

PART TWO

ALL AROUND THE HOUSE AND GARDEN: Cleaning and Organizing Room by Room

Saving money starts at home, and the tips in this section will give you simple ways to make your money go further both inside and outside your home. As you move from room to room, you'll discover how to affordably clean your home using all-natural, homemade cleaners; get rid of any kind of stain on the planet; organize like a whiz; keep your car at its best; and perform simple household repairs. You'll be amazed by some of our surprising solutions for your most stubborn problems.

CHAPTER 1

Your Living Room

Minimize Broom-Swept Dust

The trail of dust that your broom leaves behind can be eliminated: Just fill a spray bottle with three parts water and one part liquid fabric softener, and spray the broom before sweeping. The spritz makes the broom strands more pliable and helps it collect dirt more efficiently.

Quick Dusting

Instead of using a rag, wear a pair of old socks on your hands when dusting. It's efficient (you're using both hands), cheap (remember, these are old socks), and you can reuse them.

Get a Lampshade Dust Free

The trick to cleaning a pleated lampshade is to find the right tool. Stroke each pleat from top to bottom with a dry, clean paintbrush. Or use a rolling lint remover for a quicker clean.

Forget that Pricey Dustcloth

Don't bother buying fancy dustcloths that are treated to attract dust. Instead, simply sprinkle a piece of cheesecloth with a few drops of lemon oil. Let the cheesecloth air dry, and it will be just as effective as an expensive cloth.

A DIY Duster for Hard-to-Reach Spots

Wrap a paper towel around the broad end of a kitchen spatula and secure with a rubber band. Use this to reach dust trapped between radiator coils. Spray the paper towel with all-purpose cleaner to get rid of sticky spills and stains.

Another great use for a used fabric softener sheet? Run it across the TV screen. It will not only clean off the dust, but also eliminate static cling.

For a Shiny Chandelier

There's no need to buy special chandelier cleaners. When it's time to tackle this difficult job, use a cloth dripping with a solution of two parts rubbing alcohol and one part hot water. Just slop it on, and be sure to hang an umbrella upside down from the chandelier to catch the mess.

Got Old, Smelly Books?

If your books stink, try this tactic for wiping out mildew. Dust mildewed pages with corn flour, French chalk, or talcum powder. Leave it inside the closed book for several days, then brush it off.

Out of Furniture Polish? Check the Pantry!

Vegetable oil works wonderfully on wood furniture. A very light coat will nourish the wood and help protect the finish, but be sure to rub it in well so it doesn't leave a residue. Leftover brewed tea (at room temperature) can also be used on wood furniture.

Keep Wood Wonderful

Preserve the beauty of wood by rubbing the surface with boiled linseed oil. Wipe away the excess with a soft cloth.

Prevent Sun Stroke on Wood Furniture

Don't keep your good wood furniture in direct sunlight, especially during the hot summer. It damages the finish and can bleach the wood.

Who Knew? Readers' Favorite

Stale beer is a great cleanser for wooden furniture. Dampen a soft, clean cloth, wipe it on, and follow by wiping with a dry cloth.

Prevent Polish Buildup

Excess polish can build up and leave a dull finish on wooden furniture. To remove it, mix together 2 tablespoons white vinegar and 2 tablespoons water. Apply to the surface and wipe off at once. Alternatively, cornstarch will also do the trick: Sprinkle a little on the furniture and polish with a soft cloth.

Mask Scratches in Wood Furniture

If you notice a scratch, try this crafty (and delicious!) solution. Find a nut that matches the color of the wood; the most common types for this purpose are pecans, walnuts, and hazelnuts. Rub the scratched area gently with the broken edges of the nuts—using the insides, not the shells. When you're all done, enjoy a snack break.

Coffee Stains to the Rescue

Cover up scratches in wood furniture or floors with coffee! Just brew a very strong pot, and then use a cotton ball or rag to apply the coffee over the scratch. It works as a stain, and the scratch will blend in with the floor in no time!

Another Prescription for Scratches

Repair scratches in your wood furniture with shoe polish. A crayon also works. Just find a color that's a close match to the wood, then rub the crayon or polish into the scratch. Wipe off any excess wax with a credit card edge, then buff with a cotton cloth.

Who Knew? Readers' Favorite

You've probably seen those little cushions with the sticky material on the back that can be placed on the bottom of furniture legs or the backs of picture frames to keep them from scratching floors and walls. Rather than spending the money for these expensive items, buy cushions for corns and bunions instead! As long as they aren't medicated, they're the exact same thing, and usually much cheaper.

Say "Vamoose" to Water Stains on Wood

Does your wood furniture have white rings left from wet glasses? Remove them with a mixture of 2 tablespoons corn oil and enough salt to make a paste. Apply the paste to the rings and let stand for at least one hour before rubbing the area gently. If the finish on your furniture is very delicate, you can substitute baking soda for the salt (it's less abrasive). If neither of those mixtures works, give mayonnaise a shot: Rub a tiny bit (½ teaspoon) on the ring with a paper towel and let it sit overnight. In the morning, just wipe with a damp cloth and the ring should be gone! Cover with furniture polish to get the shine back.

Slipcover Secret

When washing a slipcover for a couch or chair, you should put it back on your furniture while the cover is still damp. Not only will the slipcover be easier to get on, but it won't need to be ironed. It will help keep it from shrinking, too!

A Clean Home for Your Fish

The easiest way to clean a fish bowl is to wipe the inside with a cloth soaked in white vinegar, which will help remove mineral deposits. Just make sure you rinse the bowl thoroughly before putting your fish back in.

Cure for Cat Clawing

Here's something you probably didn't know: Cats hate hot sauce. So if you can't get your cat to stop clawing at your woodwork, just rub in a little hot sauce, buff it thoroughly, and your cat will stay clear.

Easily Clean Up Pet Hair

Pet hair all over the house? The easiest way to clean it up is to rub the furniture, carpet, or any other shedding victim (including the pet himself!) with a fresh dryer sheet.

Sponge Solution

If you don't have a lint roller and just realized your couch is absolutely covered in pet hair, use a clean, dry kitchen sponge instead. Just run it slowly across the couch and the fur will cling to it!

Who Knew? Readers' Favorite

The easiest way to keep your dog or cat off of your good furniture when you're out is to place a piece of aluminum foil on it. They hate the feeling under their paws and will stay away.

Another Quick Pet Hair Remover

Uh-oh, guests are on their way and you've just realized that your beloved cat has made a cat-fur nest all over your couch. For a quick and easy way to remove pet hair from furniture, turn to your rubber dishwashing gloves. Just slip them on, then rub the offending furniture with them. The hair will stick to the gloves and you can quickly throw it away.

Sponge Bath for Soot Marks

If your beautiful candle is staining your walls with black soot marks, don't try to scrub them away—that'll only make more of a mess. Instead, remove those unsightly spots by sponging them with rubbing alcohol.

Homemade Air Fresheners

You don't have to spend hard-earned cash to keep your house smelling nice. Freshen it up with these crafty odor-fighting tricks.

- ✦ Make a great homemade air freshener with an orange: Just cut the orange in half, remove the pulp, and fill with salt. It's effective, easy—and cheap!

- ✦ If you're not a great baker, but love the smell of fresh baked goods, try this trick: Dab a few drops of vanilla extract on a cool light bulb, then turn it on. When it heats up, the smell will fill the room.

- ✦ To keep the house smelling fresh during the dog days of summer, tape fabric softener sheets onto your air conditioner filter under the grate. Not only will they exude a lovely smell, but they'll also make the filter last longer.

Refresh Potpourri

If your favorite potpourri loses its scent, it's easy to revive—with vodka. Just pour a little vodka into a spray bottle and spritz the potpourri, mixing it up so each piece is saturated.

Stop Smoky Smells

Did you know that a bowl of sliced apples will remove the smell of cigarette smoke in an enclosed space? The next time you have a smoky party, cut up some apples and leave them around the house before you go to bed.

Vacuum Off Odors

To rid your house of pet, cooking, or other smells, add a cotton ball soaked in vanilla or lavender oil to your vacuum cleaner bag, and vacuum away. It's a great way to rid your home of an offensive odor by creating a nice scent instead.

Who Knew? Readers' Favorite

Water can collect in umbrella stands. Prevent this by cutting a large sponge to fit in the bottom. Remove it and wring it out as necessary.

Clean Up Sooty Bricks with Cola

Try an old masonry trick to brighten up soot-stained brick. Mix a can of cola with 3½ fluid ounces all-purpose household cleaner and 7 pints water in a bucket. Sponge onto sooty bricks and leave for 15 minutes. Loosen the soot by scrubbing with a stiff-bristled brush. Sponge with clean water. For a stronger solution, add more cola.

Candle Scandal

Removing candle wax from your wood floors is easy if you soften the wax first with a blow dryer, then peel off. Wipe any excess with a paper towel, and then clean with a mixture of half white vinegar and half water.

Candle Cleaning

If you have some beautiful candles that have begun to get dusty, cleaning them is easy. Just ball up some old pantyhose and rub them down. Its microfiber is perfect for picking up the dirt without harming your candle.

Drop a Glass? Sacrifice a Sandwich.

If your post-party cleanup involves collecting the shattered remains of Champagne glasses—or if you've merely dropped a glass on the floor—try out this crafty tip. Dampen a piece of white bread, and dab it on the glass fragments. It's much more effective than using a broom.

Get Gleaming Wood Floors

There's no need to buy a special cleaner for your wood floors. Simply mix equal parts vegetable oil and white vinegar in a spray bottle, and apply. Then shine with a clean cloth until the solution is gone.

A Recipe for Clean Wood

Save money on wood cleaners by making your own at home. It's simple: Just combine the juice of one lemon with 2 cups vegetable or olive oil. Use it just like you would use a store-bought cleaner!

Patch Up Carpet Burns

Here's how to eliminate cigarette burns in your carpet: First, cut away the burn mark. Then, cut a bit of carpet from an area that's covered by a piece of furniture (e.g., under a couch), and glue it carefully over the burnt spot. Finally, smack the person who dropped the ashes.

Salt Does the Trick on Carpet Stains

If you spill red wine or anything else with a bright pigment on your carpet, pour salt on the area as soon as possible and watch it absorb the wine almost instantly. Wait until it dries, then vacuum it up. Salt tends to provide a special capillary attraction that will work for most liquids. Baking soda, with its high sodium content, works with wine, too. Salt also works on mud stains.

Remove Pen Marks from Leather

If your kid has decided to write a novel on your favorite leather chair, don't panic. Just blot the stain with milk until the ink disappears, then wipe it clean with a damp sponge. You can also try using egg whites.

Crayon Cleanup

Have your little Picassos taken to the walls with their crayon masterpieces? Don't fret! A great way to clean off the Crayola is by using a car paste wax: Apply it to the affected area, let it sink in and soften the crayon, then buff it off. Wipe the wall with an all-purpose cleaner and it'll look like new. If you child has drawn on your furniture with crayon, run the warm air from a hair dryer over the marks. The heat will melt the waxy marks a bit, making them easy to remove.

Spruce Up Satin and Gloss Finishes

Clean painted walls with a solution made of 4 fluid ounces white vinegar, 1 ounce washing soda, and 1 pint water. Or mix 7 ounces ammonia, 1 teaspoon dish soap, and 7 pints water.

Breathe Easy

Purify the air without an air filter by buying potted plants that naturally clean your air. Some good choices are rubber trees, corn plants, bamboo palm, ficus, mums, gerbera daisies, English ivy, peace lily, and philodendrons.

There Really Is a Use for Dryer Lint!

Use dryer lint to prevent dirt from falling out of your potted houseplants when you water them: Place some dryer lint in the pots so it covers the holes. The water will drain out, but the dirt will stay in!

Shinier, Prettier Plants

If your houseplants are dusty, gently wipe the leaves with a soft cloth and a damp sponge. If you want your plants' leaves to really shine, rub them (gently!) with a cotton ball dipped in either mayonnaise, diluted mineral oil, or a solution of half baking soda and half water. Wipe off any excess with a soft cloth.

Got Stale Milk? Use It!

Stale milk will do a great job of cleaning plant leaves. The protein in milk called "casein" has a mild cleansing effect on the plant cell walls.

Clay Flowerpot Caveat

Never place a clay pot on wooden furniture, unless you use a coaster. Clay is porous, so water will seep through and possibly damage the wood finish.

Protect Your Soil (and Your Shirt!)

To keep mud from spattering when you water plants in window boxes, top the soil with a half-inch layer of gravel. Do the same for outdoor plants to prevent mud bombs during heavy rainfalls.

Window Washing 101

If the sun is shining on your windows, wait until they are in the shade to wash them. When they dry too fast, they tend to streak.

What Works on Your Windshield, Works on Your Windows

For light window cleaning, pick up a gallon of windshield washer fluid for less than a dollar. Although it's not as pungent as Windex, it'll spiff up spotty glass for less money.

Grease Up Your Windows

Don't pull a muscle trying to shove open a stuck window. Windows will open and close more easily if you occasionally rub a bar of soap across the track.

Dusting Your Blinds

Is there any chore more annoying than dusting your Venetian blinds? Luckily, you don't have to buy one of those "blinds cleaners" found in stores. Instead, use bread crusts. Just hold a piece of crust around each slat, then run it along the length of the blinds. An old paintbrush will also do the trick, or use the brush attachment on your vacuum cleaner.

Don't Let Dust Find Your Blinds

Dusting the blinds is always a pain, so after you're done make sure you won't have to do it for a while: Spray Static Guard (usually used for clothing) onto your blinds to repel dust!

Quickly Clean Mini-Blinds

Give mini blinds a good clean by simply throwing them in a bathtub filled with water and white vinegar, or your favorite cleanser. Just give them a good shake, and hang them up wet. There may be a few streaks once they've air-dried, but they're nearly impossible to spot.

Cleaning Aluminum Blinds

Aluminum blinds are great for keeping out light, but they can be hard to clean! The easiest way to clean smudges is with a pencil eraser. Dust will come off with a few swipes of a fabric softener sheet.

For Cleaner Shades

Stubborn smudges and stains on your window shades? Lay the shades on a table or countertop and rub the spots with an art-gum eraser (which can be found at art- or office-supply stores). It will take the smudges away!

If it feels like the minute you're done dusting your glass or coffee tables you have a layer of dust covering them again, use fabric softener for a different purpose. Mix a few teaspoons in a spray bottle of water and wipe the glass surface with it. Buff with soft, dry towel, and it will keep dust away.

Clean Those Piano Keys

Don't get upset if you find your toddler wiping the piano keys with mayonnaise. It's actually a great, gentle way to get them clean. (Just make sure she doesn't move on to the sofa!)

Diaper Wipe Double-Duty

For an effective alternative to wood cleaners and polishes, use baby wipes to whip your wood furniture and paneling into shape.

No Need for Febreze

Sprinkle rugs, the couch, and upholstered chairs with baking soda before you vacuum. Give it an hour to work its magic and go to work. It will keep rugs and furniture cleaner and fresher over the long haul.

In a Minute

Alcohol wipes will easily clean off any sticky substances on your phone, stereo, or computer (surface only). This is an easy chore to tackle on commercial breaks or whenever you only have a minute.

Just Suck It Up

Trying to clean super-small spaces around the house? Don't buy additional vacuum equipment if your attachments are too big. Instead, grab a straw—preferably one of those giant straws from a fast-food chain—and insert part of it into the smallest attachment you have. Tape it in place, and you'll be able to suck up dirt and dust in the tiniest of spaces.

Clean Out the Cobwebs

Here's an easy way to clean cobwebs from corners: Cover the head of your mop or broom with a pillowcase dampened with water, vinegar, or your preferred cleaning solutions, then secure it with a rubber band and go to it.

Be a Bag Lady

When vacuuming your home, it's always annoying to find bits and pieces that are too big for your vacuum. Instead of ending up with all those icky bits in your hand, tie a plastic grocery bag to your belt loop. That way, you'll have a portable garbage can with you at all times!

Who Knew? Readers' Favorite

When sliding heavy furniture across a wooden floor, put socks on the legs. It will make for a much smoother ride and you won't scratch the floors.

Sliding Doors

If your sliding glass door is sticking, simply spray the tracks with furniture polish. It will remove dirt and give the tracks the lubrication they need to keep the door moving smoothly.

Mending Marker Mishaps

If your kids (or you) get a permanent-marker stain on furniture or the floor, don't despair! There may be hope in the form of rubbing alcohol. Test an inconspicuous area first to make sure it won't harm the finish, then apply directly to the stain with a rag or paper towel. Rub until it disappears, then wipe with a clean cloth moistened with water.

Need More Storage Space?

If your living room sofa has a skirt that reaches the floor, you have storage space you didn't even know about. Underneath the sofa is a great place to store a bin of wrapping paper and accessories, old photo albums, and other skinny items you reach for often.

The Key to Finding Keys

Always misplacing your keys around the house? Tie a brightly-colored ribbon to your keychain. It'll be much easier to spot.

Gum? Gone!

Here's another way to get gum out of fabric or upholstery (taught to me by my great aunt). Beat an egg white, rub or brush it into the gum, and let it sit for up to a half an hour, then wipe off. The egg white breaks down the gum and makes it easy to remove.

Wonder Bread

If you have a precious oil painting in your home, it's important to keep it clean without damaging it. Our surprising cleaning tool of choice is a piece of white bread! White bread has the perfect amount of moisture to pick up dust easily, without being so wet that it will ruin your painting.

Easy Electronics Cleaner

If your MP3 player has seen better days, give it a quick clean. Our favorite method? A bit of rubbing alcohol or astringent on a clean make-up sponge. Just rub it over the player and it will look as good as new!

Citrus for Ceramic

The easiest way to clean ceramic figurines is to rub them with the cut side of a lemon wedge. Leave the lemon juice on for 15 minutes, then polish up with a soft, dry cloth.

The Answer for Artificial Flowers

To clean silk flowers, try blowing off the dust with a hairdryer set on cool. You can also put the flowers in a paper bag, add some uncooked rice, and shake. The dirt will transfer to the rice. You can also clean silk flowers easily by placing them "bloom" end down, in a plastic bag with 2 tablespoons salt. Hold onto the stems, close the bag, then shake vigorously. The salt will attract the dust, leaving your flowers looking as good as the real thing!

CHAPTER 2

The Kitchen and Dining Room

The Clean Stove Trick

Save on household cleaners by keeping your stove neater. How? When cooking, cover unused burners with a baking sheet or pizza pans. The pans will catch all the splatter, and they're easy to just stick in the dishwasher afterward!

A "Hair"-brained Idea

If you're having trouble cleaning the baked-on grease and grime on your range's hood or other areas around your stove, don't resort to harsh commercial cleaners. Instead, warm it up by blasting it with your hair dryer. Once the dirt is warm, it will wipe right off with a damp cloth.

Sticky Trick

To get a pantry even your mother-in-law won't criticize, store honey and other bottles with sticky drip-potential in little bowls or all together in a baking pan that you can easily take out, wash, and replace.

Bag the Bags

With so many free plastic bags for the taking at drugstores and supermarkets, we never buy garbage bags. Instead, we use the smaller bags for all of our trash cans, and make it even easier for ourselves by affixing two self-adhesive plastic hooks upside-down on the outside of the bin. These hooks easily hold the handles, so the bags won't slip down inside.

Clean a Dusty Dust Mop

Always clean dust mops after using them. To avoid making a dust cloud, cover a dry dust mop with a damp paper bag before you shake it out. If your mop has a removable head, put it in a large mesh lingerie bag and toss it into the washer.

Naturally Deodorize Garbage Cans

Wash and deodorize trashcans with a solution of 1 teaspoon lemon juice mixed with 1 quart water. Sprinkling baking soda into the base of every garbage bag will also help keep odors at bay.

Eau de Trash?

It's easy to keep your trashcans from stinking up your home. We like to rip out those perfume strips from magazines and place one at the bottom of every trashcan throughout the house. Or try dryer sheets: They make your clothes smell fresh and wonderful, so they'll work miracles in stinky garbage pails too.

Who Knew? Readers' Favorite

There's no need to throw out your stinky old sponges. Just soak them in cold salt water, rinse, and they're good to use again.

Stretch the Life of Your Sponge

To make your kitchen sponges and brushes last longer, wash them once a week in the utensil compartment of your dishwasher with a load of dishes. This will ward off any bacteria and mildew.

Odor Eaters

All sorts of nasty odors lurk in the kitchen, whether it's expired food, a lingering trash bag, or a mix of flavors still hanging around after a meal. Next time you've got a persistent stink, try out one of these quickie odor-killing tips.

- ✦ Keep a few washed charcoal briquettes in a shallow dish on top of the refrigerator.

- ✦ To eliminate refrigerator odors, leave a small cup of fresh coffee grounds on two shelves.

- ✦ Deep-fry a small amount of cinnamon to chase all odors from your home.

Make Your Home Smell Sugar-and-Spice Nice

For a great DIY home fragrance, simmer apple cider with a cinnamon stick and a few whole cloves. Also add a bit of orange peel if you like. Isn't this what Martha Stewart smells like?

Freshen Up the Garbage Disposal

Keep your garbage disposal running at its best with this simple once-a-month trick: Grind about a dozen ice cubes made from white vinegar. The ice sharpens the blades while the vinegar deodorizes the drain.

Saline Solution

Salt will clear out the gunk that collects in the garbage disposal and the smell that goes along with it. Pour a few spoonfuls in and flush with cold water, then run the disposal.

Quick Fix for a Stinky Microwave

Microwave odors? Cut a lemon in quarters and put it in a bowl of water, then put in the microwave on high for two minutes.

Nuke the Popcorn Smell

Too bad you didn't know about this back in college when you made popcorn in the dorm lounge. A tea bag in water (even a used one) placed in the microwave for a minute is all you need to eliminate that unidentified stale smell in there.

Orange Oven

A self-cleaning oven can leave an odor after it's done its work. Eliminate the lingering smell by turning down the oven to 350°F when it's finished, then putting orange peels on a baking sheet inside. Cook the peels for a half an hour, and not only will the oven smell fresh, but your whole kitchen will, too!

Admit It, Your Fridge Sometimes Smells

Besides baking soda, a number of other foods are capable of removing odors. Pour a little vanilla extract into a bottle cap and set in the refrigerator to absorb odors. One of the best ways to eliminate odors is to hollow out a grapefruit or orange, fill it with salt, and place in the back of the fridge. Leave it there until the salt gets completely damp, and then throw the whole thing out and replace.

Time to Clean Out Your Refrigerator?

When cleaning your refrigerator, don't use chemicals that can linger on your food and produce nasty odors. After emptying the fridge, simply dissolve a cup of salt in a gallon of hot water and wipe away. Squeeze in the juice of a lemon for a nice scent.

Spruce Up Your Stainless Steel Sink

Nothing makes a kitchen look better than a shiny kitchen sink, and luckily, there are a lot of ways to clean and shine stainless steel!

✦ Club soda is a terrific way to clean stainless steel sinks, dishwashers, ranges, and other appliances.

The least expensive club soda works just as well as the pricey brands; and flat club soda works, too. Add a little flour for really stubborn stains.

✦ You've scrubbed it twice, but you can't seem to get those water spots out of your stainless steel sink! The solution? A little white vinegar. Just rub it into the spots and they'll disappear.

✦ Stainless steel can also be quickly and easily cleaned with vodka. Place a little on a sponge or paper towel and wipe. Your faucet, sink, and other stainless steel will soon be sparkling again, so pour yourself a little glass to celebrate!

✦ Instead of using a rag or a paper towel, use newspaper, which will get it even shinier. A tougher option is aluminum foil. Just crumple it up, and scour with the shiny side.

✦ For a spectacularly shiny finish on a stainless steel or aluminum sink, rub a liberal amount of baking soda in a circular motion all over its surface with a damp sponge.

✦ For the shiniest sink you've ever seen, finish off your cleaning session by buffing the sink with a touch of baby oil on a soft cloth.

Oven Cleaning Made Easy

A simple way to clean your oven is to place an oven-safe pot or bowl filled with water inside. Heat on 450°F for 20 minutes to loosen dirt and grease with the steam. Once your oven is cool, wipe off the condensation and the grease will come with it. After you're done, make a paste of water and baking soda and smear it on any enamel. The paste will dry into a protective layer that will absorb grease as you cook.

Not a Fan of Oven Fans?

Oven fans are magnets for grease. The simplest way to clean the resulting mess is to pop out the fan filter, then run it through your dishwasher on the top shelf.

Who Knew? Readers' Favorite

To clean your electric can opener, run a piece of paper towel or waxed paper through it. This will pick up the grease and some of the gunk.

Clean Your Coffee Maker

For the best tasting coffee, make sure to clean your coffee maker regularly. Just add several tablespoons of baking soda to your pot, fill it with water, and then run your coffee maker as usual. It's a good idea to run it again with just water. You can also use a denture-cleaning tablet instead of baking soda.

Now Clean Your Coffee Grinder!

Even your coffee grinder needs a good cleaning every now and then, and uncooked rice can do the job. Simply mill a handful of rice as you normally do to your coffee beans. The chopped rice cleans out the stuck coffee grounds and oils, and absorbs stale odors to boot. Afterwards, throw away the rice, wipe the grinder clean…and brew fresh coffee.

Lube Up Your Blender

To keep your blender and mixer in top working order, be sure to lubricate all moving parts every three months with a very light coating of mineral oil (not vegetable oil).

Getting Rid of Counter Stains

Stubborn stains can be removed from your countertop by applying a baking soda paste and rubbing with a warm, damp cloth. If the stain still remains, consider using a drop or two of bleach, but be careful—bleach can fade your countertop along with the stain!

Cease Grease!

Forget about buying those expensive stove cleaners to get rid of cooked-on grease stains. Just wet the stains with vinegar and cover with baking soda. After watching the fun foaming reaction, wipe with a damp sponge and buff with a dry, clean cloth.

Make a Gross Chore Easier

Eventually, it's time for one our least-favorite cleaning chores: cleaning the top of the fridge (vinegar usually does the trick). After you finish, place an old placemat on top. When it gets gross, either replace it or throw it in the washing machine for a quick clean.

Who Knew? Readers' Favorite

Ammonia is a no-nonsense cleaning essential for your kitchen. To clean a really greasy pan, add a few drops of ammonia to your soapsuds.

Great All-Purpose Cleaner

For a perfect all-purpose cleaner, mix together 1 gallon hot water, 3½ fluid ounces ammonia, 3½ fluid ounces white vinegar, and 7 ounces (1¼ cups) baking soda. Store in a tightly sealed bottle and use on glass, silver, and countertops.

Perk Up Your Floor

If you have black scuffmarks on your linoleum or vinyl flooring, you can remove them with a bit of white (non-gel) toothpaste. Simply rub the toothpaste over the scuff vigorously until it disappears.

A No. 2 Will Do

The easiest way to remove black scuffmarks from a vinyl floor? Just use a pencil eraser! It really works.

Mopping Up

If you own a mop that requires replacement cloths, substitute baby wipes instead of buying packs of those pricey cloths. Rinse the wipes off before using, and they'll get your floors just as clean. Sturdy paper towels are another solid option for ready mops—just rip small holes in the towel so the cleaning liquid still sprays through the mop.

No More Tears!

The secret to shiny laminated floors is baby shampoo. Just mix a spoonful with a gallon of warm water and mop as usual!

A Two-for-One Deal

You can save cash and storage space with this quick-fix cleaning alternative: Use a small, plastic garbage can as your mop bucket and you'll not only clean the can, but you'll never have to buy a bucket!

Make Your Ceramic Floors Gleam

There are tons of commercial cleaning products for ceramic or vinyl floors, but they're costly, toxic, and liable to irritate your skin. Luckily, they can be easily replaced with this safe, effective homemade alternative: Combine 1 cup white vinegar and 1 gallon warm water, and mop till those floors sparkle.

If your vinyl tile has loosened, simply put it back in its original place. Lay a piece of aluminum foil on top, and run a hot iron over it. In no time at all, the glue will begin to adhere. Then just stack a few books on top of the tile until the glue hardens again.

Shiny Chrome

What is chrome for, if not to be shiny? To bring back dull chrome fixtures, dampen them, then rub them with newspaper. You can also shine them up with a paste of vinegar and cream of tartar.

For the Best Potholders

Your potholders don't have to look stained and dirty. Wash frequently, and after each time you wash them, spray them with starch. Spray starch repels grease, so your potholders will stay unstained.

Conserve Steel Wool Pads

It's easy to keep your wet, soaped steel wool pads from rusting: Just wrap them in aluminum foil and store in your freezer. But before you do, cut them in half. It's economical, because they won't wear out as fast, and the frozen half will stay rust-free. And as a bonus, it's a great way to sharpen your scissors.

Handle with Care

If you've ever experienced the frustration of breaking a dish while washing it, you'll love this tip! Prevent breakages by lining your sink with a towel or rubber mat before washing.

Stuck-On Substances

If you've given up hope of ever removing stuck-on food from your pots and pans, help is on the way—in the form of a fabric softener sheet! Just cover the stain with hot water, and float a fabric softener sheet in it. Leave overnight, and in the morning, the food should wipe off easily.

Who Knew? Readers' Favorite

There's no need to buy expensive dishwashing liquid. Buy the cheapest brand you can find, then add a few tablespoons of white vinegar to the water while you're washing, and your dishes will shine. The same is true for dishwashers—just buy the least expensive detergent, and add some white vinegar to the machine. Vinegar will remove spots from glass in a flash.

Cast Iron Cure

The best way to clean cast iron pans is to cover any stain with a paste of cream of tartar and white vinegar. Apply liberally, let it sit, then scrub with a damp, soft cloth.

What if Your Nonstick Pan Sticks?

For the most part, coated pots and pans are easy to keep clean, but they do stain, and over time grease and oil may build up. This will adversely affect the efficiency of the nonstick surface, so it's important to clean and re-season any stained areas. To do so, simply mix 1 cup water, 2 tablespoons baking soda, and ½ cup white vinegar in the pot, set on the stove, and boil for 10 minutes. Wash the pot as usual, then rub vegetable oil on the surface to re-season it.

Burnt Food Be Gone

Here's another great way to remove burnt food from pans. Sprinkle baking soda, salt, and dishwasher detergent over the crusty bits, then cover with water and boil for a half an hour. Even the toughest baked-on food will wipe off easily.

For a Sparkling Coffee Pot

To remove coffee stains from inside a glass coffee pot, add 1 tablespoon water, 4 teaspoons salt, and 1 cup crushed ice. Gently swirl until it is clean, then rinse thoroughly. (Just make sure the coffee pot is at room temperature before cleaning.)

Get Rid of a Smelly Thermos

The easiest way to remove smells and stains from a thermos is by filling it with hot water and ½ cup baking soda, then letting it sit overnight. In the morning, just rinse well, and it should be good as new! Next time, place a few whole cloves or a teaspoon of salt inside before closing it up.

Remove Stubborn Stains

Get rid of really tough stains on your metal and ceramic pots, pans, mugs, and dishes by filling them with boiling water and adding a denture tablet. Let it sit overnight, and the stain should disappear.

This Cup Has Seen a Lot of Coffee!

If the inside of your coffee cup is stained from coffee or tea, it's not too late to get it to look like new. Mix a paste of coarse salt (or baking soda) and water. Scrub the mug with this, then rinse well.

Who Knew? Readers' Favorite

Cleaning a cheese grater will never be a problem if you grate a small piece of raw potato before trying to wash it out. Sometimes an old toothbrush also comes in handy for cleaning graters.

Crystal Clean

Use a paste of lemon juice and baking powder to remove small stains from crystal. Treat tougher stains by placing 2 teaspoons uncooked rice inside the crystal piece, adding water, and swirling. The small amount of abrasive action from the rice will remove the stains—perfect for vases with narrow necks.

Camouflage a Crack in Your China

Antique dealers use this trick to hide hairline cracks on china plates and cups. Simmer the piece in milk for 45 minutes. Casein, a milk protein, may fill in the crack, depending on its size. If your china is old or fragile, though, this could backfire—heat can cause pieces to expand and crack.

Nix the Nicks

Buff away a nick on the rim of a glass or your china with an emery board. Don't use a nail file or sandpaper; both are too coarse and will scratch the glass.

Everything You Need to Know to Care for Your Silver

Even if you didn't get it as a wedding present, you probably have silver cutlery that has been passed down from generation to generation. This beautiful silverware is always a nice treat on a special occasion. But as you've probably discovered, silver will eventually tarnish if exposed to air for an extended period of time, turning duller and darker as time goes on. However, you can keep your silver shiny and beautiful by polishing and storing it wisely.

✦ Never combine silver and stainless steel cutlery in the dishwasher—the silver will turn black. Any contact with dishwasher detergent will also result in black spots. Remove silver cutlery from the dishwasher immediately after the cycle ends, and dry at once to avoid stains and pitting.

✦ Sulfur compounds in the air cause silver to tarnish; to prevent this, store your silver in airtight containers, or wrap it in tarnish-proof cloths or papers. (Never wrap silver in plastic food wrap. It will keep air away, but it can also cause stains and corrosion.)

✦ If your silver does develop spots, dissolve a little salt in lemon juice, then dip a soft cloth into the mixture and rub it onto the cutlery. Rinse in warm water and finish by buffing to a shine with a chamois.

✦ You can also rub off tarnish with toothpaste. Place some white (non-gel) toothpaste on a soft cloth and use it to rub solid silver (not silver plate). Then rinse it off gently. Don't use whitening toothpaste—it can damage the surface.

✦ To remove tarnish from the tines of a fork, coat a piece of cotton string with toothpaste and run it between the tines.

✦ Polishing silver is never a neat chore, but an old sock can make it easier. Slip the sock over your hand; use one side to apply the polish and the other to buff it out.

✦ If you have large silver items that are not used with food, consider having them lacquered by a jeweler to prevent tarnishing. Candelabras, vases, and trophies are good candidates for this treatment.

✦ If you place a small piece of chalk in a silver chest, it will absorb moisture and slow tarnishing. Calcium carbonate (i.e., chalk) absorbs moisture from the air very slowly. Break up the chalk and expose the rough surface for the best results.

Who Knew? Readers' Favorite

Believe it or not, a great way to polish copper is to rub it with ketchup and let it stand for an hour. Rinse off the ketchup with hot water, then buff to an incredible shine.

Lemon for Brass and Copper

One of the best cleaners for brass and copper is a simple lemon! Cut a lemon in half, sprinkle the cut side with salt, and rub over the surface you're cleaning. Rinse with cold water and watch it shine.

For Tablecloth Blunders

If you spill wine on a tablecloth, blot up as much as you can as soon as you can with a cloth, then sponge with cool water. Wash immediately. If the fabric is not machine washable, cover the stain with a small cloth dampened with a solution of detergent, water, and vinegar, then rinse. Get the cloth to the drycleaner as soon as you can.

Keep Candleholders Clean

To prevent wax from sticking to a candleholder, rub a thin coat of olive oil on the base of the holder before lighting the candle. If your holder already has some wax buildup, mix olive oil with dish soap to clean it out.

Candlestick Fit

Most taper candles won't fit perfectly into standard candlesticks, so you'll have to do a little work to ensure your candle fits securely. (Do not light the candle and melt wax into the base— this is messy and dangerous!) First, try placing the candle base under hot water; this softens the wax and allows it to mold to its new surroundings. If this doesn't do the trick, whittle down the wax around the base of the candle with a paring knife, checking the fit as you go. Stop when you get it narrow enough to fit the holder. Apply wax adhesive around the base of the candle, and place it in the candlestick.

Who Knew? Readers' Favorite

Accidentally drip candle wax on a tablecloth? Remove it by rubbing with an ice cube and then scraping with a dull knife. Another way to remove candle wax from a tablecloth or other fabric is to place some brown paper (not newspaper) over the top and iron it on a low heat. The wax will transfer to the paper!

Cardboard Tubes for Tapers

Here's a great way to store tapered candles: Use paper towel tubes to protect them. Just wrap two candles at a time in tissue paper, then slip them into the cardboard tube. Keep tubes together with rubber bands if necessary.

Try This Tip and Call Us in the Morning

When your toddler spills your iced tea, and you don't want to waste a bunch of paper towels mopping it up, use pages ripped from last year's phone book instead. The thin (free!) pages are perfect for minor drips and spills.

A Tidy Toaster Oven

How will you get the toast just right if you can't see through the toaster oven window? Mix four parts white vinegar with four parts hydrogen peroxide and two parts dishwashing soap. You can clean directly with paper towels or else spray on first, let it go to work, and wipe clean an hour or so later.

Mended Mug

Broke a mug? Pour sand into the bottom of a little tray (Tupperware will do) to hold broken china while you line the edge with glue and stick the other piece (also lined with glue) on top. Leave the repaired cup balanced on its side to dry so the break won't have to fight gravity before the glue takes hold.

De-Gunk Your Griddler

Here's the easiest way we've found to clean a countertop grill: Unplug the grill, and put a wet paper towel inside (with the lid closed) for 10 minutes. The grease loosens up and is easy to clean off.

A Pint-Sized Space Saver

Those plastic baskets that berries come in are perfect for small items in your dishwasher. Just wedge in place and throw bottle tops, lids, and small utensils inside.

Who Knew? Readers' Favorite

You know you're not supposed to use "regular" dishwashing liquid in your dishwasher, but...what do you do when you're out of powdered detergent and company is on its way? The truth is, you can use some of the liquid kind—use only a few drops, and fill the rest of the detergent container with baking soda. It will stop the soap from producing too many suds.

For Clean Cabinet Shelves

Instead of using contact paper on your kitchen shelves, use some peel-and-stick vinyl floor tiles (cut to size if necessary). They're super easy to clean, and they're usually cheaper, too—some stores will even give you a free sample.

Liquor Is Quicker

If you're having trouble removing a pesky label, just soak the spot in rubbing alcohol. Leave on for up to a minute, then wipe right off. Don't have any rubbing alcohol? The kind of alcohol you drink—like vodka, rum, or gin—works well, too.

Getting Rid of Grease

When flushing grease down the drain, don't use hot water (like many of us were taught). The grease coats the pipes, cools, and will collect bits of debris. Instead, use cold water. It will make sure the grease solidifies in chunks that will easily get flushed through the pipes. Better yet, empty your grease into a soda can and throw it away!

Thrifty Kitchen Storage

Save space by reusing an empty six-pack holder to store aluminum foil, plastic wrap, waxed paper, and other boxes of wrap. Stand the long boxes on their ends, insert them into the plastic rings, and put them under your sink. This'll free up a valuable kitchen drawer.

A Pantry Pointer

Keep packets of sauces and gravies in one easy-to-manage spot in your pantry—we suggest using a child's empty shoebox! Stand the envelopes upright in the box, so the labels are easy to read, and the shoebox should fit perfectly on a shelf in your pantry.

Free Up Shelf Space with Hanging Cup Storage

Under-the-shelf cup holders are a clever, super-efficient way to save space in your kitchen. You can buy a slip-on cup holder for less than $10, no tools required. You'll save tons of shelf space for plates and bowls, while your cups, mugs, glasses, and cooking utensils stay out of the way.

A System for All Those Plastic Lids

Are plastic lids taking over your kitchen? We feel your pain, and can offer a solution: Store a dish drainer in your cabinet, and file the lids on their sides in size order. You'll find the lid you need in seconds, and your kitchen will seem much more organized.

Who Knew? Readers' Favorite

Plastic grocery bags have a way of multiplying and taking over kitchen drawers. A space-saving solution is to stuff all of them into an empty tissue box. You'll be amazed how many fit, and you can easily remove them one at a time when you need to.

Another Use for Cardboard Tubes

Instead of trashing cardboard tubes from paper towels or toilet paper, create a cozy storage container for all those stray plastic grocery bags. Stuff the plastic bags inside, one by one, until the tubes are full. Then you can tie several tubes together with a rubber band, and store them in a drawer or on a closet shelf.

CHAPTER 3

The Bathroom

Bathroom Quick Clean

If you can only clean one room before guests arrive, make it the bathroom. It's the only room where your guests will be alone (and possibly snooping around!), and a dirty bathroom is more unappealing than a cluttered living room. Here's how to do it in two minutes or less: Just apply a touch of baby shampoo to a wet sponge and wipe down your sink, fixtures, tiles, and bathtub. It cuts through oily residue, and smells good, too.

Steam Out a Nasty Bathroom

If you've let the bathroom get so dirty that it now resembles a gas station restroom, turn on the hot water in the shower for 10 minutes with the door closed. The steam will loosen the buildup of mildew and mold. Then get in there and clean.

Who Knew? Readers' Favorite

Looking for an easy mildew remover? Simply scrub the affected area with an old, damp toothbrush sprinkled with baking soda.

Another Use for Vodka!

For a great mold and mildew fighter, try vodka! It works especially well on the caulking around your tub. Just spray on, leave for 10 minutes, and wipe clean.

Ever-Useful Alcohol

Isopropyl alcohol, which is available at most supermarkets and drugstores, is a cheap and effective disinfectant. But it also belongs in your bathroom cabinet for more than just first-aid purposes. Use it, mixed with equal parts water, to clean the bathtub caulking and shine chrome and glass.

Clogged Showerhead?

Removing mineral deposits from a showerhead without harsh chemicals is easy. Just unscrew it and submerge in white vinegar overnight, and the clogs will disappear. It you can't unscrew it, fill a small, sturdy bag with vinegar and attach to the showerhead with duct tape. You can also brush the showerhead with vinegar using an old toothbrush to make it sparkle. To clean the screen in your showerhead, wash it with water with a dash of dishwashing liquid added.

Flour Fix

If your chrome faucets are less than sparkly, try rubbing them with flour. Rinse, then buff with a soft cloth, and they'll really shine. Vinegar also works well for cleaning chrome.

Who Knew? Readers' Favorite

Believe it or not, toothpaste makes a great polish for your faucets. Just rub on and buff off with soft cloth. The white, non-gel variety works best.

Mirror Miracle

Make your mirrors shine with a solution of equal parts vinegar and water. Use old newspapers to wipe the surface of mirrors with the mix, then add extra shine by rubbing with a clean dry-erase or blackboard eraser.

Shined to a "Tea"

Here's an all-natural way to clean your mirror that will also give a spotless shine: Wipe the mirror with a clean cloth dipped in strong, cool tea. Buff with a dry cloth and you're done!

Get Rid of Copper Stains

Removing blue-green stains caused by high copper content in your water can be challenging, even with the help of bleach. Instead, treat this stain on your shower or tub with a paste of equal parts cream of tartar and baking soda. Rub into the stain, leave for half an hour, and rinse well with water. Repeat, if necessary.

Toilet Bowl Cleaner

To remove hard-water deposits in your toilet bowl, pour 1 cup white vinegar into the bowl and allow it to sit for several hours or overnight before scrubbing. A fizzy denture tablet works well, too!

Plop-Plop, Fizz-Fizz

Oh, what a relief it is to clean the toilet this easily. Throw in two Alka-Seltzer tablets and let them soak for a half hour. Give a quick brush and follow with a flush.

Scouring Powder Substitute

The best thing about scouring powder is its abrasive action. The worst is the harsh chemical smell. Get all the benefits without the caustic chemicals by using baking soda instead. In most instances, baking soda will work just as well as scouring powder.

Another DIY Alternative

Make your own all-natural scouring powder by combining 1 cup salt with 1 cup baking soda. Store in a closed jar or can, and use it to scrub off hard water stains on your porcelain sinks and bathtub.

Soap Scum Solution

Clear soap scum away effortlessly from shower doors by wiping them with a used (dry) dryer sheet. It gets the job done quickly!

Spic-and-Span Shower Doors

Need to clean those dirty glass shower doors? You can wipe down the doors with leftover white wine (if you haven't finished it off!). Wipe the wine on with a damp sponge, leave for five minutes, then rinse off. Finish by quickly buffing with a clean, dry cloth.

Cleaning Your Shower Curtain

If your shower curtain has seen better days, wash according to the care label attached, but add a cup of vinegar to the water and it will look like new. Remove as soon as the cycle is complete and hang back in position to drip-dry without any creases.

Shower Curtain Savvy

Avoid leaving a shower curtain bunched up after use, especially in a small bathroom—the steam encourages mildew. Always close the shower curtain after use, and if small spots of mildew do appear, dab with baking soda on a damp cloth. Wash larger areas in hot water, rub with lemon juice, and dry in the sun, if possible.

Who Knew? Readers' Favorite

Need to remove mildew from a plastic shower curtain? Try washing the curtain in the washing machine with two large, white bath towels. Add a little bleach in with your usual detergent and 1 cup white vinegar to the rinse cycle to prevent future mildew growth.

In the Pink

If you have a pair of pinking shears (scissors with a zigzagging edge used in sewing), put them to good use in the bathroom. Use them to cut the bottom of your shower curtain liner: The uneven hem allows water to slide off more easily, making bottom-of-the-curtain mildew a thing of the past.

Smooth Move

Do the rings on your shower curtain squeak as they run along the rod? The solution is simple: Just rub some petroleum jelly or car wax along the rod and they'll slide right along it.

Save a Shower Curtain

Our family used to go through shower curtains like toilet paper, until we learned how to prevent the nasty culprit: mildew. Simply soak a new shower curtain in salt water for a few hours before hanging it up.

Ceramic Care

To keep them sparkling, wipe ceramic tiles regularly with a sponge dampened with water and a splash of vinegar. Avoid soapy or oily cleaners and never use abrasives, which will dull the finish and make glazed tiles more prone to dirt.

Perfect Porcelain

Steel wool and scouring powders will scratch porcelain, so if your tub or sink is made of this material, rub a freshly cut lemon around the surface to cut through grease, then rinse with running water.

Stubborn Tub Stains

No matter how hard we scrub, we never seem to get the corners of our tub clean. Luckily, we have a clever solution! Soak cotton balls in your favorite tub cleanser (or just some rubbing alcohol) and leave one in each corner of your tub overnight. By morning, they'll be as clear as day.

Fabric Softener Sheets to the Rescue (Again)

To clean chrome-plated fixtures in your bathroom instantly, always keep fabric softener sheets handy. Just wipe, and the chrome will sparkle. Rubbing alcohol also does the trick.

Grout-Buster

If you've tried milder grout cleaners and you still have black stains on your grout, it's time to bring out the big boys. Make sure to wear protective gloves and that the area is well ventilated, soak some paper towels in bleach, and place them around the grout. Leave for at least an hour, then remove the towels and enjoy your clean, white grout.

Who Knew? Readers' Favorite

When the grout stains in your bathroom have you throwing up your hands, bring on the sandpaper. The folded edge will slide into the space between tiles and around the edge. This is still a delicate job—steer clear of the tiles themselves or they'll scratch.

Get Rid of Caked-On Hair Spray

If your beauty routine includes spraying your entire 'do to keep it in place, you probably have a film of hair spray on your bathroom vanity and walls. Easily remove it with a solution of two parts water and one part liquid fabric softener. Wipe on with a damp cloth, then rub off with a clean one.

Cut Down on Cleaning

You've just spent what seemed like an entire day cleaning your bathrooms. Now keep them that way by applying mineral oil all over shower doors and tiled surfaces. This will delay build-up and cut down on future cleaning time.

Drain Maintenance

Don't wait until your drain gets clogged before you flush out grime, grease, and hair. Perform monthly maintenance with the help of a little yeast. Pour two packets of dry yeast and a pinch of salt down the drain, then follow with very hot water. Wait half an hour, then flush again with hot water. The yeast reproduces and expands, which breaks up stubborn grime and hair clogs and saves you from calling the plumber.

Down the Drain

If you have a clogged drain, try this before springing for expensive drain cleaners that are harmful to your pipes. First, remove all standing water so you can access the drain. Then pour 1 cup baking soda down the drain, immediately followed by 1 cup table salt, and then ½ cup white vinegar. Let stand for five minutes, and pour 1–2 quarts boiling water down the drain. The baking soda, salt, and vinegar will dissolve any organic matter (like hair or grease), while the water will flush it out.

Get the Most from Your Plunger

Add a little petroleum jelly to the rim of your rubber plunger. It helps achieve great suction, so the disgusting job ahead is a little bit easier.

Bar Soap Solution

Always try to keep the soap in your soap dish dry. It will last much longer that way, and let's face it—picking up a soggy piece of soap to wash your hands is a bit on the disgusting side. Choose a soap dish that allows water to escape somewhere and your soap will stay solid!

Who Knew? Readers' Favorite

Stinky litter box? A great way to keep cat litter smelling fresh is to mix in a bit of baby powder each time you change the litter.

Give Your Toothbrush a Bath

A great way to keep your toothbrush clean is to soak it overnight, every few weeks, in a solution of equal parts water and baking soda. Rinse well before brushing again.

Bring Back Your Brushes

Revive hairbrushes and combs by soaking them in a pot of warm water and 1 tablespoon baking soda or ammonia.

Frost a Window to Keep Out Prying Eyes

To create a temporary "frost" for a bathroom window, mix a solution of 1 cup beer and 4 tablespoons Epsom salts. Then paint the mixture onto the window. The paint will wash off easily.

Defogging Glass

What household item will cause mirrors or eyeglasses to stop fogging? Shaving cream! It's weird but true: just rub glass with the cream, leave on for a couple of minutes, then rub off for a fog-free finish.

Newer Nail File

Ever wondered if there's a way to clean dirty emery boards? Just press transparent tape onto them, smooth over a bit, and peel off. Metal files can be cleaned with soap and water.

Who Knew? Readers' Favorite

To create an automatic air freshener in the bathroom, we blot a bit of perfume or scented oil in the center of the toilet paper roll. Whenever someone uses it, the roll releases a pleasant whiff to keep the room smelling fresh.

Bag That Soap Scum

Keep soap scum off the walls of your shower with this easy trick: Just rub wood furniture polish onto the tile and doors, and soap scum and mildew won't stick.

Soften Up Scum

Fight soap scum in your bathroom by using a granulated water softener (such as Calgon). Water softener is a cheap, gentle, skin-safe product that is also an excellent additive for your washing machine water.

A Shining Sink

Here's a quick and easy way to clean your bathroom sink: Just dampen a cotton rag or a bit of toilet paper with hydrogen peroxide and give it a few swipes! It's even great for sink stains, too.

One Soap, Two Uses

These days, most dishwashing liquids have moisturizers in them to keep your hands smooth even after doing the dishes. They work so well that you can use dishwashing liquid as a stand-in for hand soap! Just fill an old soap dispenser with 2 tablespoons dishwashing liquid and top off with water. Shake to combine and you'll have hand soap at a fraction of the cost.

Keep Cords Tidy

From hair dryers and blenders to electric shavers, most small electrical appliances have cords that can get a little unwieldy. Keep them neat and out of the way with ponytail holders or rubber bands, or fold them up and store them in paper towel tubes—label the tubes to remind yourself which cord belongs to which appliance.

Who Knew? Readers' Favorite

If your bathroom drawers are a jumbled mess, invest in an inexpensive plastic silverware tray. It's a great way to organize the little things you've got rattling around in there.

Small-Item Storage

If you need extra storage space in your bathroom, try one of our favorite fixes: an over-the-door plastic shoe storage container. Available at home stores, these organizers are perfect for make-up, lotion, and even small appliances like curling irons.

Mirror, Mirror on the Wall

Rather than purchase a bulletin board or whiteboard for your home, write messages with dry-erase markers on the mirror in your bathroom. The bathroom gets heavy foot traffic, so it's a great place to keep notes and reminders for everyone in your family.

CHAPTER 4

The Laundry Room

Whitening Whites

White fabrics can turn yellow for any number of reasons—detergents, plastic storage containers, the oils in your skin, or simply old age. To whiten old linens, boil a pot of water, then add ¼ cup dishwasher detergent and the linens and let sit for overnight. Rinse and wash as usual. The whitening powers of the dishwasher soap will restore the brightness to your whites.

Bringing Brightness Back

If you have a white linen tablecloth or other cotton item that has turned yellow over time, bring it back to its original brightness with baking soda and salt. Just bring a gallon of water to a boil, remove from the heat, stir in ¼ cup each baking soda and salt, and add the fabric. Let it soak for at least one hour. Then rinse and launder as usual.

The Order of Things

Without order, we have chaos! Make sure to add the detergent at the proper point when doing your laundry. Your clothes will get cleaner if you turn the washer on while it's empty and add the detergent immediately. Let it dissolve and mix with the water before you add your dirty clothes. Putting detergent onto clothes that are still dry can cause dyes to fade and stains to crop up.

Color Saver

Separates that go together should be dry cleaned together so the colors will continue to match. Slight fading can add up over time to turn an elegant suit into a sloppy one!

Don't Overdo the Dry Cleaning

Just when you're done patting yourself on the back for getting your dry cleaning done on time, here's a news flash: Don't overdo it or you'll risk damaging the fabric of your favorite outfits. Suit jackets, for example, usually only need to be dry-cleaned once every three months.

Cold for Clothes

No matter which temperature you choose to wash your clothes, always use a cold-water rinse. It will help the clothes retain their shape and color, and you'll save money and energy by not taxing your water heater.

Vinegar in Your Wash

If you suspect the rinse cycle isn't getting all the soap out of your clothes, add ½ cup apple cider vinegar while they are rinsing. The vinegar will dissolve the alkalinity in detergents as well as give the clothes a pleasant fragrance.

Who Knew? Readers' Favorite

Cut your dryer sheets in half (or in quarters). You won't be able to tell the difference in your clothes, but your pocketbook will.

Sock Sorting the Easy Way

Use a mesh lingerie bag or zippered pillowcase to launder each family member's socks separately. It's an easy way to keep them together, so they'll be easier to sort later.

Make White Socks White Again

Weird but true: Discolored socks will return to their original color if you boil them in a pot of water with a few slices of lemon.

Chalk it Up

One of our laundry room must-haves? A piece of chalk. That's because chalk is great at removing grease stains. Just rub it on the stain as soon as possible at it will absorb much of the grease. Chalk can also be used to prevent ring around the collar. Rub some white chalk on your collar before ironing and it will absorb sweat before it stains your shirt.

Stop Shrinkage

Jeans are usually tight enough as it is! To minimize shrinking, wash them in cold water, dry them on medium heat for only 10 minutes, and then air dry them the rest of the way.

Who Knew? Readers' Favorite

Add a big, dry towel to the clothes dryer when drying jeans and other bulky items. It will cut the drying time significantly. It will save you time and energy costs!

Add Scented Salts for Beautiful Linens

Salt is a miracle worker when it comes to removing linen stains, and if you use scented salts in your laundry, you'll get the extra bonus of lovely-smelling sheets. Add ¼ cup scented bath salts during your washing machine's rinse cycle. Not only will your sheets smell great, but the salt acts like a starch to keep them extra crisp. Just make sure not to use bath salts with dyes on light sheets.

Don't Dry-Clean if You Don't Have To!

If a clothing label of a silk garment doesn't specify dry-cleaning only, you can wash it by hand. Silk should be hand-washed using cool water with mild liquid soap. Always air dry silk—never place it on the dryer, even on cool—and iron it from the "wrong" side of the fabric.

Wily with Wool

Dry-cleaning wool can cost some major money. Try using your washing machine instead. Wash wool with mild dishwashing liquid in cold water on the gentle cycle. If it's a blanket, air fluff to dry. If it's a garment, handle with great care, since wool fibers are very weak when wet. When getting rid of excess water, don't pull, stretch, or wring out the garment. Instead, roll it in a towel, squeeze the excess water out, and then dry flat.

Inside Out

Washing corduroy can be a nightmare, thanks to the amount of lint it attracts. To keep corduroy garments from retaining lint, wash them inside out. This technique also will keep acrylic sweaters from pilling.

Stain Quickie

Here's a great use for a cleaned-out plastic bottle (of the ketchup or salad dressing variety). Pour in a mixture of water and laundry detergent or your favorite stain remover, and use it to quickly pretreat stains on your clothing.

Fight with Fizz

If your clothes are extra greasy, add a can of lemon-lime soda to your washing machine along with detergent. The acid in the soda breaks down the oil in the greasy clothes, and your wash will sparkle.

Oh, Baby!

Forget expensive stain pretreatments for your laundry—just reach for the baby shampoo! Use as you would a pretreater, and it will work just as well for a fraction of the cost.

Blame the Fabric Softener

Does it seem as though your clothes get greasy stains on them in the laundry? It may not be your imagination. One cause: adding undiluted fabric softener. Remove these stains by pretreating the fabric with a paste made of water and detergent, or use a commercial stain remover. Next time, dilute the fabric softener before you add it, or skip the stuff altogether and use vinegar instead.

Brightly colored fabrics often run the first time you wash them, and they can accidentally dye the rest of your wash! To keep your colors from running, wash them for the first time with salt. Add 1 teaspoon salt per gallon of water (about ¼ to ½ cup for a full load) to the washing machine the first time you wash a garment and its colors won't run.

Why the Sour Face for Lace?

If you own a lace tablecloth or doily that is beginning to turn yellow, let it soak in a bucket of sour milk for a few hours to return it to its former brilliant white. Just make sure to hand-wash it in mild detergent afterward!

Wrinkle-Free Curtains

Need to wash your sheer curtains but hate the thought of ironing them afterwards? Simply dissolve a packet of clear gelatin in the final rinse when laundering, and hang them up damp afterwards. The gelatin will remove almost all the wrinkles.

Treat Ties Tenderly

Never try to remove a stain from a tie with water or rubbing, or you may create a large, hard-to-remove watermark. Blot away excess stains (salad dressing, sauces, and gravy are popular ones) with a napkin or soft, white cloth. Take it to the dry cleaner as soon as possible: stains set after 24 to 48 hours.

The Best Stain Fighters

It's not necessary to buy expensive chemicals to treat stains on your clothing! Instead, use these all-natural remedies to remove drips and spills on fabric. To remove tough stains, you may have to apply a stain remover more than once—if all else fails, just keep the garment near your washing machine and wash it over and over (applying the stain-remover each time) until the spot is gone. Just make sure the stain is gone before you put the fabric in the dryer. The heat can further set the stain.

✦ BERRIES. Soak the stain overnight in equal parts milk and white vinegar. Launder as usual.

✦ BLOOD. Soak the stained area in club soda before laundering. If the blood is fresh (ouch!), make a paste of water and either talcum powder, cornstarch, cornmeal, or meat tenderizer. Apply it to the stain. Let it dry, and then brush it off.

✦ COFFEE AND JUICE. Stretch the garment over a bowl, cover the stain with salt, and pour boiling water over the stain from a height of one to two feet. (The gravity helps.) Of course, always test first that the garment can withstand hot water (unlike, say, cashmere). Repeat a couple of times if necessary, but some of the stain (especially if it's not fresh) may remain. If so, treat with your usual spray-and-wash stain remover.

✦ **COSMETICS.** Dampen the stain with water and rub gently with a white bar soap (like Dove or Ivory), then rinse well and launder.

✦ **DEODORANTS AND ANTIPERSPIRANTS.** Apply white vinegar, then rub and rinse. If the stain remains, repeat with rubbing alcohol, then launder.

✦ **DIRT.** Rub shampoo over the area and let sit for five minutes before washing. For tougher stains, try presoaking in a mixture of one part warm water, one part ammonia, and one part laundry detergent.

✦ **GASOLINE.** Removing gasoline stains from clothing can be tricky. The most effective way we know is to apply baby oil to the stain, then launder as usual. Since gasoline is an oil-based product, it takes another oil to pull out the stain and smell.

✦ **GRASS.** You can get rid of grass stains with toothpaste. Scrub it into the fabric with a toothbrush before washing. Or rub the stain with molasses and let stand overnight, then wash with regular dish soap by itself.

✦ **GREASE.** Grease is one of the hardest stains to remove from your clothes, but if you catch it before it dries, you can remove it with baby powder. Apply baby powder to the stain, let it sit for an hour or so, and then wipe off the powder.

◆ **GUM.** Rub with ice until the gum hardens, then carefully remove it with a dull knife before laundering.

◆ **INK STAINS.** Rub the area with a cut, raw onion, letting the onion juice soak in. Let sit for two to three hours before laundering.

◆ **KETCHUP AND TOMATO PRODUCTS.** Remove excess with a dull knife, then dab with a damp, warm sponge. Apply a bit of shaving cream to the stain, and let it dry before laundering as usual.

◆ **LIPSTICK.** If you have lipstick on your collar (or anywhere else), first try getting as much as you can off by pressing some Scotch tape over the area. Then, apply petroleum jelly to the spot and let sit for 15 minutes before laundering.

◆ **MUSTARD.** Hydrogen peroxide is effective at getting rid of mustard stains. After making sure the fabric is colorfast, apply a small amount to the stain and let set for several minutes before laundering.

◆ **NAIL POLISH.** Unfortunately, the only thing that can remove nail polish is nail-polish remover. If the fabric can withstand this harsh chemical, work it in from the inside of the fabric by pressing gently with a paper towel.

✦ **OIL.** The best way to remove stains from cooking oil (olive, vegetable, canola, etc.) is with regular shampoo. Just make sure it doesn't have a built-in conditioner.

✦ **OLD OR UNKNOWN STAINS.** If a stain is so old that it's set, try softening it up with vegetable glycerin. Glycerin can be found in health-food stores, vitamin shops, and online. Apply some to the stain and let set for an hour before laundering.

✦ **PAINT.** Treat the stain while it is still wet; latex, acrylic, and water-based paints cannot be removed once dried. While the paint is wet, rinse in warm water to flush the paint out, then launder. Oil-based paints can be removed with a solvent; your best bet will be to use one recommended on the paint can. If none is mentioned, blot with turpentine, rinse, and rub with bar soap, then launder.

✦ **PERSPIRATION.** A great way to remove perspiration stains from white shirts is to crush 4 aspirin tablets into ½ cup warm water, and apply to the stain. Soak for at least three hours, and launder as usual.

✦ **RUST.** Remove rust stains by wetting the spots with lemon juice, then sprinkling with salt. Let the fabric stand in direct sunlight for 30–45 minutes.

✦ **SCORCH MARKS.** Scorch marks will come out if you rub the area with a cut, raw onion and let the onion juice soak in thoroughly—for at least two to three hours—before washing. You can also try blotting the area with hydrogen peroxide.

✦ **SHOE POLISH.** Try applying a mixture of one part rubbing alcohol and two parts water for colored fabrics and just straight rubbing alcohol for whites. Sponge on, then launder.

✦ **TAR.** Rub gently with kerosene until all the tar is dissolved, then wash as usual. Like with all stain removers, make sure to test a small area first to be sure the fabric is colorfast. If you don't have kerosene, try petroleum jelly—just rub it in until the tar is gone. The jelly itself might stain the fabric, but it's much easier to remove with a spray-and-wash stain remover.

✦ **TOBACCO.** Moisten the stain and rub with white bar soap (like Dove or Ivory), then rinse and launder.

✦ **WINE.** Blot the stain with a mixture of one part dishwashing liquid and two parts hydrogen peroxide. If this doesn't work, apply a paste made from water and cream of tartar and let sit. You can also try using shaving cream.

Lipstick prints on silk seem like disaster, but it's almost as easy to lift them off as it is to get them on there. Use transparent or masking tape to pull off the stain. Any remnants can be sprinkled with talcum powder and shaken off.

Lipstick Stain?

Lipstick on your collar? To remove a lipstick stain from fabric, cover it with petroleum jelly for five minutes, then wash as usual. The glycerin in the jelly will break down the oils in the lipstick, making it easy to wash away.

A Silly Solution

If you happened to give the kids silly string yesterday, their clothes probably now have silly string stains all over them. Easily remove them by soaking the areas in vinegar before you throw them in the wash.

"Out, Damned Spot!"

Shakespeare's Lady Macbeth probably wishes she knew this trick for getting rid of bloodstains: Make a paste from cornstarch and water to rub the stain out and simply brush it off when dry. (Cornmeal mixed with water works equally well.)

Fight the Flu—and Fabric Stains

Hand sanitizer can fight germs and stains on fabric—we always keep it on hand in case of spills. If you've dropped something on your clothes, immediately rub a generous amount of sanitizer on the spot; blot with a soft cloth or tissue, and reapply as necessary. The alcohol in the sanitizer will quickly get to work breaking up the stain.

A Dirty Job

Kids came home with fresh mud stains on their clothes? Don't apply water! Instead, let the mud dry, then use a piece of packing or duct tape to lift all of the hardened dirt you can. Then wash as usual.

Tablecloth Tragedy Averted

Did your clumsy uncle spill gravy all over your best holiday tablecloth? Not to worry! Just blot up what you can with a paper towel, then sprinkle artificial sweetener or flour over what remains on the tablecloth. After dinner, soak the tablecloth in the washer with your regular detergent for half an hour, then wash as usual.

Perspiration Elimination

You don't have to throw out shirts with embarrassing yellow stains under the arms. Mix 2 tablespoons salt with 2 cups hot water and use a little elbow grease to rub the stain out.

Sick of Sweaty Stains?

If you're sick of the sweat stains on the armpits of your white shirts, use this pretreatment to get rid of them forever. Turn the shirt inside out and sprinkle the pits with baking soda, then press with an iron on medium heat for three seconds. The pressed-on powder will absorb sweat and keep the fabric clean.

A Zipper Fix

Stuck zipper? Rub a beeswax-based candle or lip balm on the zipper, and the problem is solved! You can also try rubbing the zipper with the lead from a pencil.

To Keep Your Thimble Nimble

Do you use a thimble to sew or sort papers? If so, wet your finger before you put the thimble on. This will create suction, so the thimble stays put.

Never a Knot

To prevent thread from getting knotted when sewing on a button, first run a bar of soap over the thread. The soap will stop knots!

Shoes That Stay Put

Have you been looking for a way to make your mules stay on your feet? Spray hair spray inside to provide more traction (just be sure to let them dry before you slip them back on)!

A Citrus Refresher

Smelly shoes? Make them a thing of the past with orange rinds. Place the inside of the rinds against the soles of your shoes and they'll absorb moisture and make them smell wonderful!

Shoe Freeze

Believe it or not, a great way to get rid of smelly shoes is to store them in a plastic bag in the freezer each night. The cold slows down the growth of bacteria, which causes the funky smell.

Sneaker Keeper

During the hot summer months, don't leave your sneakers for the gym in the car. The heat can partially melt the rubber, making your shoes less supportive.

Get Rid of Wrinkles

What's the secret to wrinkle-free pants? When hanging up your pants to dry, make sure to hang them by the cuffs at the bottom. (Either use a pants hanger with clips, or just add clothespins to a hanger.) Thanks to gravity, they'll dry with few to no creases!

Pantyhose Pleaser

The easiest way to clean suede? Simply ball up some old nylons and use them to brush to suede back to its original luster.

If only because they have the word "cleaner" in their name, we're always looking for ways to use pipe cleaners that don't involve crafts! Here's a good one: To clean the holes in your iron, dip a pipe cleaner in white vinegar and poke into each hole. Just make sure the iron is cool and unplugged!

Iron Too Hot?

If you scorch a garment when ironing, cover the scorch mark with a vinegar-dampened cloth, then iron with a warm iron (not too hot). Presto! The burn is gone. For scorches on cotton garments, you can also use hydrogen peroxide or lemon juice instead. Just dab it onto the scorch and leave out in the sun to bleach away the stain.

Unclog Your Steam Iron

Another way to clean your iron is to pour equal amounts of vinegar and water into the water holder. Turn the dial to "steam" and leave it upright for five minutes. Unplug and let the iron cool down. Any loose particles should fall out when you empty the water.

Pumping Up Your Iron

The layer of starch that collects on your iron can be easily gotten rid of by ironing aluminum foil. Then put the used aluminum foil sheet under the cover of the ironing board for greater efficiency in ironing (it will reflect heat).

Sticky Iron?

If your iron is beginning to stick to fabrics, sprinkle some salt on a piece of waxed paper and iron it. The salt will absorb the stickiness.

Spring-Cleaning Prep

Get prepared for spring-cleaning by storing your cleaning products in a vinyl shoe holder, and hanging it on the back of your laundry room door. It's a great way to save space, and a reminder of the cleaning storm to come!

Who Knew? Readers' Favorite

You can make your own dehumidifier for the laundry room (or basement) without having to spend a lot in the process. Simply fill a coffee can with charcoal briquettes and punch a few holes in the lid. Place it in damp areas, and replace the charcoal once a month as it absorbs the humidity.

A Dab'll Do Ya

Are you using too much laundry detergent? Today's high-efficiency washers need a lot less detergent than you might think. To see if you're using too much, throw a clean towel into the washing machine by itself. After the wash cycle begins, take a look inside. If you see any suds, you're using too much.

A Blue Streak

Growth spurts don't have to mean new blue jeans, at least not right away. Take down the hem, then use a blue permanent marker to disguise the faded band.

Stop a Stain Before It Sets

Don't let a stain "set" even if you are running out the door. Instead, spray with stain remover or soak in water and store in a resealable plastic bag until you have time to deal with it. Once a stain dries, it's much harder to remove.

Make Your New Jeans Your Old Favorites

Got a new pair of jeans? To make them softer and more comfortable to wear, stick them in the wash with ½ cup salt in addition to your regular laundry detergent. The salt helps reduce stiffness and locks in the dye.

Break In Your Blue Jeans

New jeans are great, except for how stiff they are when you first put them on. Break them in without having to do some strange squats by throwing them into your dryer with a few tennis balls. After 15 minutes on low they'll be as good as...worn!

Who Knew? Readers' Favorite

Save on laundry products while you're saving the environment. Instead of buying fabric softener sheets, pick up a bottle of the liquid kind. Mix a solution of

½ fabric softener and ½ water, and put it into a spray
bottle. For every laundry load, spritz onto a cloth and
toss it in the dryer. A small amount (several sprays) will
go a long way.

Breaking News! No Ironing Board Needed

Save room in your utility closet by forgoing an ironing board and
using a pillowcase over stacked up newspapers. Make it as high
or low as you find comfortable.

Dyeing to Make a Change

Not happy with the color of a handbag or pair of fancy shoes?
Instead of buying new accessories, turn that unbecoming
chartreuse into an elegant black with a can of shoe color spray.
You can pick up an inexpensive can of color from a shoe repair
shop, then revamp the item yourself instead of paying someone
else to do it for you.

A Fresher Hamper

We feel bad throwing away used dryer sheets and now we don't
have to. Instead, we place them at the bottom of the hamper to
keep clothes smelling fresh (a relative term) until we're ready to
wash them.

Lean on Me

If you have a toddler or pet safety gate that you no longer need,
give it a new life in the laundry room! Lean it against the side

of your washer or the wall to make the perfect drying rack for delicates and sweaters.

Extending Your Clothesline

If you love the smell of air-dried clothing, but never have enough room on your clothesline, you'll love this ingenious trick: Pull the fabric off an old umbrella with a hooked handle. Then open it up, hang it from the line, and you'll have a bunch of spokes on which to hang your laundry overflow.

A Delicate Matter

You don't need to spend money on detergents just for delicates. Instead, use this homemade solution: 1 cup baking soda mixed with 1 cup warm water. The baking soda will clean your clothes without harming their delicate fibers.

Pin the Spot!

If you spilled something on a tablecloth or blanket, make the stain easy to find in the laundry room by clipping a bobby pin or safety pin to the location. Find the pin and you've found the stain!

To Pick Up Pills

If you have a Velcro hair roller you no longer use, repurpose it as a lint roller! It's perfect for rolling over sweaters and other clothes to pick up any stray pet hair or pills.

Care for Cotton

Make your clothes last longer by taking your cotton clothing out of the dryer 20 minutes before the cycle is about to end and letting them air-dry the rest of the way. Excess dryer heat can break down the fibers in your clothes prematurely.

Who Knew? Readers' Favorite

Repurpose an old ice cube tray as an organizational tool for your laundry room. It's perfect for keeping buttons that have fallen off your clothes and other small items you may find in your pockets.

All-Natural Fabric Softener

Fabrics made of from natural fibers do not need fabric softeners; only synthetics do. Add ¼ to ½ cup baking soda to the wash cycle to soften synthetic fabrics.

CHAPTER 5

Bedrooms

Bed Pillow Know-How

Here's an easy way to start your spring-cleaning: Begin with your bed pillows. To make them fluffy and fresh, just place them in the clothes dryer with fabric softener and two clean tennis balls for a few minutes.

Refresh Drapes and Bedspreads

The easiest way to freshen draperies and heavy bedspreads is to place them in your dryer with a damp towel, on the delicate cycle, for 30 minutes. For extra freshness, hang them outside afterward if the weather allows.

Quick Fix for a Saggy Mattress

To keep your mattress from sagging, it's a good idea to reverse it once a month. If it dips in the middle, place a few folded sheets under the center to even it out.

The Pencil Is Mightier than the Sword?

Squeaky door hinges can be fixed with a pencil. Just rub the point over the hinge. Pencils contain graphite, which is an effective lubricant. Rubbing a pencil over the ridges of a stubborn house key will also help it slide into the lock more easily.

For Brass That Shines

Shining the brass hinges and knobs of your doors is easier than you think! Apply a white, non-gel toothpaste (a mild abrasive) to door fittings with a soft cloth, then rub. Use a fresh cloth to wipe clean, and your brass will sparkle! To protect brass between cleanings, apply a light coating of olive or lemon oil.

For Sweaty Summers

On sticky summer nights, cool down by sprinkling a little baby powder between your sheets before retiring for the night.

Smell the Roses Everyday

Clean laundry loses its fresh scent quickly when sitting in stuffy drawers and closets. To get your clothes, lingerie, and linens smelling freshly washed all the time, place fabric softener sheets in your dresser drawers.

Keep Drapes Fresh

Try this nifty trick to make sure your new or recently cleaned drapes stay crisp and fresh: Spray them with a few light coats of unscented hair spray before hanging them up.

Raise Matted Carpet

If a section of your carpet has been matted down by a piece of furniture, you can raise the nap back up with this simple ice cube trick. Let the cube melt into the matted area; wait until the next day to vacuum.

If the kids have drawn all over their bedroom walls with crayons, remove the mess with a bit of WD-40 spray, which works like a charm. Afterwards, you'll need something to remove the grease—we like a mixture of dishwashing detergent and white vinegar. If you don't have any WD-40, dip a damp rag into baking soda and rub on the mark to remove it.

Time to Clean Teddy

To clean stuffed animals, just place them in a cloth bag or pillowcase, add baking soda or cornmeal, and shake. The dirt will transfer to the powder.

De-Grease Sticky Playing Cards

An oft-used deck of cards can get sticky and grimy from the oils on your hands. De-grease the cards by placing them in a plastic bag with a few blasts of baby powder. Give it a good shake before dealing the first hand.

Silence a Squeak

When a squeaky door needs grease, spray shaving cream on the offending hinge as a lubricant. Now open and listen—silence! Much easier to play hide-and-seek around the house this way.

Odors Vanish with Vanilla

Fight odors in smelly places throughout the house (closets, coolers, drawers, etc.), with this nifty trick. Place a damp paper towel in a cup and add a couple teaspoons of vanilla extract. Let it sit for a few days in the stinky spot, and the odor will vanish.

Stop a Stale Smell

Wondering how to get that stale odor out of old wooden dressers or chests? Soak a slice of white bread in a shallow dish of white distilled vinegar, and place it inside. It'll freshen up in no time.

Protecting Fine Linens

Use wax paper to separate lace handkerchiefs, doilies, and other linens in your drawers. It will block light and keep dyes from seeping between items.

Reorganize for More Storage Space

Move your bed sheets and linens from the hallway linen closet to a top shelf in your bedroom closet. That way, they'll be closer to where they're actually used, and if you fold them properly, they won't take up much room. The major bonus? You've now freed up a valuable hallway closet to store something else.

Classic Cedar Tip

Clothes moths are a pain in the neck to get rid of once they've invaded your closets. Since mothballs are toxic, pick up cedar chips at a craft store instead—cedar is an effective and safe moth repellent. Stick the chips in cheesecloth or an old nylon sock, tie it closed, and store in closets or drawers to keep the pests away.

Who Knew? Readers' Favorite

Cedar chests are wonderful because they not only look great, but their scent keeps moths away, too. But what to do when they begin to lose their scent? Get out some fine sandpaper and go to work! Gently sanding the inside of the chest will bring its scent back to life, making sure your clothes are safe and your room smells wonderful.

Keep That Candle Longer!

If your wonderfully scented candle is almost gone, it's easy to keep the smell with you! Carefully cut or break the remaining candle into pieces, then put them in an old sock or nylon and hang in your closet. The enclosed space will be filled with your candle's scent every time you open the closet door.

A New Use for Old Toys

Do your kids have lots of stuffed animals? This winter put those less-popular ones to good use: Line them up in front of their bedroom windows to prevent drafts from coming in underneath.

Hoard No More

Going through your closet or storage area and can't decide whether or not to get rid of something? Put it in a "Maybe" box and set it aside. If you haven't used it or thought about it after three months, it's a definite sign you should sell or donate it.

Alleviate Dresser Drawer Mayhem

Is your dresser drawer starting to look like someone ransacked it? Egg cartons and plastic ice cube trays make great organizational tools for jewelry, cuff links, and other trinkets, and they'll easily fit inside your drawer.

Art Supply Storage

Keep art supplies in a clear, vinyl shoe bag hung from the back of your child's door. It's a smart, space-saving way to hold paints, pens, markers, brushes, and more.

A "Cap"-ital Idea

Don't throw away caps to your hair spray, spray starch, and other cans! They make perfect organizing containers for your drawers.

Hanging Handbags

Here's a handy storage tip: Hanging purses to store them puts stress on the handles. You'll do better keeping them on shelves or in one big bag so they'll last longer.

Purse Cleaning Secret

You've cleaned out your purse, but it stills has crumbs, grime, and little pieces of god-only-knows-what at the bottom. Quickly clean it out with a lint roller. Just roll the inside and you're done!

Who Knew? Readers' Favorite

The easiest way to vacuum under a dresser? Just remove the bottom drawer, and you'll be able to suck up those dust bunnies with ease.

Sage Advice

Break up a few leaves of sage and spread them around inside your shoes. They'll kill the bacteria that causes foot odor. To cut down on how much you perspire in the first place, try drinking sage tea. Herbalists say it will take several weeks, but you'll see results!

Perfume Perfection

You probably keep your perfume bottles on your dresser or wherever else you usually apply it. But we keep ours in the refrigerator! Why? The colder temperature makes the volatile chemicals in perfume evaporate less quickly, meaning that your perfume will not only last longer, it will retain the scent it had when you fell in love with it.

CHAPTER 6

The Home Office

Clean Up Your Keys

The easiest way to clean the gunk and dust between your computer keys is with transparent tape. Just slide a two-inch strip between the rows of your keyboard, and the adhesive will pick up any debris.

Delete the Dirt

Need to clean a computer keyboard? Simply dip a cotton swab or cotton ball in hydrogen peroxide and run it between the keys.

Who Knew? Readers' Favorite

Unless it's cracked, it's usually possible to fix a skipping CD. First, eliminate any dust and dirt by holding the CD under running water and rubbing with a soft, lint-free cloth to dry. To fix any scratches, rub a little white (non-gel) toothpaste into the scratch, then wipe with the damp cloth to remove any excess. The toothpaste won't repair the CD entirely, but it will at least keep it from skipping.

Label Madness

If you're like us, you receive free address labels in the mail from time to time. Put them to good use by labeling notebooks, kid's items, and anything else you'd like to personalize.

Lost Your Ruler?

If you need to measure something and don't have a ruler, grab a dollar bill instead. A dollar is exactly six and a quarter inches long.

Cuts Like New

Rehabilitate a pair of old scissors with these simple tips. First, remove any rust by applying a paste of salt and lemon juice, leaving for 15 minutes, and then rubbing thoroughly with a dry cloth. Then, sharpen the scissors by cutting a piece of steel wool or balled-up aluminum foil 20 times or so.

Substitute Staple Remover

Need to remove a staple and don't have a staple remover? Don't risk using your fingernail. Instead, use nail clippers. They work perfectly for removing stubborn staples.

Go-To Glue Remover

To remove glue residue on almost any surface, try vegetable oil on a rag. It's also an easy-breezy way to clean off residue from sticky labels. The vegetable oil neutralizes the glue's bonds.

Get Rid of Glue Fast

If your gluing project gets a little messy, use WD-40 to lift off dried glue spots. Wipe clean and now get back to arts and crafts.

How to Get Unstuck

It's a great feeling when you save the day by breaking out the extra-strong glue. Just remember not to stick your fingers to each other! If you forget, slink off to the supply closet while you pretend everything's fine. This is yet another instance where WD-40 comes to the rescue.

Goo Be Gone

You don't want to know whether the smooshed item on your magazine, book, or page-a-day-calendar is a raisin or something worse. You just want a fast way to get it off! Blow dry (on low). The gooey substance will melt so you can effortlessly wipe it clean.

Invisible Ink

If you have ink stains on your hands from a marker or pen, try this: Just add a bit of sugar to your hands when washing with regular soap, and the granules will act as a gentle abrasive to help wash the ink away.

Who Knew? Readers' Favorite

Use a thinner font to save when you print out documents. Thinner fonts like Times New Roman and Century Gothic will use up to 30 percent less ink than Arial.

Toner Tip

Need to print out some helpful but not super-important pages (such as a grocery, chore, or to-do list)? You can conserve ink by changing the font color to gray rather than using the heavier black ink.

Shake It Up, Baby

Here's a trick used by office workers everywhere: When your printer's out of ink, remove the cartridge and shake it up for a bit. Stick it back into the printer, and you'll find it's got enough ink left for at least a few more print jobs.

Full of Hot Air

You're trying to print out a document, but you just ran out of ink! This solution will save you a trip to the store: Take out the ink cartridge, then blow hot air on it with a hair dryer. Once it's warm, put it back in the printer. The heat loosens the ink that is stuck to the side of the cartridge, often giving you enough to finish the job.

Safely Store Important Papers

The school year is over, and you need a place to store the kids' artwork and diplomas. Try rolling them tightly in paper towel tubes so they won't crease, then label the outside, so you know what's inside. The tubes can also be used to store marriage certificates and other important documents.

Mail Safety Measure

Always put outgoing bills in a post office mailbox instead of the mailbox at your front door. A thief could get to your mail before the mail carrier does, and the information provided in your envelope could lead to identity theft.

Mail Management

If you're mailing out invitations, stick them in the mailbox on Wednesday, so that they'll arrive on Friday or Saturday. People respond more quickly to mail received on the weekend—and you'll get your head count finalized sooner!

Minimize the Mail Pile

With such a busy family, it's hard to control the clutter in our house. So we try to prevent it before it even starts: We keep a small, inconspicuous trashcan near our usual mail-opening spot. That way, we can easily toss junk mail into the garbage without setting it on a table or countertop, where it will sit for weeks.

Send It "Media Mail"

Mailing books, CDs, or DVDs? The cheapest way to get them there is to take your package to the post office and ask for it to be sent "media mail." Though it will take a little longer to arrive, this low rate—reserved for mailing "media"—will save you a lot of money, especially if your package is heavy.

Postage Prescription

If you're sending a get-well card to a friend in the hospital, but aren't sure how long she'll be there, try this: Put the hospital's address on the front of the envelope, and your friend's address as the return address. That way, you're certain she'll get the card—at the hospital or once she returns home. (Just don't tell the post office!)

Unstick Stuck Stamps

If your postage stamps are stuck together, place them in the freezer for about 10 minutes. (Unfortunately, this doesn't work as well with self-adhesive stamps.)

Frozen Moments

If you discover a couple of photos stuck together, don't lose hope! They can be unstuck. Place them in the freezer for half an hour, then gently break them apart with a butter knife. You can also slowly unstick them by blowing air on them with a hairdryer set on low.

Saving Precious Memories

If a beloved book or photo album has gotten wet, it's not ruined yet. Try sprinkling baby or baking powder on each page, then placing it in a closed paper bag for up to a week. The powder should absorb the water while keeping your book safe.

Newspaper Mementos

To preserve special newspaper clippings, dissolve a milk of magnesia tablet in a shallow pan with a quart of club soda. Soak the paper for an hour, then let it lay flat to dry. Afterward, it's best to keep the paper under plastic in a photo album.

Who Knew? Readers' Favorite

If your windows or desk drawers are stuck, simply rub a candle or white soap on the runners and the problem should be solved.

Finally, a Use for Old Telephone Cords!

If your desk is a tangled mess of computer, printer, and internet cables, keep them tidy by running them through a coiled telephone cord. The coils will keep everything together neatly. You can also use a few cardboard tubes from paper towels instead of a telephone cord.

Bind Your Cords

You'll love this way to keep all the cords to your various electronic devices organized on your desk. Clasp several binder clips to the side of your desk, then slide the cord through the arms and let the plug be held by the narrower end. Instant organization!

Nonskid Drawers

A nonskid rug pad is a terrific liner for your office drawers. The tacky surface prevents paper clips, thumbtacks—anything!—from slipping around. It'll work well in your kitchen drawers, too.

Dry-Erase Board Substitute

Need a dry-erase board? Consider picking up white shower board instead—it does the job just as well, but it's less expensive. You can find it sold in sheets at most home supply stores. Just cut it down to the size you want and either frame it or hang it on the wall as is.

Cleaner Communications

The phone is a bacteria hotspot. Wipe yours down with alcohol wipes or plain alcohol on paper towels. (Don't forget the phone at work.) It not only helps the spread of colds, it will also cut down on acne along your jawline.

A Surprising Use for an Egg Carton

Forget bubble wrap and packing peanuts! For a cheaper and more environmentally sound alternative, hold on to old foam egg cartons, and use the egg cups as packing material. Store them stacked on a shelf in your closet, and you've got sturdy padding handy for your next fragile package.

Consider a Credit Union

Tired of all the fees and high interest rates at your bank? Consider joining a credit union instead. CUs are not-for-profit, member-owned institutions, thus allowing them to be more beneficial for every account holder—not just the ultra-wealthy ones. To find one in your area and to determine if it's right for you, visit NCUA.gov and select "Credit union data."

Internet Password Organizer

If you're in over your head when it comes to computer passwords, consider trying out RoboForm.com. This neat site keeps track of your passwords on one encrypted site, then enters them when you're at sites that require passwords.

Save Your Dying Cell Phone Battery

You've just realized your cell phone's battery is about to die, but you're at work at don't have your charger. Get a little more talk time by detaching the battery and placing it in your workplace's freezer, then allowing it to come back up to room temperature before you use it. The cold will keep your battery from losing any more juice.

Hey, Watch This!

The next time someone at work asks you why you bother wearing a watch anymore, show them this: Put your watch face-up on your desk and your mouse on top of it. The reflective surface will confuse the optics inside your mouse, making your computer think it's still moving. If you have a work computer that makes you log in every five minutes when you're not "active," you know how helpful this is!

Sounds Great

Have trouble hearing music through your mobile device's speakers? Just place it in a bowl (preferably an aluminum or stainless steel one). The sides of the bowl will amplify the sound.

CHAPTER 7

The Great Outdoors

Bid Adieu to Oil Stains

Cleaning oil spots off the driveway is difficult, and the cleaners can be quite expensive. Instead, sprinkle baking soda over the stains, then rub with a scrub brush soaked with hot water. The baking soda breaks apart oil particles, so with a little elbow grease you can have your driveway spot-free in no time.

Get Rid of Grease

Another way to remove a grease stain from your concrete driveway is to rub kitty litter into the stain and let it stand for one to two hours before sweeping it up. The super-absorbent litter will soak up the stain.

Tidy Up the Driveway

You can keep paved areas looking spiffy with this trick. To remove unwanted grass or weeds from sidewalk and driveway cracks, squirt them with a solution of 1 gallon vinegar, 1 cup salt, and 8 drops liquid detergent.

Sidewalk Cleanup

Want to get rid of the grass growing in the cracks of your sidewalk or patio? Make a mixture of salt and baking soda, sprinkle it on and sweep it into the cracks. Problem solved.

Stains on Stones?

If you have stains on paving stones or a concrete patio, the solution is simple. Try pouring hot water from several feet above the stone onto the stain. Repeat several times, and your stain may just disappear. If this doesn't work, try rubbing some dishwashing liquid into the spot with a toothbrush, then rinsing off. For really tough stains, add a bit of ammonia to the water.

Algae Antidote

Your birdbath used to be a hot spot for the feathered folk, but ever since it became slimy with algae, they've stayed away! Make your birdbath as fresh as new by emptying the water, then covering it with bleach-soaked paper towels or newspaper. After letting the paper sit for 5–10 minutes, remove it and rinse the bath thoroughly. Then fill it with fresh water and watch the birds enjoy. To attract even more birds to your birdbath, just cover the bottom with multi-colored marbles.

A Better Birdbath

There's a chemical in lavender that inhibits the growth of algae. Make a bundle of lavender flowers and daylily leaves for your birdbath to keep it free and clear of algae. Change every few weeks.

Slip and Slide

This idea may conjure up a cartoon chase scene, but here's a safe, natural way to feed the birds and not the squirrels: Simply rub shortening on the pole leading up to your feeder to keep the uninvited guests from letting themselves in.

No Fungus Among Us

If you have mold on your faux wicker (plastic resin) furniture, get it summer-ready by mixing a paste of lemon and salt. Polish it on in a circular motion, rinse, and leave to dry in the sun. If your patio umbrella has mold, here's another easy fix: Fill a bucket with warm water, add 2 cups of white vinegar, and a couple of generous squirts of dishwashing liquid. Let soak for a half an hour, then scrub with a cleaning brush. Rinse with water and let it dry in the sun.

Get Your Wicker Ready for Spring

Make sure your wicker furniture is front-porch ready for the spring and summer months. Blow-dry off the loose dirt, then clean with white vinegar and warm salt water, and apply a coat of lemon oil.

A Little Lube

To keep your metal deck furniture free from rust and wear all winter long, reach for the petroleum jelly. Just apply a thin layer (especially in areas where the furniture tends to rust) after cleaning the surface with simple soap and water.

Stow Your Wicker for the Winter

Before the first freeze arrives, bring all your wicker furniture inside to protect it from the cold. Freezing will cause the wicker to crack and split, which unfortunately is impossible to repair.

Frugal Furniture Covers

No space to bring outdoor furniture inside in bad weather? Instead of buying pricey furniture covers, protect lawn chairs and tables by covering them with large plastic bags.

Store Your Hose Properly for Maximum Usage

Your garden hose will last twice as long if you store it coiled, rather than folded. Try coiling it around a bucket. Note that the hose will be easiest to work with when it's neither very cold nor very hot outside.

Who Knew? Readers' Favorite

If you have an old hose you're about to throw away, here's a great second use. Cut off a two-inch section, then cut a horizontal slit all the way through it. Slide onto the handles of buckets to make them easier to carry. Reinforce with duct tape if necessary.

Keep Your Trash Bag in Place

When you're raking leaves, nothing is more frustrating than a plastic trash bag that slips down into the garbage can. Rest easy, friends: All you need to do is secure the bag with a bungee cord (or two) and get to work. Fold the open end of the bag over the rim of the trashcan and wrap the cord around the outside to hold it in place.

Tiki Torch To-Do

If you have tiki torches lighting up your backyard, here's a trick that make them burn twice as long. Before you start them blazing, soak the wick of each torch in white or apple cider vinegar for an hour, then allow them to dry. The vinegar will make the wick burn more slowly.

Guard Outdoor Light Bulbs from Winter Wear

Before it gets too cold, consider applying a thin layer of petroleum jelly to the threads of all your outdoor light bulbs. It will prevent them from rusting and make them easier to replace when they blow out.

Shovel Snow Without Killing Your Back

Shoveling wet, heavy snow is a backbreaking job, but you can make it easier with a simple tip: Just coat your shovel with vegetable shortening, car wax, or cooking spray, and the snow won't stick. If you're using a snowblower, coat the inside of the chute.

Don't Stand On Icy Ground—Melt It!

Make your winter season safer by salting icy ground in the most effective way possible. Use a lawn seeder or fertilizer spreader to distribute salt or sand in a thin, even layer. And don't forget to watch your step!

Flag FYI

You may know there are particular rules governing how to keep and fly a flag, and that includes making sure it stays clean. To do so, simply wash with a bit of liquid dish or laundry detergent in the sink. Iron to get out any wrinkles. For vintage flags or flags with tassels, get them dry-cleaned.

Proper Pyrotechnics

Setting off fireworks this Fourth of July? Make sure you keep a bucket of water on hand in case of fire, and never try to relight a firecracker that malfunctioned or didn't go off for some reason. Only light fireworks on a smooth, flat surface away from others.

Who Knew? Readers' Favorite

If there is too much chlorine in your pool, don't buy expensive treatments that will just have you balancing and counter-balancing chemicals for the rest of the summer. Simply don't put the cover on the pool for several days. The sun will naturally lower the chlorine content, and after a bit of evaporation, you can add more fresh water.

Cleaner Containers

We haven't figured out why our storage containers always seem to be covered with a sticky substance when we take them out of the garage. But we have figured out a way to prevent it! Simply spray them with cooking spray and sticky substances will be less likely to cling.

A Clever Catch-All

When you're clearing out leaves this fall, make a sturdy leaf bag with this smart trick: Cut out the bottom of a hard plastic laundry basket, and stick the bottomless basket into your leaf bag. It'll hold the bag in place so you can dump leaves into it without worrying about spills. Just remove the basket when the bag is ready for the trash.

Proper Use of Paving Stones

Never use decorative paving stones near your home. Certain kinds of ants love to make their homes underneath them! Use them away from your house to be sure ants won't decide to come in for a visit.

Padlock Protection

Have a padlock on your shed or another outdoor structure? Keep it from rusting by protecting it from the elements. Slice open the side of a tennis ball (carefully!) and slip it over the lock.

CHAPTER 8

Home Repair

Thaw Frozen Pipes Before They Burst

When temps drop to freezing, be on alert for frozen pipes in your walls, attic, or basement. Should a pipe burst, you might be left with some serious and costly damage. If your pipes are frozen but haven't yet burst, find the suspected area (often in an exterior wall), turn on your faucets, and use a blow-dryer to thaw it out. As always, though, take care that the hair dryer doesn't get wet.

Moving Marble

If you're moving a large piece of marble, such as a tabletop, always transport it upright. If you carry it flat, it can crack under its own weight.

Repurpose Wine Corks

Slice old corks into thin disks, then glue them to the feet of your heavy furniture. It's a great way to protect your floors, and it makes moving the furniture a bit easier.

Walls Have Cavities, Too!

Small holes in your white wall? It's toothpaste to the rescue! Simply dab a small amount of white (non-gel) toothpaste into the hole, and you'll never notice it again—or at least your guests won't!

Who Knew? Readers' Favorite

Before driving a nail into a plaster wall, place a small piece of tape over the spot you're working on. This simple prep step will prevent cracking.

Got Grease Stains on Your Wall?

If grease is still visible on the wall after removing wallpaper, apply a coat of clear varnish to the spots. The grease won't soak through to the new wallpaper.

Wallpaper 101

Hanging wallpaper? Try using a paint roller to apply paste, instead of a sponge, and then use a separate clean paint roller to smooth it out afterward. You'll get more coverage per stroke.

A Sour Solution for Old Wallpaper

You're renovating the kitchen, and step one is taking down that old wallpaper. To make your job easier, use a sponge or spray bottle to saturate the wallpaper with vinegar first. Wait a few minutes and it will peel right off.

Border Patrol

Redoing a room with a wallpaper border? Easily remove it by blowing hot hair from a hair dryer on it. The heat will loosen the glue and it will peel right off.

Speed Up a Paint Job

Quicken your interior paint jobs by mixing a quart of semigloss latex paint into a gallon of flat latex paint. The finish won't shine more than it would with straight flat paint, but the paint will glide on and cover much more easily.

When painting your house, it's always a good idea to keep track of paint colors—you may need them to match future paint jobs or to help you coordinate other items in the house. Create swatches by dipping a 3-by-5-inch index card into your paint can and writing down the details.

Don't Let Your White Paint Yellow

Some white paints can yellow in a matter of months, making a new paint job look much older and staler than it really is. Keep your white walls white by adding 7–10 drops of black paint to each quart. Also, when selecting your paint colors, note that white paint will age better if exposed to natural light.

Get Rid of Paint Smell

If you hate the smell of drying paint, fix it before you start. Simply add 1½ teaspoons vanilla extract to a gallon of paint, and your drying walls will smell delicious.

This Tip is Old News

When painting a windowsill, forget the edging tape: It's expensive, and it can pull up the paint you already have on the sill. Instead, use strips of newspaper. Dampen them and wring out as much excess moisture as you can without ruining the paper, then use them in lieu of tape. They'll stick as long as they're wet, but won't pull up any paint when you're done.

Remove a Painting Mistake

You've just painted your window trim and got a big glob of "country yellow" on the glass pane. There's no need to use a dangerous razor blade to remove the paint that spilled on the glass. Instead, remove the paint safely and easily with a pencil eraser. If the paint has dried, or is old, dab on some nail polish remover, wait a minute, then erase.

No Cleaning Necessary (for Now)

If you want to avoid cleaning a paint roller, wrap it in foil or a plastic bag and place it in the refrigerator. This will keep the roller moist and usable for a few days, so you can finish where you left off later.

The Art of Paintbrush Maintenance

Old, crusty paintbrushes put a cramp in our paint projects. To soften those bristles, we soak them in full-strength white vinegar and then clean them with a comb. To prevent brushes from hardening in the first place, rub a few drops of vegetable oil into freshly cleaned bristles to keep them soft.

Keep Your Paint Fresh for Longer

If you've got leftover paint, you can prevent it from drying up with this crafty maneuver: Blow up a balloon until it's about the size of the remaining space in the can. Then put it inside the can and close the lid. This will reduce the amount of air in the can, thus prolonging the paint's freshness.

Want your paint to last longer in the can? First, place a piece of plastic wrap under the paint can's lid, then make certain the lid is on tight before you turn the can over. The paint is exposed to less oxygen this way and will last much, much longer.

Avoid That Icky Paint Skin

If you've ever stored a partially used paint can, you've probably noticed that a skin of dried-up paint forms at the top of the can. To prevent this, place a piece of waxed paper the size of the opening on top of the remaining paint.

Strain Out Lumpy Paint

If you have lumps in your paint, cut a piece of window screen just slightly smaller than the circumference of the can. Place it inside the can and let it settle to the bottom. It'll carry the lumps with it.

Guard Your Work (and Your Shirt) from Dripping Paint

To catch drips while you paint, try this makeshift drip cup: Cut a tennis ball in half and slice a thin slot in the bottom bowl of one half. Then slide your brush handle through the slot so the bristles stick out of the open side. A small paper plate or cup works too.

Prevent a Dripping Paint Can

You know that little groove along the rim of a paint can that tends to fill up and spill paint all over the place? Using a nail or an awl, notch a few holes in there to create a drain for the paint, so it drips back into the can instead of dripping down the outside. Alternatively, you can place masking tape on the rim of the paint can before pouring—remove the tape later and the rim will be clean.

Who Knew? Readers' Favorite

Painting doors? Avoid getting paint on the hinges by coating them lightly with petroleum jelly before you start.

Paint Roller Pan Liner

There's no need to spend your money on disposable paint liners for your roller pan. It's just as easy to line the pan with aluminum foil—and a lot cheaper, too.

Perfect Pan Liner

Here's yet another use for larger plastic bags you get from the store: Put one over a roller tray whenever you're painting with a roller. When the job is done, just pull off the bag and turn inside-out to throw away, and the tray is ready to be used again!

Quick Clean for a Paintbrush

The fastest way to clean a paintbrush? Put ½ cup liquid fabric softener in a gallon of water and vigorously swirl the brush in it for 20 seconds.

Revive Old Paintbrushes

Don't throw out old paintbrushes. Just soak them in hot vinegar for 20 minutes, then wash with dish soap and warm water. They'll be close to brand new again.

For Paint-Covered Hands

It's hard not to get paint all over yourself when painting a room. And old household trick is to wipe turpentine on your hands to get the paint off, but there's a much less smelly way! Simply rub your hands with olive oil, let it sit a couple of seconds, then rub off with a damp, soapy sponge. Not only will the olive oil remove the paint, but it's great for your skin, too! For enamel or oil paint, rub your hands with floor paste wax, and then wash with soap and water.

Sticky Fingers (and How to Unstick Them)

If you glue your fingers together when working with a quick-bonding glue or epoxy, nail polish remover will do the trick. If you get stuck working with rubber cement, try lacquer thinner; you may need to let the thinner soak in for a few minutes before gently pulling your fingers apart.

Looking for a Stud? (In a Wall, That Is)

If you'd like to hang a heavy mirror or piece of art, you'll first have to locate a wall stud. Don't own a stud finder? No worries. Studs are normally 16 inches apart, so measure 17 inches from a corner to find your first stud. Keep measuring out by 16 inches until you find the stud nearest your desired spot. Alternatively, you can use a compass. Hold a compass level with the floor and at a right angle to the wall, and then slowly move the compass along the surface of the wall. When the needle moves, that's where you will find a stud.

When's Your Wood Smooth Enough to Use?

If you're sanding wood and want to know when it's smooth enough, use the pantyhose test: Slip an old nylon stocking over your hand and run it over the wood. You'll have no trouble finding the slightest rough spot. Just don't wear those nylons afterwards!

Aged Wood Absorbs Stains Best

If you allow wood to "weather" before you apply a stain, the stain will last years longer. It's a case where patience pays off.

For a Smooth Varnish

Stir varnish thoroughly from the bottom of the can, but don't stir vigorously. Stirring can create air bubbles, which can ruin a smooth finish. If you notice air bubbles, brush them out while the varnish is still wet. If it's already dry, gently buff them out with very fine steel wool.

Flour Power

If you're painting old woodwork and need to patch small holes, fill them with flour and then paint. It will harden without being noticeable.

Who Knew? Readers' Favorite

If you need to repair a hole in a piece of wood, add a small amount of instant coffee to the Spackle, or to a thick paste made from a laundry starch and warm water. The coffee tints the paste to camouflage the patched-up spot.

Window Screen Fix-Up

To repair small holes in window screens, cover them with a few of layers of clear nail polish. It will keep the hole from becoming bigger and prevent insects from coming through.

Tighten Droopy Cane Chairs

A chair's caning can loosen and begin to droop. If you let it go long enough, you might even fall through the seat and hurt your bum (not to mention your ego). But, no fear! You can tighten it easily and cheaply. Apply very hot water to the underside, then dry the chair in direct sunlight.

A Safe Ladder, with a Coffee to Go

Save up your used coffee cans for your next home-maintenance project. If you need to use a ladder on soft earth, set the legs inside those empty cans so they won't sink from your weight.

Saw Safety

Keeping your saws safely stored is easy. Use a split piece of old garden hose to cover the sharp teeth whenever they're not in use.

Nip Rust in the Bud

Prevent your tools from rusting now, and avoid the annoying rust-removal process later. Place a few mothballs, a piece of chalk, or a piece of charcoal in your toolbox—all three eliminate moisture and fight rust before it begins. If you've got nuts and bolts that are rusted together, just submerge them in cola for a day and they'll come apart easily.

Loosen a Rusty Nut or Bolt

To remove that pesky rusted nut or bolt, put a few drops of ammonia or hydrogen peroxide on it, and wait 30 minutes. If you're out of both, try a little bit of cola instead.

Squeaky floorboards? Make them a thing of the past by sprinkling a little talcum powder between the boards.

Squeak Tweak

Squeaky doors and cabinet hinges, as well as sticky locks, benefit from a light spritz of a nonstick cooking spray. And it's cheaper than WD-40, too!

Safely Remove a Busted Light Bulb

To remove a broken light bulb from the socket, first turn off the electricity or unplug the lamp, and then push half of a raw potato or small apple into the broken bulb's base. Turn it to unscrew the base. Just don't eat it afterward!

Fix a Glass Scratch

Don't tell the kids this, but scratches in the window and breakfront glass don't have to be permanent. Rub a little white toothpaste into the mark and buff. Wipe clean and coat with a solution of 1 tablespoon vinegar and ½ cup water.

Patch It Up

Patch up little holes and imperfections in your walls with a natural paste made from 2 tablespoons salt, 2 tablespoons cornstarch, and 5 teaspoons water. Sand first, then spread the paste over the areas you want to revitalize.

Careful Nail Removal

If you do more damage than good when removing nails with the claw of a hammer, you can use a spatula as a guard, holding it between the claw and the wall each time you yank.

Got a Screw Loose?

Are the knobs to your drawers and cabinets coming loose? To fix the problem forever, remove the knob and coat the end of the screw with nail polish (use clear if you're a bit messy), then screw the knob back on before the polish dries.

Chalk Talk

Chalk is good for more than just writing! If your kids have outgrown sidewalk chalk, or you happen to have some around, place it in the damp areas of your home (like your basement) to absorb excess moisture and repel mildew. Use a container that allows air to get through it, like a mesh bag, a coffee can, or a paper bag with holes poked in it.

Who Knew? Readers' Favorite

You need a Phillips-head screwdriver, but your search through your junk drawer was fruitless. A great replacement in a pinch is a metal potato peeler. The curved top edge will fit into the x-shaped groove of the screw.

A Nutty Idea

The next time someone sends you a box full of packing peanuts, save a few and throw them in your toolbox. They're great for getting screws into stripped holes. Just stuff the packing peanut into the hole, and then turn the screw into its dense Styrofoam. Cut away any pieces of the peanut that remain outside the hole.

Fix a Chip

If you've chipped a vase, stop swearing at yourself and go get your kid's biggest box of crayons. Then very carefully hold a flame under the tip of the crayon, letting the melted wax drip onto the chip. Once it has cooled but not hardened, smooth it out and your vase will be almost as good as new.

Open a Sealed Window

If humidity has sealed your window shut, here's how to get it open again: Hold a block of wood up against the frame, and tap it gently a few times with a hammer. Then move to a different place on the frame until you've tapped all the around the edges. You should now be able to easily pull it up.

Must Buster

Does your basement smell like, well, a basement? Try this: Cut an onion in half, and put it on a plate near where you smell the mildew. It will smell like an onion for a bit, but afterwards, the mildew odor will be gone!

There's a blackout, and you just realized your flashlight is out of D batteries. Even if you don't have any of these jumbo batteries around the house, there may be a solution: Place a couple of C-sized batteries inside and fill up the extra space with a ball of aluminum foil. You won't get as bright of a light, but it will help shine the way.

Temporary Screen Fix

Don't leave a hole in your screen door just because you don't have the right tools to fix it. Instead use rubber cement to affix a small piece of pantyhose around the area. It's easy to remove but will keep ugly flying things out of your house in the meantime (at least the ones that don't live there).

Light the Way

We were nostalgic about our boys' dinosaur nightlights, but—like many relics from their baby years—they were ready to toss them without so much as a backward glance. What to do? Turns out a nightlight on an extension cord can serve as a perfect work light for a small, dark space so we held on to all of them. Dragons do live forever!

CHAPTER 9

Your Car

For a Better Car Battery

The corrosion around your car battery posts can be cleaned easily with a thick solution of baking soda and water. Let it stand for 10–15 minutes before washing it off.

Is Your Car Winter-Ready?

Winterize your car battery so you don't get stuck in the cold. Pour a can of cola over the battery posts; let it sit for a half hour, then wipe it clean. Rub petroleum jelly on the posts before reattaching the battery cables. You should be good to go for the winter!

Tar on Your Car

It's easy to remove tar from the outside of your car. Make a paste of baking soda and water, then apply it to the tar with a soft cloth. Let it dry, then rinse off with warm water.

Clean Car with Cornstarch

To clean dirty windows or your car's windshield, mix a tablespoon of cornstarch to about ½ gallon of warm water, and dry with a soft cloth. It's amazing how quickly the dirt is removed—and no streaking, either!

Club Soda Saver

One thing that never leaves our cluttered trunk (except when we're using it) is a spray bottle filled with club soda. Club soda does wonders for getting grime, bird droppings, and bug guts off your windshield. Just spray on, wait a few minutes, and turn on the wipers.

Smeary Windshield Wipers

Messy wipers are a safety hazard, and they're also pretty annoying. To fix the problem, wipe the blades with some rubbing alcohol.

Make Car Cleaning Easier

One of the dirtiest parts of your car is usually the wheels, thanks to all the dark brake dust that accumulates there. Next time you clean your car's wheels, spray them with a light coat of vegetable oil when you're done. It will keep the dust from clinging, and you'll be able to wipe off the dust easily. Use steel wool pads for cleaning whitewalls.

Gross Grille?

Don't you hate the smashed-up insects that seem to cover your car grille in the summer? The only thing worse than looking at them is trying to scrape them off, unless you try this trick: Spray a light coating of vegetable oil or nonstick cooking spray on your grille, and the revolting bugs will wipe off easily.

Who Knew? Readers' Favorite

Got a bunch of bug guts on your windshield after a road trip? Easily remove them with a pair of old pantyhose and some vinegar. Just bunch up the hose and wet it with white vinegar, then easily scrub away.

Zap the Sap!

Tree sap dripping on your car is one of the hazards of summer, but you can remove it easily with butter or margarine. Just rub the butter onto the sap with a soft cloth, and it comes right off.

De-Rust Your Bumper

The best way to remove rust from your car's chrome bumper? Just rub the rusted area with a shiny piece of crumpled aluminum foil that has been dipped in cola.

A Surefire Way to Wipe Away Window Decals

Transparent decals may be easily removed using a solution of lukewarm water and white vinegar. Place the solution on a sponge and dampen the area thoroughly for a few minutes. If this doesn't work, saturate the decal with straight vinegar and let stand for 15 minutes.

Who Knew? Readers' Favorite

Is it finally time to get rid of your "Gore 2000" bumper sticker? Try this: Set your blow-dryer on high and run it back and forth over the sticker until the adhesive softens. Then apply a bit of vegetable oil. Carefully lift a corner with a credit card, and peel it off.

Make Dashboard Scratches Disappear

Got scuffs and scratches on your odometer? You can eliminate the marks on dashboard plastic by rubbing them with a bit of baby oil.

Got a Stink in Your Car?

Instead of buying a commercial air freshener, repurpose a dryer sheet to sweeten the air. Place sheets under the seats, in door pockets, or in the trunk to keep your car smelling fresh.

Forget the Ice Scraper

When the forecast calls for ice or snow, protect your car by placing two old bath towels across your windshield. When it's time to drive, simply pull off the towels and you're ready to go!

Ice Proof Your Windshield

If an ice storm is in the forecast, coat your windshield with a solution of one part water to three parts white vinegar. It will keep your windshield ice-free.

Ice Ain't Nice

In the winter months, the only thing worst than having ice all over your windshield is having to spend a lot for a windshield deicer. Here's an inexpensive, yet effective, alternative to deice your windshield and windows: 1 part antifreeze, 4½ parts alcohol, and 4½ parts water.

Prepare Your Car for Winter Weather

Before winter hits, fill a few old milk cartons with sand or kitty litter and keep them in your car's trunk. If you get stuck, sprinkle the sand on the ice to improve the tires' traction.

Who Knew? Readers' Favorite

If your car doors freeze shut during the frigid winter months, try this preventative measure: Rub vegetable oil on the rubber moldings around your doors. Since it's the rubber, not the metal, in your doors that freezes, lubing it with oil should do the trick.

Stuck in the Mud?

If you get stuck in snow or mud, try using your car floor mat for traction. Better yet, be prepared and keep a blanket in the trunk for this very purpose.

Be Careful with Cruise Control

Important safety tip! While cruise control is a great fuel-conserving feature on your car, make sure it's turned off when the roads are wet or icy. If your tires start to hydroplane, the cruise control may continue to accelerate, and you might end up skidding and losing control of the wheel when your tires catch the ground again.

Spend Less on Car Washes

Specialty items used to clean cars are often found in big box and hardware stores. However, you'll find the same items—squeegees, shams, and sponges—for much less in the cleaning aisle of your local grocery store.

And No One Will Be the Wiser

Misjudge how much room you had backing out of a parking spot? Just whip out a can of WD-40 and spray whichever car got left with a paint stain. Wipe with a clean cloth or tissue and the paint will come right off.

Safe from Spit Up

Taking a road trip? If your baby tends to lose most of her food on your car's upholstery, don't forget to guard it with a towel, tablecloth, or bath mat before you leave.

Fantastic Air Freshener

We love this cheap, environmentally friendly air freshener for the car. All you need is an old, burned-up candle with a strong scent. Chop the leftover wax into chunks, slip it into an unused (but clean!) sock, and tie the sock closed. Stick it in the side pockets of your car door or under the seat during cooler months.

Who Knew? Readers' Favorite

When your car's keyless remote needs a new battery, don't head to the dealership for a replacement—

depending on the kind of car you have, it could cost anywhere from $50 to $150. Instead, pry open your remote and check the size and type of battery you need. Then head to a hardware or electronics store for a much-cheaper alternative.

Boost Your Remote

Want to know how to increase the range of your car's keyless entry by 30 percent? Just press it against your head as you use it. It will conduct the (perfectly safe) radio signal through your body, giving its travel power a boost. Strange but true!

A Penny for Your Thoughts?

Does your car need new tires? To find out, put Abe Lincoln to work! Place a penny in your tire's shallowest tread, with Abe facing the hubcap. If you can see the hair on top of the president's head, the tread is worn down to the point that you should buy new tires.

Saved a Scorched Cell Phone

Left your cell phone in your hot car, and now it won't work? Just turn on the car's air-conditioner, and direct it at the phone. When you get home, continue cooling the phone until it is no longer hot to the touch, and then put it in an airtight bag in the fridge (not freezer) for five minutes. Your phone should work fine again now!

Control the Clutter

Your daughter is suddenly too cool for her Dora the Explorer backpack. It's not even worn out, but it's not really your look, either. A great way to repurpose it is to use it as storage in your car! It will easily hang on the back of one of the front seats to store all those odds and ends that usually litter the floor.

Who Knew? Readers' Favorite

Chips in your car's paint job can be expensive to fix, so before you head to the auto body shop, see if you can find a crayon that closely matches the color of your car. Fill in the nick with the crayon, and then buff gently. This works especially well with minor scratches!

Frugal Fueling

The cheapest days to refuel your car are Tuesdays and Wednesdays. People fuel up on Thursdays and Fridays for weekend trips, and on Monday for their workweek. Therefore, most gas stations do their weekly price changes on Tuesdays or Wednesdays.

Don't Tempt Fate

If you park your car on the street, make sure to remove any electronics from your car, as well as the holders. Thieves will often break into cars if they see a GPS holder attached to the windshield, assuming that the unit is in the glove compartment.

PART THREE

MORE WAYS TO SAVE

In this section, we pull out all the stops to help you make the most of your budget—on your schedule. You'll find out how to get rid of pests that invade your home using ingredients you already have; get more goodies from your garden; haggle like a hero; beat the airlines at their own game; keep the kids under control, and much, much more. Whether you're a novice at saving money or you consider yourself scrimping royalty, you're bound to find lots of tricks and tips that will have you saying, "Who knew?"

CHAPTER 1

Getting Rid of Pests

Killing Roaches the Green Way

Nothing is more revolting than roaches, except perhaps the chemicals we use to kill them. Try this natural pesticide: Make a mixture of equal parts cornstarch and plaster of paris, and sprinkle it in the cracks where roaches appear. They'll soon be a thing of the past.

A Safer Roach Spray

Chasing, banging with a shoe, and squishing—none of these is a fail-safe method when it comes to getting rid of roaches. Go for the kill by zapping them with WD-40 instead of bug spray.

A Spoonful of Sugar...

Sugar and baking powder are a great one-two punch when it comes to getting rid of roaches. Mix in equal parts and shake over any area where you've had a sighting or suspect entry. Clean and replace at regular intervals. Sugar attracts, baking soda (strangely) kills.

Who Knew? Readers' Favorite

Another great method for eliminating cockroaches is to fill a large bowl with cheap wine, then place it under the sink or wherever you see the revolting little bugs. The pests drink the wine, get drunk, and drown.

Say Bye to the Flies

The easiest way to get rid of fruit flies is to limit their access to their favorite foods. Let your fresh fruit ripen in closed paper bags. Then when it's ripe, store it in the refrigerator.

Fruit Fly Formula

To eliminate fruit flies naturally, fill a spray bottle with 10 parts water and one part rubbing alcohol, and spray away. It's about as effective as an insecticide, but not nearly as harmful to your family.

Vengeance with Vinegar

Have a fruit fly problem? Add a couple of drops of dishwashing liquid to a bowl of apple cider vinegar and leave it where you see flies. The smell of the vinegar attracts the flies, while the dish soap breaks the surface tension of the vinegar and causes the little nuisances to drown.

Herbal Help

A number of herbs will ward off crawling insects. The most potent are fresh or dried bay leaves, sage, and cloves. Place any of these herbs in locations where a problem exists, and the critters will do an about-face and leave the premises. Ants, roaches, and spiders may be more difficult to get rid of. If these herbs don't work, try mixing 2 cups borax with an equal amount of sugar in a large container, and then sprinkle the mixture in areas that you know the pests frequent. When crawling insects cross a fine powder, they lose the waterproof layer from their bodies, causing water loss and, ultimately, death.

Repel Flying Insects

Basil is not just for pesto! If you have a problem with any type of flying insect, keep a basil plant or two around the house. You can also dry the leaves and hang them in small muslin bags to repel flying insects—they hate the sweet aroma.

Clove's the Way

Silverfish are disgusting, down to each and every one of their little legs. An effective, natural way to repel them is with whole cloves. Just sprinkle a few in drawers and other areas where you see them.

So Long, Silverfish

Silverfish like to hang around damp places, but they'll slither away if you decorate with spiced sachets. Try combining sage, bay leaves, and apple pie spice in fabric bags and hanging in the kitchen, bathroom, basement, and other moist areas.

Who Knew? Readers' Favorite

If you can figure out where ants are entering your house, you can keep them out. Simply sprinkle salt, cinnamon, chalk dust, or ashes on their path of entry, and they'll turn around and go elsewhere.

A Not-So-Happy Ending for Carpenter Ants

Get rid of carpenter ants naturally with this formula: Mix one packet dry yeast with ½ cup molasses and ½ cup sugar, and spread on a piece of cardboard. Leave this sticky trap wherever you see the ants; they'll come in droves to the sweet smell. Unfortunately for them, they'll also get stuck. Wait until your molasses mixture is covered with the creepy pests, then throw away. We've also had readers tell us they've used this method for catching wasps!

Mealworm Menace

Keep a few sticks of wrapped spearmint chewing gum near any open packages of pasta, and they'll never get infested with mealworms.

A Mouse's Favorite Food

Though cartoons would have us believe otherwise, mice love the flavor of peanut butter even more than cheese. If you're having problems trapping a mouse with cheese, try smearing peanut butter on the trap instead.

Mice Hate Mint

If you're suffering from a mouse infestation and can see the mouse holes, smear a bit of mint toothpaste nearby and the smell will deter them. You can also rub toothpaste along the bottom of your baseboards and anywhere else mice may get into your home.

Peppermint for Pests

In addition to mice, moles, squirrels, gophers, and rats also hate the aroma of peppermint. Try planting mint near your home—chances are you will never see one of these pests again! For a preexisting gopher problem, soak cotton balls in peppermint oil and then drop them down a gopher hole.

Who Knew? Readers' Favorite

If you're squeamish about having to pick up the remains of a rodent you've set a trap for, place the baited trap inside a brown paper lunch bag. Rodents like exploring small spaces, and once the trap has done its trick, you can scoop it right up and throw it way.

Keep Flies Away from Their Favorite Places

If you don't keep trashcans and compactors sealed tightly, you can quickly end up with a swarm of flies. Luckily, flies are repelled by lavender oil. Soak a few cotton balls with the oil and toss them into your garbage at the beginning of each week. The flies will stay away and your garbage won't smell as bad! Other natural repellents that will send flies in the other direction are oil of cloves and wintergreen mint sprigs.

Keep Plants Pest-Free

When watering outdoor plants, place a few drops of dishwashing liquid into the water, and make sure it gets on your plants' leaves. The detergent will keep bugs away, making sure your plants remain healthy and beautiful.

Do Battle with an Army of Ants

If your yard or garden is infested with pesky ants, sprinkle artificial sweetener (anything with aspartame) over the affected areas. Or try oats, cornmeal, instant grits, or cream of wheat. The ants will eat the dry cereal, which will then absorb all the moisture in their bodies and kill them.

Solve a Snail or Slug Problem

Need to get rid of snails or slugs in your garden? Find the cheapest beer you can, then pour it into several shallow containers (shoeboxes lined with aluminum foil work well). Dig a few shallow holes in your garden and place the containers inside so that they are at ground level. Leave overnight, and the next morning you'll find dozens of dead (or drunk) snails and slugs instead. These critters are attracted to beer (who isn't!), but it has a diuretic effect on them, causing them to lose vital liquids and die.

Clear Out Slugs with Cabbage

If you're having problems with slugs eating your flowers and nothing else seems to work, your best solution might be in the form of distraction. Slugs love cabbage, so planting a few in your garden will ensure they stay away from your flowers and go for the cabbage instead.

Save Your Plants

If you want to keep bugs off your plants, try spraying the leaves with a solution of 10 parts weak tea and one part ammonia. Try it first on a few leaves to test for damage, and make sure pets and children don't try to eat or lick the leaves (hey, they've done weirder things!).

For Crawling Critters

Sometimes, getting rid of insects is as easy as making it hard for them to get where they're going. Smear petroleum jelly around the base of plant stems, and ants and other crawling insects will slide right off, protecting your plants.

Buh-Bye, Bambi!

Hang small pieces of a deodorant bar soap on trees to keep deer from munching on them. Or, try a piece of your clothing that you've worn for several days—deer don't like the smell of humans.

Who Knew? Readers' Favorite

Spray your garbage cans with a mixture of one part ammonia and three parts water on a regular basis to keep squirrels, raccoons, dogs, and other critters from rummaging through the cans.

Rotten Eggs Are Good for Something!

It's a breeze to keep deer, antelope, elk, and other large animals away from your garden and trees by using eggs that have gone bad. Just break them open (outside of the house!) around the area that you want to keep the critters away from. The smell of hydrogen sulfide from the rotten eggs will keep them away long after the offending odor has dissipated.

Strip Tease

If birds or other critters are nibbling at your fruit trees, try hanging long strips of aluminum foil from the branches. They'll be attracted to its shiny surface, but once they bite it, they'll fly away.

Get Rid of Bothersome Bees

Don't you hate having to worry about a bee hijacking your soda while you're having a drink outside? So sip in confidence by covering the top of your drink with aluminum foil, then sticking a straw through the top.

Picnic Peace

To win the war against ants at your picnic, place the picnic table's legs in old coffee cans filled with water. The ants won't be able to climb up the table, and your food will stay safe.

Wasp Reduction

If you find a large wasp's nest, have it removed professionally. But for smaller numbers of these freaky fliers, fill a jar with half jam and half water. Cover with paper punctured with holes to attract, trap, and drown them.

Wary of Wasps?

Is there anything worse than coming upon a swarm of wasps when you're enjoying your garden? If you find that wasps are building a nest in the same spot year after year, spray the area with white vinegar several times in the beginning of the spring, and they'll find somewhere else to roost.

Great Trick for Window Boxes

If you keep plants in window boxes, paint them white first. The bright, reflective surface will deter insects and reduce the risk of dry rot. It looks great, too!

Give Flies the Brush-Off

If you prefer not to use chemicals to get rid of flies, and you're not the most accurate fly swatter, invest in a strong fan. Scientists say that flies' wings are unable to operate in a breeze above nine miles per hour, so open the windows, turn the fan to full power, and they'll soon buzz off. This is also a great trick for an outdoor party—just aim a few fans at the center of the action instead of spraying down your yard with awful smelling repellant.

Free a Bee, Don't Smack It

If a bee or other stinging insect gets trapped in the car with you, do not swat at it! Instead, pull your car off to the side of the road, open all the windows or doors, and let the critter fly out.

Moth Trap

Trap moths by mixing one part molasses with two parts white vinegar and placing the mixture in a bright yellow container. The moths will be attracted to the color and the smell, then drown inside.

Who Knew? Readers' Favorite

Placing your woolen clothes in a well-sealed bag isn't always enough to keep moths away, as any eggs laid in them beforehand will hatch—and the new moths will have a field day. To make sure all the eggs die before you put your clothes in storage, place the airtight bag of clothes in the freezer for 24 hours.

Keep Clothes Safe with Soap

When winter rolls around, do your sweaters smell like mothballs? Ick. Mothballs work great, but leave a nasty odor. When you're storing winter clothes next year, put a few leftover soap slivers in a vented plastic bag, and add it to your closet or cedar chest instead of mothballs. The soap will keep moths from damaging your clothes, and it smells fresh, too.

Flea Flicker

Fleas can be eliminated from upholstery and carpets by using a high-powered vacuum cleaner (ideally one with a canister) with a bag that seals well. Remove the bag and dispose of it outside as soon as you finish.

A Good Night's Sleep for Your Pet

To ward off fleas from a pet's sleeping area, try sprinkling a few drops of lavender oil in the area. Fleas hate the smell of lavender oil and will find somewhere else to hide. Your pet, meanwhile, can enjoy a good night's sleep—and smell great in the morning.

Spray to Lead Bugs Astray

If flies or bees have invaded your home, and you want to get them away from you fast, squirt a little hair spray into the air. They hate the stuff and will go elsewhere.

Repel Bugs Naturally

Don't spend money on bug sprays. Their main ingredient is usually alcohol, so save some money by simply making a mixture of one part rubbing alcohol and four parts water, then spraying it on as you would bug spray. Another natural (and great-smelling) alternative is equal parts water and pure vanilla extract.

Dryer Sheet Wonder

Is there anything a dryer sheet can't do? Many people report that keeping dryer sheets in your pockets will help repel mosquitoes and other bugs. This may be because of a citronella-like ingredient they contain.

A Use for Pencil Shavings!

Add pencil shavings to your plants if they suffer from bug infestation. Bugs don't like the smell of the cedar in pencils. Just mix in with the soil, mostly at the bottom.

Fooled by Fake Flowers

If your child is being bitten by a lot of bugs this summer, it may be because of his or her colorful clothing. Believe it or not, bugs are fooled by bright colors and floral prints. They think they're real flowers, then bite your kids instead when they fly close.

Who Knew? Readers' Favorite

Flour mixed with cayenne pepper makes a great barrier to ants in your cabinets. You can also sprinkle it outside wherever ants are infesting your garden or yard. Ants will run for shelter and you can sweep up the powder. Try ½ tablespoon pepper together with ½ cup white flour (sifted makes it easier).

Stopping Slugs

If slugs are finding their way into your container plants, cover the bottom hole with used sanding disks or circle of sandpaper. Slugs hate the scratchy surface and won't cross it.

Chalk It Up

Draw a line ants won't cross...with chalk! Ants think chalk is ash and won't cross it (because it may be a sign of fire). Use their tiny brains against them by drawing a thick line of chalk along windowsills, cabinets, or anywhere else they enter your home. You can even draw a line on your picnic table!

An Ace Solution for Aphids

If aphids are infesting your plants, here's an easy solution. Cover a tennis ball with petroleum jelly and leave it nearby. The bugs will be attracted to its bright color, and then get stuck on its side.

Can't You Smell That Smell?

Citronella candles are great for repelling insects, but they can be pricey. Get the same effect for much less by mixing garlic with water and spraying it near all your outdoor light bulbs. As the bulbs heat up, they'll spread a faint garlicky scent across your yard, which will keep mosquitoes and other bugs away.

Send Peter Rabbit Packing

Are rabbits overrunning your garden? Keep them away with the help of some vinegar. First poke a few holes in a pill bottle, then soak 3–4 cotton balls with vinegar and place them inside. Bury the bottle just under the soil and the smell will keep rabbits away.

CHAPTER 2

Energy-Saving Tips

A Truly Bright Idea

Dusting a light bulb can increase the light in a room by up to 50 percent.

Electrical Insulation

Did you know that you could be losing warm (or cold) air through your electrical outlets? We placed some fireproof foam insulation under our outlet covers and switch plates and saved several dollars a month on our utility bill.

Vacuum Those Vents

Make sure to vacuum your heating and air conditioning vents regularly. When the vents get caked up with dust, your furnace or air conditioner has to work much harder!

Slow and Steady with the Heat

When it's time to turn on the heat, be patient. Your house won't heat up any faster if you crank the thermostat way up, but you are likely to forget to turn it down, which can be a huge energy waster.

Who Knew? Readers' Favorite

Don't let your fan go to waste just because it's no longer hot outside. To stay toasty during the frigid days of winter, hit the reverse switch to push hot air down into your room.

Feed Plants from Your Fish Tank

If you have an aquarium, save the water each time you change it, and use it to water your houseplants. The fishy water contains nitrogen, potassium, and phosphorus—all three function as natural fertilizers for plants. You'll be amazed at the results.

Set Up an Efficient Kitchen

Organize your kitchen so your hot appliances (an oven or dishwasher) don't sit near your cold appliances (the fridge and freezer). Otherwise, they'll have to work harder to do their jobs. Also, make sure your refrigerator isn't exposed to direct sunlight or heat vents. These simple tips will help keep your kitchen in tip-top shape and your energy costs down.

Ease Your Energy Bill

Even when you're not using appliances, they still continue to use energy. So pull the plug when you're done with the blender, toaster, food processor, even your television—everything except appliances that need constant power to preserve a special setting.

Energy Saving Tips for Your Fridge

Clean the condenser coils on the back of your refrigerator twice a year, and you'll use less energy while increasing the life of the appliance. It's also important to keep your freezer packed—even with bags of ice if necessary—because a full freezer is much more efficient than a half-empty one.

Microwave Safety

Microwave doors may become misaligned, especially if you pull down on them when opening them. When the doors don't close properly, they can leak radiation, making your food take longer to cook. Check them periodically with a small, inexpensive detector, which can be purchased in any hardware store.

Battery Booster

Batteries will last longer if they're stored in the refrigerator. To boost their energy, place them in the sun for a day before you use them.

Warm-Weather Dishwasher Tip

Here's a terrific tip to use during warm weather: Turn off your dishwasher after the rinse cycle, open it up, and let your dishes drip-dry. You'll save a lot by avoiding the heat-drying cycle on your machine.

Keep a Tight Seal

If your refrigerator is more than a few years old, its seal is probably not as tight as it used to be. To save energy and keep your food cooler, first clean the door's gasket (that rubber lining that goes around it), then rub it with petroleum jelly to ensure a tighter seal.

Radiator Energy Saver

Here's a great energy-saving tip for cold winter nights: If you have cast-iron radiators, tape aluminum foil to a sheet of cardboard (shiny side out) and place it behind the radiator. The radiant heat will bounce back into your room instead of being absorbed into the wall.

Lengthen Laptop Battery Power

If you clean the battery contacts on your laptop and cordless phone, the charge will last for a longer time. Use the tip of a cotton swab dipped in rubbing alcohol to clean the connection points.

Save Water in the Shower

When it comes to saving water, a short shower is better than a bath, but even still, lots of water gets wasted. Collect as much as you can with buckets to use for the lawn (or water play later on in the day, if you have young kids).

CHAPTER 3

The Art of Decorating

All Decked Out

When it's time to repaint your deck or porch, why not get creative and paint a piece of artwork? Try painting a "rug" by using a different color than the main base color for an inside rectangle, along with stencils for a border. If you skip the acrylic topcoat, you'll get a worn look that will add to the tromp l'oeil effect.

The Floss Fix

To hang lightweight artwork that's not in a heavy frame, there's no need to buy picture wire. Unwaxed dental floss will do the trick.

Picture This

Hanging a picture? Make it easy by first taping a thumbtack (pointy side out) to the back below the hanging bracket. Perfectly position your picture, then give it a bit of a push into the wall.

Bookshelf Decorating Done Easily

A pair of wine bottles, either full or empty, makes great bookends for your shelf—especially if there are cookbooks on it!

Who Knew? Readers' Favorite

When slipping curtains over a metal rod, first place a plastic freezer or sandwich bag over the metal end. This will help you avoid snagging the curtains so they go on easily.

If You Never Use Paper Napkins

If you have a set of pretty cloth napkins you never use, consider making them into an equally pretty throw pillow. Fill it with pillow foam, an old mattress egg crate, cotton stuffing, old fabrics, or nylon stockings.

Stuff It

Tired of the way your expensive valances seem to hang limply at the windows? Get that magazine look by stuffing plastic grocery bags into your draperies to get them to pouf out more.

Upright Candles

Do your candles slide around in their holders like a kid wearing his dad's pants? Wrap the bottom with tape to get the right fit.

Magazine Management

Are magazines piling up around your home? Make some decorative and functional magazine holders by cutting cereal boxes at angles and covering them with wrapping paper. Cover with some craft lacquer for a durable finish.

Everything in Its Place

Here's an unusual way to get a put-together look in your kitchen. Outline your small appliances with weather stripping to keep them stationary on the counter. This works well for the phone, blender, coffee machine, toaster oven—anything you permanently leave out.

From the Frying Pan

You treasure your grandmother's antique cast-iron pans, but you hate cooking in them! Repurpose these kitchen classics as magnet boards by hanging them from hooks and using some refrigerator magnets to hang recipe cards, postcards, artwork, and more.

Put on a Pedestal

Cake stands are perfect for displaying much more than cakes. Use them to show off trinkets or collections, or simply use as a just-in-the-door clutter catcher for keys and change. Now you finally know what to do with all those cake stands you got for wedding presents!

Do-It-Yourself Headboard

To perk up your bedroom with a splash of color, get crafty with a DIY faux-headboard. Find a colorful sheet that complements the décor of your room; any fabric will work, so consider cotton, linen, velvet, and even fur! First, consider the width of your bed; a headboard should be slightly wider than your mattress. Then decide what style of headboard you like best, and cut your fabric to the right size and shape. Either wrap your fabric around a foam base and hang it on the wall, or hang it up on its own.

A terrific way to hang posters in your kid's room without leaving holes or stains is with white, non-gel toothpaste. Just put a generous drop on the back of each corner, press to the wall, and watch it stick.

Your Poster Child

If your teenager loves tacking posters up on his bedroom wall, here's a great tip to keep the corners hole-free. Place a binder clip on each corner, then slip them over nails or thumb tacks. As an added bonus, get shiny or colorful binder clips.

A Great Use for Old Jewelry

Do you have too many brooches and pins to ever get around to wearing them all? Repurpose them by turning them into unique magnets that get noticed! Just use wire cutters to clip off the pin on the back, then glue a magnet (available at craft stores) on the back.

CHAPTER 4

Fantastically Frugal Kid Tips

Never Buy a Baby Wipe Again

If you have a baby, you know that one costly item that's impossible to use less of is baby wipes. When we had babies, we saved hundreds per year by making our own diaper wipes! They are easy to make and can be kept in an old baby wipes container, a plastic storage bin with a lid, or a resealable plastic bag. Here's how to do it: combine 2 tablespoons each of baby oil and baby shampoo (or baby wash) with 2 cups boiled and cooled water and 1–2 drops of your favorite essential oil for scent (optional). Remove the cardboard roll from a package of paper towels, then cut the entire roll in half (you can also tear off sheets by hand and stack them in a pile). Put some of the liquid mixture at the bottom of your container, then place the half-roll in the container. Pour the rest of the liquid over your paper towels and voilà—homemade baby wipes! Let the wipes sit for about an hour to absorb all the liquid, and your baby will never know the difference.

Freshen Up Stinky Diapers

If you get a nasty whiff every time you open the diaper pail, drop a few charcoal briquettes under the pail's liner. You'll be amazed at what you don't smell.

A Trick Worthy of the Lucky Charms Leprechaun

If you're one of those super-parents who don't let their kids eat sugary cereal, have you thought about using it as a reward? Kids not used to having a morning sugar fix normally like sugary cereal brands as much as they like candy, so why not use it instead? That way, when kids are getting a sugary treat for being good, they'll at least get it from a food that is also enriched with vitamins. And if you want to wean your children off the sugary stuff in the morning, this might be a good way to start!

An Idea You'll Love

Uh-oh, it's Valentine's Day, and you forgot to buy cards for your kid's class. Don't despair! Just head over to FreePrintableValentines.net, a site that gives you dozens of valentine designs to print out instantly.

Pretty Cool Prank

We can't help but share our favorite harmless prank. Add a couple of drops of food coloring (we like green) to your milk carton before your child goes to pour the milk. (Make sure to shake it up.) He'll get a surprise and a big kick out of the color!

Who Knew? Readers' Favorite

Sneak some calcium into your kids' food by adding powdered milk to their meals. It'll be inconspicuous to them in dishes such as mashed potatoes, meatballs, and peanut butter sandwiches (mixed in with the peanut butter).

The Right Bike

Before you get your kid that bike he's been begging for, make sure it's the proper size. When sitting on the seat with hands on the handlebar, your child should be able to place the balls of both feet on the ground. He should also be able to straddle the center bar standing up with an inch or so of clearance.

Toy Tamer

You could pay 50¢ a pop for links that secure your child's toys to his stroller. But for a less expensive substitute, try using shower curtain rings, which are available in 12-packs for less than $2.

Keep 'Em Guessing

We like to add a little more excitement and surprise to the holidays by labeling our kids' gifts with colorful stickers rather than gift tags. The stickers are color-coded for each recipient, and we don't reveal the code until gift-opening time on Christmas Day. It's a clever, fun, and inexpensive way to keep the kids guessing.

Add a Splash of Color

Make your kids' bath time colorful with this easy alternative to store-bought bath crystals: Simply put a few drops of food coloring into the bath water. Whatever color you choose, your children will still emerge from the bath squeaky-clean.

Placement Fun

We love these unique placements for your kids: Buy an inexpensive or secondhand picture book, then pull out the pages and laminate them using clear contact paper. They're waterproof, original, and cheaper than store-bought placemats.

Tone Down the TP Usage

If your potty-trained toddler enjoys pulling toilet paper off the roll, use this trick to keep his TP usage in line: Before putting the roll on the dispenser, squeeze the tube so that it flattens slightly. This will keep the roll from turning too easily, thus keeping the amount that comes off the roll manageable.

A Nutty Facial

If you're looking for a way to entertain your kids, put them to work with this fun chore. You can "wash" the faces of your daughter's dolls by smearing peanut butter on them, then wiping it off. The oils in the butter seep into the plastic, removing every last bit of grime.

Save Those Pennies

Teaching the kids about saving their money? An ice cream container makes a great piggy bank. Just clean it, cut a slot in the lid, and decorate the outside with wrapping paper, stickers, and ribbon.

Who Knew? Readers' Favorite

Almost all soft rubber balls, including tennis balls, can be brought back to life by spending a night in the oven with only the pilot light on. The heat causes the air inside the ball to expand. Just be sure to remove the balls before you turn the oven on!

DIY Finger Paints for Little Da Vincis

Keep your kids busy and encourage their creativity with homemade finger paints: Start by mixing two cups cold water with ¼ cup cornstarch, then boil until the liquid is as thick as, um, finger paints. Pour into small containers, swirl in some food coloring, and watch them create their masterpieces (just keep those colorful fingers away from walls!).

Dryer Lint Dough

Make a Play-Doh substitute for your kids with an unlikely ingredient: dryer lint! First save up 3 cups of dryer lint, then stick it into a pot with 2 cups water, 1 cup flour, and ½ teaspoon vegetable or canola oil. Cook, stirring constantly, over low heat until the mixture is smooth. Then pour onto a sheet of wax paper to cool.

Homemade Bubbles!

Summertime is bubble season for kids who want some outdoor fun. Here's an inexpensive homemade solution for blowing bubbles: Mix 1 tablespoon glycerin with 2 tablespoons powdered laundry detergent in 1 cup warm water. Any unpainted piece of metal wire can be turned into a bubble wand: Just shape one end of the wire into a circle. Blowing into the mixture with a straw will make smaller bubbles float into the air. For colored bubbles, add food coloring.

CHAPTER 5

Vacations and Family Activities

Flight days flexible? Try searching for trips that begin and end on a Tuesday or Wednesday, when we've found that flights throughout the US and Canada are cheaper.

Keep Checking Those Rates

Just because you've booked your flight doesn't mean you can't still save. Make sure to keep an eye on airfare prices, and rebook your flight if necessary. Even if your airline charges you $75 to cancel a ticket, you'll still save a bundle if a rival airline is offering tickets at $150 less than what you paid.

Go Direct

Planning a trip to a far-away locale? Before buying plane tickets, check out booking sites such as Expedia.com, Kayak.com, or Orbitz.com, which show the cheapest deals from every airline. Once you've found the best prices, check the airline websites directly. They'll offer either the price you've found online or an even lower one, and you'll save on the internet booking fees.

Get Past the Sponsors

When searching for travel deals online, make sure to scroll through a few pages of results before making your pick. Many sites have "sponsored results," which means that companies have paid to be featured at the top of search results.

Your Ticket to the Lowest Price

After you buy a plane ticket, visit Yapta.com. Enter your flight details and they'll email you if the price goes down. Even if you have to pay a fee to change your ticket, you'll find that fares often fluctuate by hundreds of dollars. This is an easy way to make sure you're getting the cheapest price.

The Five-Day Outlook for Travel

Farecast.com is one of our favorite sites for planning a trip. If your travel dates are flexible, it will tell you the cheapest days to travel. If you know exactly when you're coming or going, it will predict whether or not the price will go up or down. The coolest part is, it's not affiliated with a particular airline or travel site, so the advice is unbiased. If you want to lock in the price the site gives you, you can buy "insurance" for a small fee.

Last-Minute Deals in Travel

If you're looking for the best deals in travel, head over to AirfareWatchdog.com, which catalogs the cheapest fares as they are listed on travel and airline sites. This site requires a bit of work—you have to click through to other sites to find the rate yourself, but the "watch dog" will tell you which days of the week to search and in what date range. If you normally spend a lot of time trying different combinations of travel dates and nearby airports, this site will take a lot of the guesswork out of it for you.

If you've been to an airport lately, you've probably noticed that the ticket counters are staffed by fewer people than ever before. It's annoying on a regular travel day, but if there are lots of flight cancellations, this can mean a two-hour-plus wait in line. Save yourself a lot of time by skipping the line all together. Instead, call the customer service number for your airline and rebook your cancelled flight right over the phone.

Time To Get A Passport

In these bad economic times, it's hard to see a silver lining, but here's one for anyone who loves an exotic vacation: It's now cheaper than ever to travel to many fascinating destinations around the world like Reykjavik, Iceland; Montreal, Canada; and Sydney, Australia. Check out vacation packages on sites like Expedia.com and Orbitz.com or ask a travel agent for hot deals to faraway lands.

International Travel Tip

Before you travel internationally, pack a spare passport photo and write down your passport number and the date it was issued. If you lose your passport while abroad, you'll have all the materials you need to get a new one. Bring your photo and passport info to a nearby US Embassy: It'll take much less time to process your request if you come prepared.

Save in Europe

If you're aged 12–26, if you're a student of any age, or you're a teacher or faculty member, you qualify for the International Student ID Card , which gives you amazing savings in Europe. Available at ISECard.com, the card costs $25, but with it you get discounts on trains, rental cards, tourist attractions, and more. Best of all, they'll provide medical travel insurance up to $2,000.

Pile Up the Points

Traveling a lot this summer? Check out Points.com, a site that lets you keep track of your airline miles and other rewards points, all in one place. Better yet, you can swap points from one reward program to another!

Don't Pay for Location

Save money on car rental by not renting at the airport, which charges rental car companies concession fees. Instead, take a cab to a nearby location—even with the fare factored in, you'll be surprised how much you save.

—*Drey Luca, CA*

The Cheapest Rental Cars

When looking for great deals, Hotwire.com is a good place to turn. The downside to this site is that you don't know which airline you're flying or which hotel you're staying at until after you've booked. While we aren't always a fan of this format for flights or lodging, for cars, who cares what dealer it is, as long as it's at the airport?

Rent a Wreck

If you're renting a car for your vacation this year, try Rent-a-Wreck (RentAWreck.com), which offers older cars (that are far from being wrecks, by our standards!) at discounted prices. You can also try asking at local dealerships to see if they rent cars—many have begun to in an attempt to make extra cash!

An Alternative to Airport Parking

Find out the cheapest place to park at your nearby airport by visiting BestParking.com. You'll discover lots close to the airport that aren't run by the airport itself—and are often half the price.

Who Knew? Readers' Favorite

When digging for discounts on rental cars and hotels, always call the hotel or rental company directly. If the only phone number you have is a national, toll-free one, look up the local number for that particular location and speak to them directly instead. The closer you get to your travel date, the better—in fact, don't be afraid to call the day before to confirm your reservation and ask for a better rate.

Fun Website for Travelers

For ideas of inexpensive places to visit while on vacation, visit Localyte.com. Localyte is a free website that connects travelers with locals in the know. Post a question about your destination, and have it answered by a local expert!

Forgo The Foliage

The best summer vacation you'll ever take might not be in the summer. As soon as Labor Day goes by, the rates go down drastically on hotels and airfare to most vacation destinations. Some of the most-discounted areas are the Caribbean, Hawaii, California, and anywhere else there's a beach. In a warm climate, it will still be as hot as ever on the sand. But the price will be much less, and you'll get the added benefit of having a smaller crowd. Check out a travel site like Travelocity.com for good deals to your dream destinations.

Where to Find Cheap Cruises

If you're dying to get away on a cruise, check out CruiseDeals. com, which has packages to Alaska, the Bahamas, Hawaii, Mexico, and just about anywhere else you'd want to go on a boat. The company negotiates with some of the world's biggest lines to bring their customers the best rates on cruises. If you want to hit the water, this is the best place to start.

Timeshares

If you're staying somewhere for a week or longer, you may be able to save money on your accommodations by renting a timeshare. Timeshares are properties owned jointly by several different families, who split up their time at the property during vacation months. You'll often find people renting out their time, or landlords who rent out their properties on a week-to-week basis over the summer in tourist-filled areas. To find a cheap timeshare in your destination, search on Craig's List or Ebay. You can also try SellMyTimeshareNow.com and TimesharesOnly.com.

When you're on vacation, use your digital camera for more than just snapshots in front of the sights! Take photos of street signs and the fronts of stores to remember favorite shops you visited, and snap a photo of needed subway maps, too. That way, when you're looking for the subway you don't have to pull out a map and look like a tourist—just look at your photo!

Planning a Road Trip?

Find out exactly how much you need to budget for gas at FuelCostCalculator.com. Enter the make and model of your car and your origin and destination, and AAA will calculate how much it will cost you using the Environmental Protection Agency's fuel economy ratings and its own gasoline prices report. With rising gas prices and fluctuating airfare, this is a great site to visit if you're not sure taking the car will save you money.

Keep 'Em Fed

Going on a road trip? Make sure to pack plenty of food before you leave to cut down on meal expenses along the way. Periodically handing out food is also a great way to keep kids quiet(er)! Have several different types of snacks on hand so they don't get bored.

Make a Single-Night Stop Easy

Time for a family road trip? If you have an overnight stop on your journey, prepare for it by packing small, individual bags for each family member. That way, you won't have to dig around in the car for pajamas and toiletries for the one-night stay.

Going the Distance

Planning a road trip this summer? When it's time to fill up on gas, drive a little farther off the highway exit before choosing a station. The gas stations closest to the highway will often charge more per gallon than the ones located a bit off your course—you could save a few bucks by going the extra distance.

Save on Souvenirs

When you're on vacation, save money on souvenirs by staying away from gift shops and stores close to tourist areas. Instead, visit a local grocery store, where you'll usually find locally themed postcards, maps, key chains, magnets, t-shirts, and more, normally at discount prices.

Bring Some Easy Mac and Ramen When You Go

When booking a hotel for your summer vacation, make sure to choose one that offers a free breakfast or an in-room refrigerator and microwave. Eating a couple of meals at the hotel is one of the easiest ways to save while you're away.

—*Rita Guerrero, Middlebury, VT*

Packing with Pantyhose

Use a pair of nylons to store your socks and underwear. Keep the clean ones in one leg, then switch them to the other leg after you've worn them. It will make it super easy to find clean socks and undies in your suitcase.

Just in Case

When packing a suitcase for a trip, put at least one outfit in the suitcase of your spouse (or other travel buddy). If the airline loses your luggage, you'll have at least a few items of clothing to tide you over until it's found.

Who Knew? Readers' Favorite

Packing for vacation? Consider packing clothes in the same color family, and pants that can go with a lot of different shirts. You can more easily mix and match them, so you'll have to pack less. This trick will also come in handy when you spill something on yourself—if your blue shirt is soiled, you still have another in your suitcase.

A Hot Idea

A hair dryer can serve double-duty while you're traveling: It'll dry your hair and stand in for an iron. Wet the clothing you'd like to de-wrinkle and lay it on a table or other level surface. Smooth the wrinkles out with your hand while blowing warm air on the spot with the dryer.

Packing Presents?

When you have to pack tons of presents, it's usually more frugal to pay to ship the contents of your suitcase to your destination ahead of time. Most airlines charge between $15 and $30 for the first checked bag and much more for the second, while it only costs around $14 to mail up to 70 pounds via the post office.

Keep Your Necklaces Looking Nice

Don't waste any more time untangling necklace chains. Before packing them, cover each side with tape. If you didn't think ahead, use baby oil and a straight pin to work out the knots.

Another Neat Necklace Trick

Packing for a trip? Keep your necklaces safe and tangle-free by taping them to some bubble wrap. Then roll the wrap up and pack safely in your suitcase.

Shower Caps for Shoes

When you get plastic shower caps at hotels, save them for your suitcase. They make the perfect covers for dirty shoes!

Perfect for Accessories

Repurpose a plastic daily vitamin/pill container into a jewelry box that's perfect for trips. Rings, earrings, and even necklaces fit perfectly inside. You'll be accessorized for each day you're away!

When you're packing for a trip, keep some plastic wrap nearby. Before you pack shampoo, sunscreen, or other toiletries, take off the caps, place a layer of plastic wrap over the mouth of the container, and twist the cap back on. The plastic wrap will give you double the protection against suitcase spills.

A Sweet Solution!

If you use artificial sweetener for your coffee, you know what brand is your favorite! Make sure you always have some with you by using a business card holder to keep packets in your bag or purse.

Lighten the Load

Don't over-pack your vacation luggage—it could cause more pain than pleasure during your travels. To prevent a sore back, test the packing job before you leave: Pack your suitcase completely, and walk around the house with it for a few minutes. If it's too heavy, unload a bit or split your stuff into two lighter bags.

Keep Burglars Away

If you're concerned about your house being broken into while you're away, don't stop at automatic light switches. Ask your neighbor to park a car in your driveway, so robbers will think someone's at home.

Put Your Plants on Autopilot
While You're Away

Place a large container of water near your plant (or if you have several plants, gather them into one spot to make it easy). Then place one end of a long piece of yarn into the water, and stick the other end into the plant's soil, near the roots. Lay the strand across the stalks of the plant. This will keep it moist until you return.

Plant Sitter

Now there's one less thing to worry about when you're on vacation. Water your plants yourself in absentia with this handy trick. Fill an ordinary plastic drink bottle with water and punch a little hole toward the bottom. Turn on its side and place on the soil near the plant stem to give a continual slow drip. Now go enjoy your trip and know you won't come home to a bunch of withering geraniums.

Save While You're Away

Many newspapers and magazines will allow you to suspend your home delivery or subscription. If you're going on a long vacation, make sure to call them up and stop service for the time you'll be away. You can also often do this for online movie rental and other services. You won't miss them while you're gone, and then you'll get an extra week or two when your subscription would normally be up.

Be A Day-Tripper

The most expensive part of any vacation is transportation and lodging, so consider taking several day trips during the summer rather than one week-long one. Commuter rail lines often offer discounts on train fare and tickets to theme parks and other attractions, or you may be overdue to take a drive to that nearby state park. For ideas of where to take day trips in your area, call your state's tourist board or type your state's name and "day trips" into a search engine.

For the Ski Buff

Like skiing? You'll love Liftopia.com. It offers discounts on lift tickets for more than 100 ski resorts across the United States and Canada. You can search by destination, or by categories like "good for beginners" and "nighttime skiing." You can also sign up for an email newsletter that will let you know about upcoming deals.

Smoother Skis

When you're getting ready to hit the slopes for the first time this year, take a few minutes to spray WD-40 on the bottom of your skis and snowboards before you scrape off the old wax. It will make your job much easier.

Keep Your Keys

If your vacation plans involve a boating excursion (or several), prevent drowned keys by sticking a few corks onto your key chain. Should the keys fall into the water, you'll find the corks bobbing along the surface.

Time to Go Camping!

Waking up to the sights, sounds, and smells of the forest can be one of the most peaceful things you'll ever experience—not to mention, the most inexpensive vacation you'll take in years. If you've never gone camping, it's time to start! If you don't have any equipment, ask friends if you can borrow theirs in exchange for lending them something of yours. You and your kids will enjoy working together while roughing it (and don't worry, "roughing it" can involve bathrooms and showers, electricity hook-ups, and even wireless internet). Best of all, with all that hard work each day, plus all the room in the world to run around in, your kids will get exhausted fast! To find campsites across the United States and Canada, visit ReserveAmerica.com, and for a great article for first-time campers, go to RoadAndTravel.com/adventuretravel/campingforfirsttimers.htm.

More Fun Activities Than You Ever Thought Possible

All you need to know when you're searching for fun things to do at Goby.com is what you're interested in and where you are (and, if you want, when you're going). Whether it's getting coffee, going to a playground, hitting up a museum, or more adventurous activities like sailing and horseback riding, Goby will tell you what's out there, and even give you a map to see where it is. The best thing about Goby is its straightforward, user-friendly design: no huge ads, no "sponsored results," no long loading times or signing up. For those of us who have spent a lot of time searching for things online, it's a welcome respite.

Cable: Not Always A Rip-Off

If you have cable, you may have movies and television shows available on-demand for free. Many cable systems offer a wide variety of old movies, as well as recent TV shows, that cable channels are trying to promote. Every system is different, but take a look and see if there is an option on your On-Demand menu that says "Free Movies," "Free Shows," or "Free On-Demand." You may also have to look through the shows and see which are listed as $0.

Who Knew? Readers' Favorite

The easiest place to get free DVDs may be at the homes of your friends! Try starting a movie-lending circle with friends or neighbors who also watch a lot of movies. Each person has another person they give movies to, and someone they receive them from. When you get your own movie back, it's time to pick a new one! You may want to pick a timeframe to exchange the movie—for example, before each weekend or at a weekly book club or school-related meeting. Movie-lending circles are a great way to discover movies you might not have picked out yourself, but really enjoy.

Going to the Movies

Even if you don't plan on getting snacks at the theater, it's hard to say "no" once you smell that popcorn popping! Always eat before you arrive; that way you'll be safe from snacking—and from spending. Find out which theaters in your area offer matinees, and also check to see if any membership programs you belong to offer free or discounted days. In some areas, Cablevision (also known as Optimum) offers free movies once a week for customers who sign up for cable, internet, and phone service.

Rent on the Cheap

What would the weekend be without a trip to the video store? With so many options for movie and video game rentals, the supply is up, so it's time to demand! Compare rates at your local video stores, and see if the store with the best perks—like being close to your home and letting you rent for the longest amount of time—will match the lowest price you can find. Since fewer and fewer people have VCRs these days, if you are still renting VHS cassettes, see if you can get a discount or a longer rental period when renting tapes instead of DVDs. Finally, keep an eye out for Redbox machines, which can be found in many drug and discount stores, where you can rent a DVD for one night for as low as $1.

Find Cheap Tickets More Easily

If you find Ticketmaster and other ticket sites as annoying as we do, you'll love ZebraTickets.com. Zebra Tickets collects ticket prices from around the web for sporting events, concerts, and plays, so you'll be sure to know which site is offering the best deal.

Free Summer Fun

For ideas on fun, free activities to do over the summer, try checking out your community center or park district. Most towns have tons of free summertime events, from sports clinics for kids to free concerts for adults. See if they have a website or pick up a calendar at your local branch.

Who Knew? Readers' Favorite

Even if they normally have high admission prices, most museums offer opportunities for you to visit for free. If a museum gets money from the government, they're usually required to either offer free admission one day a week or charge admission as a "suggested donation"—that is, you only have to pay what you want. Other museums have late hours that are free to visitors once a week or month. If you like looking at art, also check out galleries, where you can find cool, local art displayed for free in the hopes that someone will buy it.

TV: Live and In-Person!

If you live near a big city, especially Los Angeles or New York, one of the most fun free activities you can do is attend a TV taping. Talk shows, sitcoms, and game shows are always looking for studio audience members, and it's not only a blast to see a show live, but also to get a peek at what happens behind the scenes. To get tickets to shows, visit TVTickets.com for shows in LA, or NYC.com for events and shows in New York (click on "TV show tapings" under "Top attractions."). NYTix.com offers an even wider range of New York tapings, but requires you pay $3 to take advantage of their "special relationships" with the shows. If a show you know and like is being taped in your area, try looking it or its network up online or seeing if there is a phone number at the end of the show to call for audience tickets.

Because a Good Game Is a Good Game

If you love going to see sports, but don't love the price tag of taking your whole family to a professional game, consider amateur sports instead. Colleges as well as intramural leagues have games every weekend for free or a few bucks. It's great to support local teams, and younger kids won't even know the difference in skill between a pro player and a Division Three league anyway.

Theme Park Savings

Nothing's more fun than taking the kids to an amusement park, especially when they've been begging you to do it for two summers now. Whether you're going to a local, Six Flags–type of park, or going all out for that Disney World vacation, here are some tips to keep your costs down.

✦ A lot of organizations offer discount packages to local and national theme parks. Check with any organizations you belong to, such as the AARP, AAA, wholesale clubs like BJ's or Costco, or a branch of the military. Also look for promotions mailed out with your credit card bill.

✦ Ask for a group discount. If you have at least 15 people in your party, you can usually get a good deal, depending on the time of year.

✦ Visit AmusementPark.com, which has great deals on tickets to amusement parks around the country. They also have savings on local tours, dinner cruises, museums, and tourist attractions.

✦ Keep an eye out for merchandise tie-ins. Many products—especially soda and chips—offer easy discounts such as bringing the wrapper or can to the park to get several dollars off.

✦ Check out the packages. Large theme parks such as Universal Studios and Disney World always offer package deals on—for example—a flight, hotel, and park tickets. These aren't usually significantly cheaper than buying tickets online through a site like Expedia.com or Orbitz.com, but they do often offer added incentives like free transportation or breakfasts.

✦ Call the park and ask them! Most parks (or their automated representative) will tell you about current deals being offered, and may offer promotions of their own. Also check the website of the individual park you're visiting.

✦ Before you get to the park, consider the real money-wasters: food and souvenirs. Bring lunches from home, and give each child a certain amount to spend at gift shops. For more indecisive kids afraid of hitting their limit, make sure to offer them the chance to go back for an item in a store if they don't find anything they like more (they usually will).

Who Knew? Readers' Favorite

Many concert venues, theaters, and museums hire volunteers in exchange for free admission. Doing a bit of volunteer work will help you get away from the kids for a bit and meet new people. Then bring your family back for the savings!

Keep It Cool on the Beach

Packing up your cooler for a day on the beach? Make sure it's at least 25 percent full of ice or cold packs. Otherwise, it won't be cold enough to keep your perishables cool.

A Shinier Straw Hat

Keep your straw beach hat looking like new with hair spray. Spray evenly over the entire hat, then rub your hand gently over it to push in any fraying ends. The hair spray will keep them all in place, and your hat will look shinier than ever before!

For Sand-Free Hands

Baby powder is the only known substance to immediately shake sand loose from human skin! Throw a cupful in a Ziploc bag and take it on your next ocean outing. When it's time to eat, dip your hands in the bag and rub off the sand. It works on other body parts as well.

Beachy Clean

Make homemade ice packs go further with this awesome trick. When you use up body wash or shampoo, add a bit of hand soap to the bottle and then fill with water. Keep in the freezer until you're headed to the park or the beach, then put in your cooler to keep everything cool. When it's time to leave, use the soapy water for quick cleanup!

Fog-Free Goggles

Goggles are necessary when swimming laps, but it's annoying when they fog over. Luckily, the solution is simple. Just coat the inside and outside of each lens with a layer of shaving cream. Leave on for a couple of minutes, then wipe away. The shaving cream leaves an imperceptible film that repels fog.

The Key to Keeping a Blanket in Place

Here's a great use for old keys: Use some thread or yarn to sew them to the corners of your beach and picnic blanket. It will help it stay put once you've laid it on the ground, even on the windiest days.

Who Knew? Readers' Favorite

When you're headed to the beach, make sure to keep your electronics in plastic freezer bags. Sand can easily get inside them, so the plastic makes the perfect see-through barrier, and you'll still be able to manipulate a touch-screen through the plastic.

Belly Up

As if you needed another excuse to sit at the bar, here's one more: many restaurants offer the same food at the bar as in the main restaurant, but for cheaper prices. You may have to order a few dishes to share since the portions may be smaller, but your savings will still be substantial. And since most restaurants also have table service in the bar area, you can still take the kids.

Daily Deals

Many chain restaurants have certain days each week on which they offer deals on particular entrees. Deals are especially easy to find for seniors and kids, but some restaurants offer buy-one-get-one-free options or discounts on appetizers for everyone. Know the "special days" at your local restaurants by visiting their websites or asking your waiter, and try to plan any dinners out so you're never paying full price for a meal.

A Big Week of Savings

Almost all big cities offer a "restaurant week" once or twice per year. During this week, you can dine at some of the nicest restaurants in town for the cost of eating at Applebee's! Most restaurants will offer a three-course fixed price, or "prix fixe," menu that allows you to choose from several different options for your lunch or dinner. This is an excellent opportunity to try that fancy restaurant you've read about or seen on TV, but could never afford. Just make sure you don't order off-menu! That cup of coffee could cost you half of what you just paid for your entire meal!

Winning Ways with Wine

The easiest way to make a dinner out an expensive one is to order a bottle of wine—but who can resist a little pinot with their pasta? Get rid of this extra expense by going to a BYOB (Bring Your Own Bottle) restaurant, which doesn't serve alcohol but will happily de-cork (or de-cap) yours and pour it into a glass. Restaurants that serve alcohol also often allow guests to bring their own anyway—call ahead and ask. Some will charge you a "corkage fee," but it's usually a smidgen of what you would pay ordering off the menu. If you'd only like one glass of wine, try asking if there's a "house wine" available. Many restaurants will pour you whatever is left in a bottle from behind the bar for as little as $3.

Who Knew? Readers' Favorite

If you often order take-out food, consider visiting your favorite restaurants at lunchtime. Most take-out joints offer lunch specials that are the same food as dinner for less money. They'll usually come in smaller sizes, but we've found that we usually don't need what the restaurant considers dinner-sized portions. Buy in the afternoon, stash in the fridge, and then reheat at dinner for savings!

Try Take-Out

How much do you spend each week eating out? To cut costs, find out if your favorite restaurants offer take-out, which is sometimes cheaper and will at least save you the tip. Pick it up on your way home from work and you'll have a restaurant-caliber meal without the temptation of impulse purchases like another drink or dessert. You'll just have to supply the silverware.

Get Your Coffee with Some Co-Eds

If you're a coffee fiend like we are, you know how costly those delicious coffee-shop lattes can be. If there's a college or university near your home, check out the campus coffee shop for your caffeine fix—they're less expensive and just as good as the local Starbucks.

Bistro Bargain

Want to try the that restaurant or cafe that just opened up down the street, but don't want to pay full price? Head over to Restaurant.com first, where you can find $25 gift cards to a wide array of restaurants for only $10 apiece. Many of the big chain restaurants aren't available, but if you like trying out local, family-owned restaurants, you have to check this website out!

CHAPTER 6

Holiday How-To

Bring Back the Mix Tape

You may not have made someone a mix tape since high school, but a collection of handpicked tunes can be a great, free Valentine's treat. Make a custom, romantic playlist to show your sweetie you care! If music isn't your thing, photocopy some of your favorite short stories or poems to present to your loved one as a "literary playlist."

DIY Easter Egg Dye

It's easy to make natural Easter egg dyes. Just add colorful ingredients to the water while you boil your eggs. Use grass for green, onionskins for yellow and deep orange, and beets for pink. If you plan to eat the eggs, be sure to use plants that haven't been treated with pesticides or other chemicals.

Better Than a Basket

The perfect holder for an Easter egg? The upside-down tops to soda and water bottles! For a little extra flair, glue a piece of Easter ribbon around the outside of them.

Halloween Pumpkin Preserver

A problem we used to have every Halloween was that our pumpkins got soft and mushy soon after they were carved. It turns out that this happens because air comes in contact with the inside flesh, allowing bacteria to grow. So to solve the problem of every jack-o'-lantern looking like an old man, we now spray the inside of the hollowed-out pumpkin with an antiseptic spray to slow down the bacterial growth and increase the time it takes for the pumpkin to deteriorate. Just make sure no one eats it!

Tart Trick for Jack-O'-Lanterns

To keep your jack-o'-lanterns fresh this Halloween, rub the insides with lemon juice before you put the lights inside. The lemon juice will prevent your pumpkin from rotting.

Make That Toothy Grin Last

Happy Halloween! Make this year's pumpkin last even longer by coating it with WD-40. It will stave off rot and keep critters from gnawing on it.

Save on Your Tree Skirt

Don't waste your money on an expensive tree skirt this Christmas. Instead, look for a small, round table cloth from a department store—they usually have a big selection and they're inexpensive, too. Cut a round opening in the center for the tree stand, and a straight line to one edge. Place the opening in the back of the tree and you're done.

Who Knew? Readers' Favorite

Making a popcorn garland for the holidays? Use dental floss! It's stronger than regular string and less likely to break when you wrap it around the tree.

A Personalized Calendar

For the holidays, consider giving a personalized calendar of your children's artwork as a gift. Pick up free calendars distributed by local companies, then paste drawings or paintings from the past year on top of each month's image. Your kids will feel proud of their work, and their grandparent, uncle, or godparent will love their new calendar.

A Twist on the Advent Calendar

Count down the days until Christmas with this fun family activity: Pull together all your holiday-themed books and wrap them as individual gifts. Let your children open one gift per night, and read the book together. Save "The Night Before Christmas" for the 24th. The pre-holiday festivities might keep your kids satiated enough to lay off the presents under the tree until Christmas!

An Exchange for a Change

If you have a large family, don't break the bank this holiday season by buying gifts for everyone. Plan a gift exchange instead: Have family members write their names on slips of paper, along with a few "wish list" items. Place the names into a bag and ask each person to draw one recipient. Everyone is sure to receive a good gift, and no one will go bankrupt!

Take Wrapping Presents in a New Direction

This holiday season, get creative (and thrifty) with your gift wrap. Got any travelers in the family? If you have old, unused maps sitting around the house, give them new life as wrapping paper. Mark any previous journeys on the map to add an extra-personal touch.

Wrapping Christmas presents? Make sure you save those little bits of unusable wrapping paper. When you've collected a good amount of scraps, run them through a paper shredder for a colorful, inexpensive alternative to bubble wrap or packing peanuts.

Festive Holiday Lights

Make your holiday lights even more festive by poking each bulb through a cupcake liner. The foil kind will make them even sparklier, while the paper kind will give off a soft light.

Long Live Christmas

We've been known to keep our Christmas tree up until well into January, and with this little trick, you can enjoy the holidays a little longer, too. Add a small amount of sugar or Pine-Sol to the water to extend the life of your tree.

Strand Storage

Once Christmas has come and gone, it's time to think about taking down the tree! When you're storing Christmas tree lights, wind each strand around a piece of cardboard cut to fit in a plastic bin, and they'll stay perfectly untangled. Think of the time you'll save next year!

Safe Storage for Holiday Decorations

When it's time to bring down the tree and lights, take great care with the delicate ornaments. Slip them into old socks or nylons; then for extra safety, place them in disposable plastic cups before storing. Old egg cartons are another ultra-safe (and eco-friendly) way to store bulbs and glass trinkets.

The Windup on Christmas Lights

When you take down your Christmas tree, always wrap the lights around the outside of a cardboard tube (try the tube from a roll of paper towels or wrapping paper) and secure with masking tape. They'll be easy to unwind next year, and you'll never have another nightmarish day of untangling all the lights while the kids wait to decorate the tree.

Zap the Sap

Pinecones are a family favorite during Christmastime, whether they're hanging on the tree, from a stocking, or simply radiating their delicious piney fragrance. But sometimes they're just too sticky to handle. To remove some of that sticky sap, place the pinecones in the oven at 300°F for 10 minutes.

Smells Like Christmas

Make your home smell wonderful during the holidays without buying manufactured home fragrances—customize your own spice potpourri instead! Select a few favorite spices from your kitchen, place them in an old nylon stocking, and tie the ends closed. Store the sachet near a cracked-open window, fan, or heating vent, and savor the spices of the season.

Ornament Storage Solution

If you ever get one of those plastic containers apples sometimes come in, make sure to save it for your Christmastime storage. They're the perfect holders for holiday ornaments, especially the classic glass orbs.

Festive Storage

Taking down the Christmas tree makes for a depressing afternoon. Make it a little less dreary this year by wrapping the ornaments. Dribs and drabs of holiday wrapping paper are a festive way to protect fragile angels and eggshell nativities for storage until next year. Plus, by skipping the newspaper route, you won't have to be reminded of last year's bad news at next year's tree-decorating party.

Ribbon Dispenser

Even if you don't have cats in the house, spools of ribbon can come undone (and tangled) up very easily. Keep your ribbon spools in a shoebox with holes cut in the sides for the end of each ribbon to go through.

Perfect Padding

Another great use for those self-multiplying plastic grocery bags—gift padding when you don't have bubble wrap or newspapers on hand. Bonus: they squeeze into all kinds of oddly shaped places.

Eco-Friendly Gifting

Say "no" to Styrofoam popcorn! Instead, save your old egg cartons for the holiday season—they'll come in handy when packing up gifts to mail. Cut them up and use the pieces as packing material. It's cheap and environmentally friendly.

Add Your Own Special Stamp

Mailing a gift and want to do something creative for that extra-special touch? Visit your local coin and stamp dealer to find unique, vintage postage sold at face value or less. Many dealers sell old yet valid stamps that aren't worth much to collectors, so you're likely to find a bargain on cool, old-fashioned postage.

CHAPTER 7

Pets

Feline-Friendly Food

Cats tend to get upset stomachs from super-cold food. Prevent tummy aches (and, more importantly, vomiting) by letting the food warm to room temperature before feeding.

Never Pay for a Milk-Bone Again

When getting a "treat" for being good, most dogs are just excited about a special snack, not that it's in the shape of a bone. The truth is, doggie treats have almost the exact same ingredients as dog food, and most dogs can't tell the difference. Instead of paying extra for dog treats, keep a separate container of dog food where you normally keep the treats, then give your dog a small handful when he's done something reward-worthy.

Remove Fur Stains

Our niece's white dog was always getting stains under her runny eyes until we tried applying our miracle liquid: vinegar. Rub a little vinegar into white fur to remove yellow or brown spots.

Sap Trap

Whether your dog is covered in sap or your cat's been hanging out under the car (or you have no idea what they've been up to!), use shampoo to remove that sticky substance from your pet's fur. Dab on a little and work it toward the edge. Pull out and rinse with water.

Quick Pick (Fur) Up

If you have pets, you probably also have pet hair all over your house. Help stop it before it starts with a dryer sheet. Just rub it over your pet and it will pick up any loose hairs thanks to static cling. It will also keep your pets smelling fresher!

Brew Up an Odor Buster

Here's a fantastic use for used tea bags. Let them dry, then cut them open. Mixed the used tea with your kitty litter to keep it smelling extra fresh.

Who Knew? Readers' Favorite

Crushed red pepper shaken onto tape and affixed to furniture is an effective "Keep Out" sign for cats. The noxious smell trumps the desire to scratch. (Just remember that you may have some explaining to do to your guests!)

Less Pricey Prescriptions

Pet medications are often insanely expensive. Luckily, we've discovered Omaha Vaccine, a website that offers great deals on meds that cost more elsewhere. Visit OmahaVaccine.com to search for your pets' medications, and get free shipping for orders over $49.

Kitty First Aid

If you accidentally cut your cat's claw too short, and it bleeds, fill a small bowl with cinnamon, and dip the paw in really quick. The cinnamon acts as a coagulant and the cat will clench its paw tighter and help stop the bleeding. Then go to the vet.

—Beth Peters, Waltham, MA

Make a Moat

Do ants keep sneaking into your pet's food? Secret tip: Ants can't swim! Place the bowl of dog or cat food into a shallow bowl filled with water.

Cooler Collar

No need to buy a fancy nighttime collar for your furry friends. Simply cover a regular collar with reflector tape and watch Rover roam all over, even in the dark.

Don't Be a Litterbug

If your cat leaves trails of litter around the house, set a sisal mat just outside her litter box, where she enters and exits the box. The fibers and grooves in the mat will catch any flyaway litter before it hits your floor.

Probiotics for Pets

Give cats and dogs yogurt to help their GI systems. Mix a few spoonfuls with their regular food once a day. Seek a veterinarian's attention if problems persist.

A Better Bath

If your dog hates taking baths, try placing a towel at the bottom of the tub before you fill it up. It will be much less slippery under your dog's paws, and that will help keep him calm.

Soothe Your Dog to Sleep

If it takes your dog a while to go to sleep, particularly on a cold winter night, use heat to ease her into slumber. Throw a large towel into the dryer for 5–10 minutes on high, then wrap around your dog's bedding. Dogs (especially older ones) will love the feeling of heat on their muscles and will settle down faster.

A Dandruff Deterrent

If your pet is suffering from dandruff, add some omega-3 fatty acids to his diet. Luckily, it's easy: Buy a can of sardines in oil, and chop up a few and add to his food. He'll love the taste, and his coat will love the nutrients. (Just be sure to check with your vet first.)

Who Knew? Readers' Favorite

In the hot summer months, you'd like to be able to give your dog a drink of water when you're out for a walk, but you haven't yet perfected how to train him to drink from a water fountain. Solve the problem by bringing a plastic shower cap with you. When you fill it with water, it will expand enough that you can hold it out as a bowl.

Keep Cats Away from Electrical Cords

If your cat likes chewing on electrical cords, we know you need a solution, and fast! Here it is: Unplug the electronics, then rub the cords with a wedge of lemon. Once they've dried, you can plug them back in. Cats hate the taste of lemon and will steer clear.

Help for Digging Dogs

If your dog likes to dig up plants in your yard (gee, thanks, Fido), sprinkle some cayenne pepper in his favorite spots. Dogs hate the smell, and will stay away.

Fat Cat?

Help your cat slim down by sprinkling a teaspoon of crushed wheat bran cereal on her food each day. It's low-fat, high-fiber content will keep her full. (Just make sure to check with your vet before changing your pet's diet.)

Decoration Dangers

Cat lovers, beware! When it's time to trim the tree, never use tinsel if you have a pet kitty. Cats love to play with tinsel and eat it, and it can be deadly if it gets stuck in their digestive system.

Laser-Sharp

A great way to keep your indoor cat mentally and physically fit is to keep a laser pointer next to your TV remote. Every time you watch TV you'll be reminded to shine a laser light for the cat to chase. This allows you to be a lot lazier than your cat, for once!

—Justin Ott, Weehawken, NJ

Vitamin Water

Vitamins and minerals are very important to your pet's health. Save the water from steamed or boiled vegetables or liquid from a slow cooker and mix it with your animal's food for additional nutrients—and a "human food" treat they'll love!

Quick Fix for Messy Paws

Forget about using soap and water on your dog's messy paws. It's faster and easier to simply wipe his paws with a baby wipe. It's a great way to remove dirt and mud—before he cuddles up with you on the couch.

Quieter Dog Days

It's great that your loyal canine is always by your side, but you could do without the accompanying jingle jangle of his ID and rabies tags. The same colorful vinyl caps that you use to easily identify keys will work to silence those ringing tags. Now the dogs can be like the kids—seen and not heard. (We can dream.)

CHAPTER 8

Your Green Thumb

Longer-Lasting Blooms

There are quite a few ways to prolong the life of fresh flowers. First, change the water and trim the stems every day. In addition, add a solution of 2 tablespoons white vinegar and 2 tablespoons sugar to a quart of water—or add ½ cup baking soda to a quart of water. When you get the flowers, submerge the stems in water, and trim an inch off the ends. This will ensure no air bubbles get caught in the stems, which will inhibit their ability to drink water. If you have roses, you can even crush the stems at the ends to encourage water absorption. If you have tulips, make a series of small holes down the length of their stems with a pin instead. And if you're displaying carnations, place them in carbonated lemonade (not the diet variety) rather than water. Change every four days.

Keep Your Overpriced Flowers Fresh

You've probably noticed that florists often keep flowers in refrigerated cases. That's because the lower temperature keeps them alive for longer. If you have a beautiful bouquet you'd like to keep around for as long as possible, place it in your refrigerator each night before you go to bed. Your flowers will age more slowly while you're not there to enjoy them. (Too bad we can't put ourselves in the fridge!)

Flat Soda for Flowers

The little bit of flat soda left in your can will revitalize and sustain fresh flowers. Pour it into the vase and let the sugar go to work keeping the flowers in bloom. Clear soda works best for a clear vase.

Vinegar for Vases

Don't put a beautiful bouquet of flowers in a cloudy vase! To make it shine like new, just pour a little white vinegar and uncooked rice inside, swish it around, and watch the clouds disappear.

Flower Arranging Done Easily

When arranging flowers, apply transparent tape in the shape of a grid across the mouth of the vase. Not only will it be easier to decide where to put each flower, but they'll stay more upright with the tape to lean against.

Who Knew? Readers' Favorite

Daffodils are one of our favorite flowers. Just remember not to mix them with other flowers when making an arrangement, as daffodils produce a toxin that kills other blooms!

A Fair Exchange

Do you have leftover vases from flowers that are long gone? Ask your local florist if she'd take them off your hands, and don't be surprised if you get a fresh bouquet of flowers in return!

Treat Your Flowers to a Cocktail

Add a drop or two of clear liquor like vodka or gin to a vase of flowers, and it will keep bacteria away from the flowers' stems, so they'll last longer!

A Beautiful Bud Vase

Finished with that glass bottle of salad dressing? Clean out the inside and peel off the label, and now you've got a brand-new vase! It'll be great for smaller bouquets, and no one will notice the difference—just tie some yarn or ribbon around the screw top and set your flowers in place.

Plants Love Starch

Your houseplants need nourishment, particularly in the dead of winter when the sunlight is limited, yet there's no need to buy expensive plant food. Just remember to save the water in which you boil potatoes or pasta, let it cool, and use it to water your plants. They love the starchy solution.

Humidity Helper

Wintertime is tough on houseplants—not only is there decreased sunlight, but there's the dry air from your furnace. If your plants are languishing, consider buying a furnace humidifier, or try a humidity tent: After watering, place a clear plastic bag over the plant, and tie the ends down around the pot with string.

Safe Transport for Your Plants

When transplanting, always use lightly moistened soil and peat moss to help retain moisture in the roots. If the soil is dry, it won't hold together well during the transplant, which might result in a messy move at best and a plant casualty at worst.

Who Knew? Readers' Favorite

If you are going to re-pot a plant, place a small coffee filter on the bottom of the new pot to keep the soil from leaking out the drainage holes. Not a coffee drinker? Try a paper towel or napkin instead.

The Right Pot for the Job

Small plants often don't do well in big pots, because the water seeps down to the bottom, below the roots. But if you only have a large pot, fill it three-quarters full with soil, then place a layer of plastic wrap on top and fill with more soil and your plant. The wrap will keep the water on the surface, but when your plant grows larger, its roots will poke through.

Soak It Up

Put a wet sponge in flowerpots before you fill them with soil. When you forget to water them, or are out of town for a day or two, the extra moisture will protect the plants from drying out.

The Garden News

Old newspapers make terrific weed screens when planting your garden. Just spread the paper on the dirt, hose it down, and cover with mulch or more dirt. Plant your garden right on top and the newspaper will keep weeds from invading your space.

Grow Your Seeds in the Daily Rag

What's black and white and warm all over? If you're a seed, the answer is newspaper. Seeds need warmth, but not light, to germinate, so if you place newspaper (black and white only) over a newly sown area, it will keep the seeds warm and block out the light.

Who Knew? Readers' Favorite

Eggshells are a great fertilizer for seedlings. Get a head start on your garden by first sowing them indoors in eggshell halves. Let them grow in an egg container, and when it's time to transplant them outdoors, just dig a hole for the shells.

Another Reason to Save Those Eggshells

Save eggshells for your garden plants. Just spread around the stems of your vegetables or flowers, and they'll help keep slugs and snails away.

Fruity Seed Starters

Save orange and grapefruit halves for use in your garden. They make great containers for starting seeds. Just fill them with soil and seeds, and plant them. After the seeds germinate, the holders will decompose, leaving nutrients in the ground.

Smarter Seed Planting

The next time you're planting seeds, save time and energy by marking one-inch measurements on the handles of your tools instead of using a ruler.

Garden To Go

Clear plastic take-out containers make great makeshift holders to jumpstart seed growing. Fill the container about halfway with soil, add the seeds, water, and close the lid. Seeds should sprout in no time when the container is left in the sun.

Soil-Free Seedlings

Grow seeds effortlessly! All you need is a wet sponge (squeezed out), a windowsill, seeds, and a misting bottle. Place the seeds in the holes of the sponge. They'll get a good start in life if you mist three times a week. Transfer to soil when your plants are an inch high.

Seed Spacing

Here's the perfect way to sow seeds while making sure they're perfectly spaced. Fill an old salt or spice shaker with the seeds and some sand, then sprinkle the mixture into the dirt when it's time to plant.

Spice Up Your Life

Here's a fun way to save money on your grocery bill while also coercing the kids into helping you around the house: grow a spice garden. Getting even a small variety of easy-to-grow herbs such as basil, mint, oregano, and thyme can save money and give you fresher ingredients to work with. (For a feline-friendly treat, try catnip, too!) Find the seeds at a home and garden center, or buy the plant starts at a nursery or farmer's market. Get the kids involved by putting the plants somewhere they can reach, and help them water them when necessary. Add the leaves—either fresh or dried—to elevate simple dishes to the next level. If your kids really get into it, you may even convince them to do a vegetable garden next year!

Who Knew? Readers' Favorite

If you have old seeds that may or may not be ripe for planting, test them out first: Pour a handful onto a moist napkin or paper towel, and cover with plastic wrap. Wait until the germination time has passed (check the wrapper for the correct time), and take a look at your seeds. If some are growing, the seeds are usable—just sow them heavily.

Storing Extra Seeds

If you have more seeds than you can use this spring, store them in a sealed container in your freezer. The cold will keep them fresh until next year.

Easy Plant Labels

Here's a cheap, easy idea for labeling plants—especially herbs, veggies, or anything you might consume. Use white or beige plastic knives, the kind you may have stashed from fast-food restaurants. Simply write the name of the plant on the knife with a permanent marker and stick into the ground. They're waterproof, and last forever.

Grow Your Own Garlic

Do you have a sprouting head of garlic? Put the whole bulb (sprout/pointy end up) in your garden and cover with an inch of soil. It will continue to send up shoots, and in a few months, a whole new bulb of garlic will have grown under the soil's surface. Best of all, garlic repels bugs in your garden!

Clear the Way for Lilacs

Lilacs hate grass. More specifically, they must compete with grass and any other vegetation for food and water. To help your lilacs flower beautifully, keep a 16- to 24-inch circle around the base free from grass. Lime and manure are great fertilizers for lilacs.

Give Pansies a Boost

If you've got pansies in your garden, take the time to pinch out the early buds. It encourages the flowers to grow, and you'll ultimately get more flowers this way.

Feed Your Fern

Banana skins and eggshells are excellent natural fertilizers for ferns, and the minerals they provide are not readily found in many synthetic fertilizers. Flat club soda is another great option for your garden: To perk up colors, give your plants an occasional sip or two.

Roses Look Better with a Little Fat On Them

Want to give your roses an extra dose of fuel? A small amount of fat drippings placed at the base of a rose bush will keep it healthier and make it bloom more frequently.

Gone Bananas

Rose bushes love potassium. Luckily, they're easy to come by in the form of banana peels. Bury the peels just under the soil near your rose's roots and it will feed your plant and help it resist disease.

Put Some Tea on Your Tea Roses

The tea that comforts you can also nurture your roses. Place tea bags or sprinkle loose tea in your rose garden, cover with mulch, and enjoy.

Take care when pruning your roses and other thorny plants in the garden—you don't want to prick your fingers. Try holding the branches with a pair of kitchen tongs while you snip.

Watch That Hose!

When watering your garden with a hose, you don't want to drag the hose over your plants. Place a few short, heavy stakes in your garden to create an alleyway for the hose, which will restrain it from rolling around and distressing the delicate plants. If you don't have stakes, simply cut a wire hanger into six-inch pieces, bend them into arches, and use them to guide your hose.

Wooden Tools Need Love, Too

Care for wooden garden tools as you would your skin and your plants—moisturize! Over time, wood dries out and splinters. Apply a thin coat of linseed oil to wooden handles on rakes and shovels; it'll keep them safe and usable. A little goes a long way, so use the oil sparingly.

Don't Spread Disease

Use a solution of bleach and water to disinfect pruning sheers after you're done so you don't spread diseases among plants. Rinse with tepid water until the bleach is gone.

Shear Genius

Make sure your garden shears never rust by adding a little car wax. Just rub a little paste over the shears (including the hinge) to prevent them from getting stuck again.

Garden Caddy

Not sure what to do with that old golf club bag? Don't throw it away or stick it in the garage sale pile just yet. It's perfect for carting garden tools around your yard!

Tie Up Your Plants with Stuff You Don't Need

If you still have old, unused cassette tapes lying around, pull out the tape and use it to tie up your plants. Better yet, try old pantyhose: Just cut the nylons into narrow strips. This works even better than plastic ties because the pantyhose expands as the plant grows.

Turn Old Nylons Into Plant Holders

Got an unwearable pair of pantyhose? Don't trash 'em yet! Nylon stockings make excellent storage containers for plant bulbs. Air is able to circulate, which helps prevent mold. Store the bulbs in a cool, dry location.

For a Colorful, Sunny Garden

Be bold when planting flowers in sunny spots. Pastel-colored flowers can look washed out in bright sun, so consider red and orange blooms.

We don't like to be too sappy, especially on our hands! The easiest way to remove sticky tree sap from skin is with butter. Simply rub butter or margarine into the spots and wash with water.

Get Rid of Garden Stains

To remove dirt, grass, and other garden stains from your hands, add ½ teaspoon sugar to the soap lather before you wash your hands. You'll be amazed how easily the stains come off!

Remedy for Super-Dirty Hands

Kids playing in the mud? Powdered laundry detergent makes an excellent hand cleaner for very dirty hands. It's specially formulated to get rid of grease and oil, and the powder will work as a mild abrasive.

Some Oat Action

Are your hands dirty from working in the garden? Keep some dry oatmeal handy, and add to your soaped-up hands. The oats' abrasive action will get your hands cleaner quicker. And don't forget—always scrape your fingernails along a bar of white soap before gardening, to keep dirt from getting under your nails!

Maintain Your Manicure

If you have a green thumb, but beautiful pink nails, try putting cotton balls into each finger of your gardening gloves to make your manicure last as long as possible. Rotate new ones in every few days or so (depending on how often you garden).

Weed Whacker

Bull and Russian thistle sound powerful, but they're no match for WD-40. When you need to get the prickly plants out of your way, give them a spray with this all-purpose formula. Our kids like to help with this chore, perhaps because spraying WD-40 in the garden feels somehow illicit!

Share the Wealth

You've heard of clothing and cookie swaps. How about plant swaps, where you share cuttings and roots with gardening friends? Make it an annual tradition and watch friendships grow along with your garden.

Who Knew? Readers' Favorite

In our family, we're never all ready to go at the same time. Since we love to garden, we keep a few pairs of garden gloves by the door so the early birds can pull out a few weeds while they're waiting. It prevents having to take the time to pull the weeds later—and keeps a certain someone from yelling at everyone else to hurry up!

After the Rain

Weeding is easier when the plants are wet. Save this dull task for post-rain or watering. When you give a yank, you'll be able to remove the whole weed down to the root.

Garden Cart

This gardening season, use your kids' winter sled as a handy cart for your garden. You won't have to buy a new one from a gardening or home supply store, and the sled's smooth bottom will allow it to slide easily over grass.

Soil Test

Good for you for remembering to water your garden! Just make sure you're not overdoing it. Here's a simple test. When you're finished with the hose, dig down half a foot or so and feel the soil. Moist is fine, but muddy means you should use a lighter hand.

Compile Your Compost

If you've been putting off having a compost pile because of the hassle of always having to tromp to the other side of the yard, simply keep scraps in your freezer until you're ready to compost. Banana peels, apple cores, eggshells, coffee grinds, etc. can all go right into a plastic container to wait until you're not feeling so lazy.

A Free Caffeine Fix for Your Compost Pile

Coffee grounds are a great fertilizer for plants that need a lot of nitrogen, like carrots and tomatoes. But even if you're not a coffee drinker, you can still get the grounds for free! Many Starbucks give away used grounds as part of their "Grounds for Your Garden" program. Just ask at your local Starbucks.

Stick a Toothpick in It

A leaky garden hose can easily be repaired with a toothpick stuck into the hole. (The hole itself should be easy to find—for obvious reasons.) Break off the part of the toothpick that hangs out and tape over the hole. Wood expands when wet so it will fit nicely after the first trial run.

Who Knew? Readers' Favorite

Got a hose that's full of holes? Turn it into a soaker hose for your garden by buying a cap for the end at a hardware store, repairing any large cracks with duct tape, and then using a fine nail to poke holes throughout its length.

Mulch with Grass Trimmings

Take extra care of your plants by laying grass trimmings around them. The grass provides nutrients and moisture, and also prevents nasty weeds.

All in a Row

Here's a tip if you have trouble planting your garden in neat rows. Run a hose in a straight line, then plant your new seedlings along the hose. Remove the hose and you'll have a perfect-looking flowerbed!

Drainage Booster

If you break a terra-cotta pot, don't toss it out—use it to help your garden drain more easily! Break it into tiny pieces, then mix with your soil to promote drainage. If they could, we're sure your plants would thank you!

Let Your Lawn Grow to Starve Weeds

Try to keep your lawn about three inches high. The higher the grass, the less direct sunlight for pesky weeds.

A Lazy Lawn

Did you know you can actually have a lazy lawn? If you feed your lawn too much, the roots won't need to reach down to find food. When it's hot, they'll dry out right away. The trick is to feed it once a year—in spring or fall. When the roots aren't pampered, they'll grow deeper and become stronger. Just like people.

A Greener Lawn

Don't worry about collecting clippings when you mow your lawn. It's a waste of landfill space, and you'll deprive your lawn of nutrients it can use through natural composting. Instead, take off the bag and leave the clippings in the grass.

A Great Grass Alternative

Patches of dirt in your yard where grass refuses to sprout? Try morning glory, wintercreeper, or lily-of-the-valley in hard-to-mow areas, or wherever grass has trouble growing. Forcing a picket-fence-green lawn is a waste of water and a missed chance to be a little more creative.

A Lawn to Inspire Envy

Make your lawn sparkle this summer with this nutritious homemade fertilizer: 1 cup baby shampoo, 1 can of beer, and enough ammonia to fill the rest of your hose-end sprayer. Shake it up, then follow the instructions on your sprayer for 2,000 square feet of lawn. Repeat once a month.

Who Knew? Readers' Favorite

The rain stopped just in time for your outdoor party, but not in enough time for the grass to dry before you want to mow it. To solve this problem, simply spray the blades of your lawnmower with vegetable oil, and the grass won't stick!

More Moss

We always thought moss looked quaint in between cracks in our sidewalk, so we learned how to grow our own. Pull up some common lawn moss and blend it with active-culture yogurt. Find a cool spot with lots of shade and paint it into nooks and crannies, stone walls, and flower pots.

CHAPTER 9

Shop 'Til You Drop

Haggling 101

Sure, you've always been able to haggle at car dealerships and mom-and-pop stores. But did you know that "big box" stores such as Home Depot and Best Buy are getting in on the act, too? With sales slipping, the staffs of chain stores are now being told that bargaining is OK. Here are some tips to make sure you get the most bang for your buck.

✦ To add extra ammo to your asking price, do a little preliminary research at competing stores or on the internet. If you can tell a salesperson that a nearby store is offering the same item for less, you'll be more likely to get it at that price.

✦ Be aware of "extras" that competing stores are offering. Even if you're not interested in an extended warranty or free engraving at the other place, you can use the incentive to your advantage when bargaining.

✦ Take a spouse or friend. One of the best methods for negotiating is the "good cop, bad cop" strategy. One of you acts really interested in the product, while the other continually points out the flaws and negative aspects. Because of the "good cop," the salesperson will remain hopeful that he can sell the product, but "bad cop" will make him work for it.

◆ Find stores where there is no commission. A salesperson will be less likely to give you a discount if he will earn less from the transaction. But if it's only company money that will be lost, there's a higher chance he'll bow to your demands.

◆ Buy accessories, too. Most stores have a higher mark-up on accessories for top-selling items. If you're buying a memory card and a carrying case for your new camera, you're more likely to get a discount on the camera itself.

Need Wood?

Looking for inexpensive, quality building supplies? Check out one of Habitat for Humanities' ReStores, which sell used and surplus materials for low prices. To find a location nearest you, visit Habitat.org/env/restores.

Reverse Wish List

To save money and space, keep a wish list for things you want now, but might not want in a few months. Whenever you get the urge to buy something, write it down, but don't buy it. Every few months, read through your list. Do you still want that leopard-print Snuggie, ultimate pet stroller, or personalized yoga mat? Chances are, you're willing to let most of them go. It's amazing how fast "I absolutely have to have this" turns into "That's so 2009."

—*Mara Berke*

You're shopping in your favorite store and notice that there are tons of markdowns. After you fill your arms with bargains, go home and mark the day on your calendar! Most stores receive shipments of new goods every 9–12 weeks and discount current merchandise to make room for the new stuff. Return to the store during that time frame to find more deals.

The Cure for Shopaholics

If you often find yourself making impulse buys, use this simple trick to cut back on spending: Once you've gathered everything you'd like to purchase, find a place to sit down for a couple of minutes and take a break. Make a phone call, play a game on your cell phone, or just sit back and relax. You'll find that clearing your mind will help you be more rational about what you really need and what you'll later regret buying.

The Best Discounts in Town

If you are an educator, a member of the military, or a government employee, always ask if there is a discount available to you! You'll often find travel and admission discounts offered to these groups. If you're over 60, of course, never ever buy anything without asking if there's a senior discount! Some discounts even start for those 50 and over. Even if you don't look your age, you might as well take advantage of the savings available to you!

The Best Places to Find Clothes Online

Shopping online is one the easiest and best ways to save money on clothing. Here are some of our favorite sites to find good, inexpensive clothes on the web.

✦ 15DollarStore.com is exactly what it sounds like—a store where all clothing is $15 or less. In addition to a large selection of women's clothing, the site also has belts, handbags, sunglasses, watches, jewelry, and some children's clothing.

✦ If you're trying to save money, it's probably a good idea to try to stay away from designer fashion labels. But if you just can't help yourself, Bluefly.com is the best place to go for a bargain. You'll find discounted prices on men's and women's designer clothing, including labels such as Kenneth Cole, Burberry, Armani, Marc Jacobs, Calvin Klein, and Prada. Just try to keep it to a couple outfits and a handbag!

✦ At Zappos.com, you'll find more shoes than you ever imagined possible, including men's, women's, and kids' sneakers; dress shoes; boots; and sandals. Not only do they have free shipping, but they also include a return shipping label with your order, so if you don't like the shoes once you try them on, you can easily return them for free.

- ✦ 6pm.com is where Zappos shoes go when they're on sale, so it's a great place to score some good deals on your favorite brands. You do have to pay for shipping, but the savings can be worth it because the selection and prices are usually quite good.

- ✦ If you love style, check out GoJane.com. Their focus is high-fashion clothing without the designer label or price tag.

Take It to the Tailor

Going to a tailor may seem like an expensive proposition, but it's often worth it if you unearth a good deal on a suit or other item that doesn't quite fit. Found some jeans for ten bucks that look great but are an inch too long? A jacket that's a steal, but a bit too baggy in the arms? For a low price, you can get these items custom-fitted at a tailor. And you'll still be saving a bundle from what the normal retail price would be.

The Seasonal Shopping Secret

For the best deals on clothes, always shop in the off-season. Buy spring and summer clothing in July and August, and fall and winter clothing in January and February. (You can often find the best sales right after the holiday season.) It's sometimes a bummer to buy something you're not going to be able to wear for six months, but when the time comes to switch seasons, you'll be happy you already have some new clothes to wear—all of which were purchased on sale!

Keep It Simple

When you're buying clothes, always go for classic looks rather than modern, trendy ones. A blue V-neck T-shirt will be fashionable year after year, while something with more exotic colors or patterns will go out of style quickly. By choosing the basics, you won't have to buy as many new articles of clothing each season.

Your Own Personal Shopper

At ShopItToMe.com, you enter your favorite brands of clothes and they do all the online searching for you. When items come up for sale on a department store's site, they'll send you an email, alerting you of the discount. The best part is, you can specify your size, so you won't have to waste your time wading through links only to find that the store is all out of extra-large!

Who Knew? Readers' Favorite

Here's an online shopping secret that can save you hundreds. When you're visiting a company's online store, make sure to hit up the "sale" section first. Many sites will also keep sale items in their original locations—without the prices marked down. Look in the sale section first to make sure you're getting the best price.

Thrifty? Try Shopping at Thrift Shops

Many people are intimidated by shopping at thrift shops. What's the best way to wade through all those clothes, organized in no particular order? How do you know you're getting something good? And what should you be wary of? First of all, it's more intuitive than you might think. If you're browsing through a thrift shop, and the clothes seem dingy or dirty, find a different shop. But for the most part, you'll find perfectly good clothes that are simply one or two seasons old. Make sure to check each item closely for rips or stains, and keep in mind that it may be worth it to buy something if you think you (or a tailor) can easily repair it. Many resale shops are organized by the color of the clothing, but most also use some kind of color-coded tag system (so that all items with a red tag are 50 percent off, for instance). Best of all, you can usually exchange your clothes for money or store credit. Make sure to ask if the store offers you more "money" for your item if you opt for credit rather than cash. And have fun looking for bargains! You never know what fantastic find you're going to get.

Take from the Rich

When going shopping at second-hand shops, try visiting wealthier neighborhoods for the best finds. Not only do they shop at these stores less often (leaving more goodies for you), they have nicer things to give away!

—*Lori McNaughton, Newport Beach, RI*

Begin in the (Bargain) Basement

How many times have you purchased an $80 sweater, only to find a nearly identical one later for much less? When you begin to look for clothes for the new season, always start at the least expensive store first. Since most clothing stores carry similar items each season, you'll make sure to get each piece for the best price. You should also try to buy most of your basics—solid-color T-shirts, socks, and so forth—at the cheaper stores. Save the expensive stores for the uniquely designed and patterned clothes, where you can see the difference in quality.

Befriend Those in the Know

If you have a favorite shop you find yourself spending a lot of time in, make sure to get friendly with the sales staff! Clothing stores often have unannounced sales, or they regularly begin sales on certain days of the week. If you're down with the people who work there, they'll often you tip you off. And if they really like you, they may let you put an item on layaway until it goes on sale a few days later.

The Mall Is a Money Pit

If you or your teen is looking for something to do, stay away from shopping malls! Although they're popular hangouts, they'll always lead you to spend money. Skip the stores and go to the park, a pool, or a matinee instead.

Don't Go into the Red on Black Friday

It's Black Friday—the craziest shopping day of the year. Before you head out to the mall, hit up FatWallet.com first. They keep track of each store's Black Friday deals, so you can keep an eye out for promised bargains and make a plan of attack for your day of shopping.

Your Site For Salon Savings

Addicted to fancy shampoo? Find all the same brands you buy at your salon for much less at SalonSavings.com. Shampoo and hair-care products are 10–80 percent off, and skincare products and fragrances are offered at much less as well. This site is also a great place to check if you have a favorite beauty product that has been discontinued.

Who Knew? Readers' Favorite

When trying to compare a pricey cosmetic with a less-expensive one, you only have to look at one thing: the active ingredients list. Products that have the same active ingredients are going to do almost the exact same thing, even if the percentages are a bit off. (The only thing you might have to worry about is which smells better.) You'll be surprised how many expensive brands—especially hair products like shampoo—have the exact same ingredients in them for vastly higher prices.

Never Pay Too Much for Cosmetics

When shopping for make-up and other cosmetics, avoid the department stores! Because of commissions for the salespeople and the cost to rent the space at the store, they're never a bargain. Instead, check out your local grocery store or discount store such as Walmart or Target—they almost always have similar brands for much less. If you can't find your favorites there, try a cosmetics discount outlet such as Ulta, or search for "discount cosmetics" online. If you still can't find your brand, consider switching to another brand you can find. Choose one a good friend uses, and ask her if she'd be willing to buy it from you if you don't like it. It shouldn't be too hard to find an affordable alternative.

Make-Up Must-Have

Most make-up is exactly the same, except for whether they call that shade of red you love "cherries jubilee" or "red crush." Make shopping for make-up easier by keeping an index card with your favorite colors on hand. Rub a bit of lipstick, blush, or eye shadow on the card, then mark down the brand and what the color is called. When it's time for more make-up, you can easily compare the colors of the sale brand with your card. Then write down what that color is called on your card. You'll soon have a list of all your favorite colors from each brand.

—*Arlene DeSantos*

Good Make-Up Doesn't Have to Be Expensive

For a great deal on cosmetics, head over to EyesLipsFace.com, where they have everything from lip gloss to nail polish for only a dollar apiece. They also have a great "Gifts" section, with cute box sets for unbelievable prices. For instance, you can find eye shadow, mascara, eyeliner, a brush, and an eyelash curler for only $5!

Who Knew? Readers' Favorite

Did you know that up to 30 percent of consumers never get around to returning items that they meant to take back to the store? If you're unsure about an item while you're in the dressing room, the best thing to do is to put it back on the rack. Once we began following this policy, we were shocked at how few never-worn garments ended up in our closets.

Use Your Phone to Check Prices

If you're lucky enough to own an iPhone, Android, or other smartphone, you're also lucky to have access to applications that make shopping easier. Once the applications are installed, you can use your phone's camera to take a snapshot of the barcode, or enter the UPC numbers underneath. Your phone will then give you a list of how much the item costs at locations near you and online. Search your phone's app store for Barcode Scanner on iPhone and Android, ScanLife on Blackberry, and ShopSavvy for

Windows phones. If you don't have a smartphone, you can still easily compare prices online. You don't get to use your phone as a scanner (which is half the fun), but you can enter the UPC code of any product to get prices from around the web by using Google's Product Search (Products.Google.com). Just type in the numbers found near the barcode and away you go!

Shopping for Electronics?

If you're in the market for a new TV, DVD player, portable music player, or other electronic device, the best time to buy is in the late spring and early summer. Prices will drop because new products are usually introduced in the late summer and early fall. New computers are also often released in February, so shop in January for savings.

Stream Free and Easy

Before you buy an expensive "streaming video" unit or get talked into buying a video game system "just so we can watch streaming Netflix on the TV," investigate your TV's hook-up options. Many TVs allow you to hook them right up to your laptop as a "second monitor." You may need to buy a couple of new cords, but they'll likely be much cheaper than new electronics.

Cheap Computing

Buying a new computer? Netbooks are smaller versions of laptops, and although they don't have nearly as many features as a full-size computer, they still work well for the basics (word processing, watching videos, searching the internet) and cost only about $500.

This may seem counterintuitive, but if you're buying a printer, try to buy one that uses as many different toner cartridges as possible. Not every household uses the same amount of every color, so you may be forced to throw away a tri-color cartridge that's out of, say, magenta, but still has plenty of yellow and cyan left. Printers with separate cartridges for each color solve that problem by ensuring that no toner is wasted. It's also a good idea, when printing, to specify a black-and-white printout in instances where color isn't really necessary.

Rah-Rah for Refurbs

If you're like most people, you probably shy away from buying refurbished electronics, but you shouldn't. We go out of our way to buy refurbs, which not only save cash, but also provide more or less the same level of reliability as brand-new items. Whether it's a cell phone, laptop, gaming console, or television, a refurbished item is arguably less likely to be defective than a new one, because these items are tested at the factory before they're resold. And in the rare instance where a refurb does fail, all of the other refurbs you've bought will have saved you enough money to replace it. Contrary to popular opinion, most refurbished units aren't simply broken items that have been repaired. They may have been returned to the maker for any number of other reasons. A customer may have returned a gift he didn't want, the packaging (but not the actual item) may have been damaged in shipping, the item might have a cosmetic blemish, or may have been missing a nonessential accessory. If you can live with those things, then refurbished items are definitely for you. Many of them even come with the original manufacturer's warranty intact.

A Game of Telephone

The most expensive place to buy a cell phone is at a cell phone store, even one run by your mobile provider. These stores count on foot traffic and impulse purchases, and usually price phones higher. When it's time to get a new phone, check out your phone company's online offerings, which will include several free or heavily discounted phones that the stores no longer carry.

Mobile Money

If you're buying a new cell phone, what should you do with the old one? Get cash, of course! Visit Cell4Cash.com and enter the brand and model of your old phone. The site will tell you if they're offering any money for it, and if they're not, they still allow you to send it in to be recycled. Plus, the shipping is free!

The Price You Pay

Looking to change your cell phone provider but aren't sure how much you're going to have to pay to get out of your contract? Head over to CellTradeUSA.com, which will tell you how much it will cost to cancel. The site also allows you to transfer your contract to another CellTrade user, if your cell company allows it.

Deals on Wheels

The internet can be a great resource for buying a car, particularly a new one. Instead of relying on a salesman's sketchy pitch, do your own online research on the pros and cons of each model. Go test-drive one to make sure you like it, but don't buy it right then. Instead, go home and hunt around for the best price among dealers in your region. Even if the dealership offering the best price is located far away, you may still come out ahead by having them deliver the car to you. We once paid $500 to have an out-of-state dealer ship a vehicle to us—and that was still $1,000 cheaper than buying the car locally.

—*Jerri Thompson Barry*

Buying Plants?

Always buy houseplants in the spring, when you'll find a better selection and prices that are 20–60 percent cheaper.

Who Knew? Readers' Favorite

If you're sending flowers for a special occasion, skip the national delivery services and websites. Instead, find a flower shop that is local to the recipient and call them directly. Most national services simply charge you a fee, then contact these very same stores themselves.

When to Buy Home Appliances

If you're looking for large appliances or household furnishings like a washing machine, dryer, dishwasher, refrigerator, or sofa, the best time to buy is in October. At this time of year, businesses are busy making room for their holiday inventory, so you'll find tons of sales on last year's merchandise. Go ahead, celebrate a little early!

Finding the Best Deals on Furniture

The best way to save on furniture is to browse your local store, then buy online. Seeing it in person will allow you to try it out and see its dimensions up-close, but buying online can give you a huge discount. If you see something you like, write down the manufacturer's name and, if available, the model number. Then do a search for the same piece and see what low prices you find.

Stop Squinting!

If you need new glasses and aren't sure how you're going to afford them, check out 39DollarGlasses.com. For around $45 (with shipping), you can get attractive (though bare-bones) glasses, including the lenses! Walmart also offers good deals on frames and lenses. If you've got to maintain your hipster image, try WarbyParker.com. They sell stylish $95 glasses including the prescription lenses with free shipping and returns. They'll even ship several frames to your house to try on and return. Plus, you can try out their glasses online "virtually" by uploading a picture of yourself. As a bonus, they donate a pair of glasses to someone in need for every pair that is sold.

Candle-Buying Benefits

If you like decorating your home with candles, buy them on clearance at after-holiday sales. There's nothing wrong with burning a pumpkin-scented candle in spring or a pine-scented one in August. If that feels weird, though, just stash the seasonal scents in the closet until next year's holidays come around.

Buy at Auction

Every month, hundreds of cars and other items are confiscated by the police. And hey, just because a criminal used it doesn't make that $100 laptop any less useful. Look in the classifieds section of your newspaper to find local auctions, or check out PropertyRoom.com or PoliceAuctions.com to find unbelievable deals on tools, electronics, bicycles, video games, and more, not to mention some truly bizarre items like a Freon tank, "assorted copper tubing," night vision goggles, and an adorable cement frog. And if you're OK with not telling the recipient where it came from, you should know that auctions are also one of the least expensive places to buy beautiful jewelry and gemstones.

Cheap Checks

When pawing through the coupon inserts in your Sunday paper, make sure to save the advertisements for checks. These companies aren't just for people who like cartoon characters next to "Pay to the order of." They're also for people who like to save! You'll always get them more cheaply than simply ordering them through your bank, and don't you give your bank enough money as it is?

Save, Then Spend

As Veruca Salt said in Willy Wonka and the Chocolate Factory, "I want it, and I want it now!" It's hard to break the habit of buying expensive items when we want them, then paying them off over the next several months. But saving up ahead of time has numerous benefits.

✦ First of all, you'll make sure you really want the item. If you have to save up for six months for a new TV, you'll have plenty of time to reconsider if the old 20-inch is good enough. And trust us, once you do finally have the money, it feels so much better to go home with a piece of merchandise that's bought and paid for, rather than one that has just put you further into the hole.

✦ When you open a new store credit card to pay for a big-ticket item, this credit card will pop up on your credit report as being opened and immediately maxed out. Obviously, this isn't good news for your credit score.

✦ Finally, not having to pay something off after the fact means no interest payments. And many mom-and-pop stores will give you a lower price if you pay all in cash.

Throw in the Towels

When you're shopping for towels in a superstore, skip housewares and go straight to the automotive section. You'll find packs of 12 white terrycloth towels, often for as little as $5. They're durable and can be used anywhere in the house.

Rent What You Rarely Use

Instead of buying something you'll only need rarely, how about renting it? Zilok.com puts you in touch with local businesses and individuals who are renting cars, vacation homes, tools, TVs, video game consoles, and more. Better yet, you can list your own items to rent! (Unfortunately, you can't rent out your kids.)

Built for the Battlefield—and the Playground

This school season, consider replacing your kids' flimsy backpacks with a sturdier (and cooler) alternative: military backpacks. These bags are built to last in the battlefields, so they'll certainly stand up to the wear and tear of the school year. You can find them in any Army/Navy Surplus store.

Don't Buy Hangers

In need of some new hangers? Try your local department store. When making a purchase, let the sales clerk know that you'd like to take the hangers, too. If you notice any empty hangers lying around the cash-out area, ask for those as well—it couldn't hurt!

Casino Coin Count

When you need to cash in loose change, avoid bank fees by taking your change to a nearby casino instead! Seem counterproductive? It's not. Bring your coins to the cashier, who will exchange them free of charge, then hustle out past the video poker machines to escape that urge to play!

Save Big

Save up the old-fashioned way by sticking money in a drawer on a regular basis. But instead of loose change in a piggy bank, stow a few dollar bills at the end of each day. Better yet, set up a "splurge fund" for your next big purchase or vacation—it'll give you incentive to be prudent with your cash.

Dump an Old Deal

That half-off Groupon deal for your boyfriend's favorite restaurant seemed like a good idea—until the two of you broke up. Luckily, all is not lost (at least in terms of your finances). Off-load your unwanted deals from sites like Groupon, Living Social, and Scoopst.com at CoupRecoup.com. And of course, if you're looking to get a great deal, this the place the visit first!

The Check Is in the Mail

Get free cash back just for shopping online at Ebates.com. Before you shop at your favorite sites (including HomeDepot.com, BN.com, Kohls.com, Target.com, and more), log in at Ebates.com. Then click through to your desired website. You get a certain percentage of cash back on each site, and a check will be mailed to you every three months. It's that easy!

Go Straight to Savings

If you're looking for deals online, your first stop should be PriceGrabber.com. It lets you see what's on sale in various categories, then takes you right to the site to get the bargain. Best of all, you can see the prices at different sites side-by-side, including sales tax and shipping!

Be a Membership Mooch

Just because you don't belong to a wholesale club like Costco, BJ's, or Sam's Club doesn't always mean you can't take advantage of their savings. Have a friend who is a member get you a gift card, and they'll let you shop there without a membership! (Make sure to check first.) Just show the gift card at the front desk.

Frugal Photo Printing

If you usually print out your digital photos using an online service, you know that there are a lot of them, and they often have promotions and sales. To help you figure out which one can give you the best deal right now, check out PrintRates.com. You indicate the number of prints and sizes you need, and it will tell you where to find the best deal.

Know the Code

Ever see that little box for "promo code" when you're buying something online? Always have something to put there with RetailMeNot.com, which has coupon codes for thousands of online retailers. Some stores offer more online codes than others, but you can usually find one that at least offers free shipping or a small discount.

Coupons for the Taking

Did you know that the websites of many malls now offer coupons? If you're headed to the mall, check their site for exclusive coupons and links to the coupons offered by the websites of the various stores inside.

Savings, Forwarded

Looking for coupons for big-ticket items for your home like washing machines, TVs, and more? Stop by your local post office and grab a packet for people who are moving and would like their mail forwarded. Even if you don't fill out the forwarding card, these packets often contain coupons from stores targeting those who have recently moved.

CHAPTER 10

Natural Remedies and First Aid

Longer Than Big Red

Bad breath? Eat some yogurt! The "good" bacteria in yogurt has been found to be effective in targeting the odor-causing bacteria in your mouth. Make sure you go for the plain kind, no sugar. Breath mints and sprays mask the odor but they don't help the underlying problem—eating yogurt does.

Great Breath Fast

You don't need expensive mouthwashes to get better breath. Simply gargle with a mixture of 1 cup water, ½ teaspoon baking soda, and ½ teaspoon salt. This combo will knock out any germs that are causing your bad breath.

Water, Water, Everywhere

How much water is enough water? Divide you body weight in half. The number you come up with is how many ounces of water you should be drinking daily. For example, if you weigh 150 pounds, you should consume 75 ounces of water each day.

Pepper Your Dishes

Why not use a sprinkling of cayenne pepper to help season your sauces? Derived from the plant Capsicum annuum, it has been reported to not only make you lose weight by elevating body temperature, but to improve circulation and to lower cholesterol. As it's a mild stimulant, it can also be added to hot water with lemon juice as an alternative to coffee.

Sage Advice

To cut down on how much you perspire, try drinking sage tea. Herbalists say it will take several weeks, but you'll see results!

Detox with Lemon

Lemon juice not only smells great, it tastes delicious, too. Mix it with hot water and try it as an alternative to hot tea and coffee. You may find it wakes you up just as well, and your body will thank you.

Kick Your Sweet Tooth's Habit

Here are two quick tricks to eliminate the craving for sweets (without hitting the fridge). One way is to place a small amount of salt on your tongue and let it slowly dissolve. The second: dissolve about a teaspoon of baking soda in a glass of warm water, then rinse your mouth out and spit (don't swallow). The salt or baking soda tends to stimulate the production of saliva, which eliminates your sweet craving.

Lutein for Healthy Eyes

Many people suffer from farsightedness, cataracts, glaucoma and other eye problems as they age. To keep your eyes healthy, increase your level of lutein—available in vegetables such as carrots, broccoli, spinach, Brussels sprouts and kale. Lutein can decrease the risk of cataracts and macular degeneration.

The All-Natural Prozac

The herbal supplement St. John's Wort can help ease feelings of depression and lift black moods. It is thought to increase the activity and prolong the action of the neurotransmitters serotonin and noradrenalin in a similar way to standard antidepressants, and will need to be taken for a few weeks before it starts working.

A Breath of Fresh Air

This is simple advice we've all heard before, but how often do we put it into practice? When you're feeling anxious or overwhelmed, take a deep breath. Take five, as a matter of fact. Start in your belly—envision blowing up a balloon there—and move to your chest, filling your lungs to their capacity. Exhale slowly. This is also a great method if you're having trouble falling asleep, since it signals to your nervous system that it's time to relax.

Furry Friends

Playing with or petting your pet is known to reduce blood pressure, improve your mood, and reduce stress. It been proven to work with all pets: dogs, cats, hamsters—everything but dust bunnies.

Relieve Stress in a Pinch

Many people hold stress in the area between their eyebrows, and in time, vertical stress lines will develop here. When you feel your brow knit together with concentration or stress, take a moment to pinch the muscle there, working from the center of the brow along the brow-line in each direction with a thumb and bent forefinger.

A Good, Stiff Drink

If you find you're often stiff after exercising, you probably just need more water. Dehydration is a major cause of post-exercise muscle soreness. Drinking water regularly while you work out should keep water levels high enough to combat pain.

Contrast Showers

You'll love the feeling of this simple routine that will help boost your immune and circulatory systems and even relieve stress. Toward the end of your shower, turn it up as hot as you can stand it and allow it to warm your body for three minutes. Then turn it down so the water is cool, and let it run over your body for 30–60 seconds. Repeat as many times as you like, ending on cold. When you get out of the shower, rub yourself vigorously with a towel to encourage circulation. Do not continue the contrasting temperatures, however, if you feel dizzy, nauseated, or excessively chilled.

Salt Sedation

Having trouble sleeping? We love this all-natural insomnia cure. At bedtime drink a glass of water, then let a pinch of salt dissolve on your tongue. (Just make sure the salt doesn't touch the roof of your mouth). Studies show the combination of salt and water can induce a deep sleep.

Rx, Vinegar

White vinegar stops nosebleeds. Just dampen a cotton ball and plug the nostril. The acetic acid in the vinegar cauterizes the wound. Who knew?

Cures for Canker Sores

Hydrogen peroxide may help reduce and relieve canker sores. Simply mix one part peroxide with one part water, then dab on any affected areas several times a day or swish around in your mouth for as long as possible. If you feel a canker sore coming on but it hasn't erupted yet, hold a slice of fresh garlic to the spot for ten minutes. It'll make your breath stink but it will also stop the sore from forming.

Get Rid of Cold Sores

If you have a cold sore, tea can help, thanks to the tannic acid in tea that helps relieve inflammation. Place a used tea bag on affected areas for 3 minutes. To make it feel even better, place the tea bag in the freezer for 10 minutes beforehand.

Homemade Heating Pad

Don't spend your money on an aromatherapy pillow! Instead, add uncooked, long-grain rice to a sock and tie it shut. Whenever you need a little heat after a long day, stick it in the microwave on high for 1–2 minutes and you'll have soothing warmth. To add a little scent to the pillow, add a few drops of your favorite essential oil to the rice.

Tiny Ice Packs

Get rid of the hundreds of condiment packets in your junk drawer and help ease the pain of smaller bruises, scrapes, and burns by keeping the packets in your freezer, then taping them to ouches with scotch or medical tape.

Soothe Bruises

If you have a bruise, soak a cotton ball in white vinegar, then apply it to the bruise for an hour. It will reduce the blueness of the bruise and speed up the healing process.

Toothpaste for Burns

Toothpaste is a great household helper, and it even comes in handy with burns. If you've sustained a minor burn, cover it with white, non-gel toothpaste to ease the pain and help it heal.

Slippery Solution

Soothe and help heal minor bruises and scrapes by using the inside of a banana peel to gently rub the injury. Treat as fast as possible to reduce bruising.

Try Honey, Honey

The ancient Egyptians relied on honey for cuts and burns long before antibiotics were around. Besides offering a soothing protective layer over minor wounds, the honey provides a natural antibiotic. Put a layer of pure honey on before a bandage.

Sanitize a Cut

You just got a nasty cut on your hand, but don't have anything to clean it out with before you put the bandage on. Luckily, there's something in your medicine cabinet that you may not have thought of—mouthwash. The alcohol-based formula for mouthwash was originally used as an antiseptic during surgeries, so it will definitely work for your cut, too.

Splinter Removal

Splinters used to be major events at our house until we discovered this trick: Vegetable oil softens the skin and helps the offending piece of wood slide back out. You can also put a drop of white glue over the offending piece of wood, let it dry, and then peel off the dried glue. The splinter will stick to the glue and come right out.

Keeping Finger Bandages Dry

You put a Band-Aid on your finger to cover up a scratch, but you still have to go through your day full of hand-washing, child-bathing, and dishes-doing. To keep the bandage dry while you work, cover it with a non-inflated balloon—any color will do!

PB&B

The blisters are gone but the Band-Aid tracks remain. Use peanut butter to get rid of the black marks and stop distracting everyone from your lovely pedicure!

Be Callous to Calluses

To remove hard calluses from your feet, try this old-fashioned but effective remedy: Grind a few aspirin tablets into a paste with equal parts lemon juice and water. Apply it to the calluses, then wrap your feet in a hot towel, cover in plastic bags, and stay off your feet for 30 minutes. When you unwrap your feet, the calluses will be soft and ready to be filed off with a nail file or pumice stone.

Another Cure for Calluses

Ugly callus got you down? Remove it easily and naturally with this simple fix: Take a piece of a lemon peel and tape it (yellow side up) over the callus using medical tape or packaging tape. Leave overnight, then remove and rub with an emery board or pumice stone in the morning. Repeat for a week and your callus will be gone!

No Need to Be Corny

To get rid of corns, soak a Band-Aid in apple cider vinegar, and apply it to the corn for a day or two. You can also try soaking your feet in a shallow pan of warm water with half a cup of vinegar. Either way, finish by rubbing the corn with a clean pumice stone or old nail file (just don't use it on your nails again).

Bee Careful

If you're stung by a bee, carefully grasp the stinger and pull it out as fast as you can. The less venom that enters your body, the smaller and less painful the resulting welt will be. Ice the area immediately to reduce the swelling. If it still hurts, try cutting an onion in half and applying the fleshy side to the sting. It should help ease the pain.

Help for Stings

Believe it or not, meat tenderizer works wonders on all sorts of stings—bee, wasp, even jellyfish. That's because it contains papain, which helps break down the proteins in venom. Make a paste with the tenderizer by adding a few drops of water at a time, then rub on the affected area.

Be Itch-Free

A great way to treat mosquito bites is with a dab of ammonia, which stops them from itching. In fact, ammonia is the main ingredient in many of the itch-relief products currently on the market. You can also try a dab of rubbing alcohol.

Getting Rid of Lice Naturally

Nothing strikes fear in the hearts of parents like the words "lice outbreak." The harsh chemicals that are used to fight lice are almost as bad as the lice themselves. Luckily, there is a cheap, more natural alternative, and it's as close as your refrigerator. Cover your child's head (or yours, if the little buggers have gotten you!) with a thick conditioner like Pantene Pro V. Put on a Disney movie to keep your kid busy, then get a wide-toothed metal comb.

Dip the comb into rubbing alcohol and comb through the hair, staying close to the scalp. Between each swipe, wipe the comb on a white paper towel to make sure you're getting the lice. Dip the comb in the alcohol again and keep going. Cover the hair with baking soda, and then repeat the process with the alcohol and the comb. Wash hair thoroughly when finished, and repeat this procedure each day for a week or until the lice are gone.

Poison Ivy?

To help relieve the itching of a rash caused by poison ivy, soak the affected area in a strong salt bath. Make sure the water is warm to fully get the itch out.

Diaper Rash Ointment

When your baby gets diaper rash, nix those pricey ointments and try a homemade remedy instead. Make a paste with about ¼ cup petroleum jelly and 1 tablespoon cornstarch, then spread it along your baby's irritated skin. Or try adding a cup of baking soda to your baby's bathwater.

Don't Horse Around with Aches and Pains

If you're suffering from aching muscles (either from illness or too much exercise), try this homemade cure. Mix 1 tablespoon horseradish with 1 cup olive oil. Let sit for 30 minutes, then apply it to aching areas.

Aid Arthritis with Oatmeal

Believe it or not, you can help relieve arthritis pain with oatmeal. Just mix 2 cups oatmeal with 1 cup water, warm the mixture in the microwave, and apply to the affected area.

Soothing Back Pain

If you have chronic back pain—especially associated with arthritis—or other sore muscles, try adding yellow mustard to a hot bath. Add a few tablespoons for mild pain, and up to a whole 8-ounce bottle if the pain is severe. The bathwater may look strange, but your aching back will thank you.

Help for an Stomach Ache

If your stomach is upset due to indigestion or a hang-over, try drinking a glass of club soda with a dash of bitters. It should help ease your pain.

Rub Away the Bloat

Feeling bloated? It could just be trapped gas. Encourage it to move by gently stroking from your right hip up towards your ribs, then across the bottom of your ribcage and down towards your left hip. Repeat several times.

Relieve Nausea Naturally

Nothing's worse than a bad bout of nausea. Try this simple trick to help relieve your discomfort: Drink a little ginger ale, then chew a handful of crushed ice, and finally sniff a piece of black-and-white newspaper. It may seem like an old wives' tale, but it works!

Root Out Morning Sickness

Ginger root, taken as a powder or in tea, works directly in the gastrointestinal tract by interfering with the feedback mechanisms that send sickness messages to the brain. Take some when you're feeling nauseated to help alleviate your symptoms.

Stop Motion Sickness in Its Tracks

If you get nauseated every time you ride in a car, boat, or train, take some lemon wedges with you. Suck on them as you ride to relieve nausea.

Sore Throat?

Aspirin does more than just relieve headaches! If you have a sore throat, dissolve two non-coated tablets in a glass of water and gargle. Just make sure to note that this only works with aspirin— don't try it with other pain relievers like ibuprofen.

Tasty Remedy

Relieve your sore throat with a time-tested home remedy. Slice one-third of a lemon off, then take the two-thirds-sized piece and place it on a shish kebab skewer or barbecue fork. Set your gas stove to high and roast the lemon over the open flame until the peel acquires a golden brown color. (This works on electric stoves too, although not quite as well.) Let the lemon cool off for a moment, then squeeze the juice into the smallest cup you have. Add one teaspoon of honey, mix well, and swallow.

Better than a Bloody Mary

In the peak of sore throat season, get a reprieve by gargling with this spicy mix: 1/3 cup tomato juice, 1/2 cup hot water, 5 drops pepper sauce. Gargle. It works even better if you gargle with lukewarm saltwater first. If you prefer sweet to salty, fill a shot glass with honey, then warm it in the microwave for about 10 seconds on high. Stir in 1/4 teaspoon cinnamon, then drink.

Scallion Cure

Stuffy nose? Don't spend money on decongestant—head to your fridge instead. Cut the "root" end of two scallions and carefully insert the white ends into your nose (being cautious not to shove them too high!). You may look silly, but your nose will start to clear in a couple of minutes.

Onion Earmuffs

Oil found in raw onion is anti-microbial, which makes onions great cures for upper respiratory ailments. If you have a minor earache such as swimmer's ear, onion may help. Slice a fresh onion and heat it in the microwave on high for one minute. Wrap it in cheesecloth or another thin cloth so that it doesn't burn your skin, and then hold it against the ailing ear for 20–30 minutes. See a doctor if the pain gets worse or continues for longer than 24 hours.

Steam Away a Cold

Steam is a wonderful household remedy for colds, especially with some aromatherapy oils mixed in. Try pouring hot water into a bowl and breathing in as you lean over it. Stick your tongue out as you do it—this will open the throat and allow more steam through, which prevents membranes from drying out. Add aromatherapy oils to the water that are especially known to alleviate the symptoms of congestion, such as black pepper, eucalyptus, hyssop, pine, and sweet thyme.

Ancient Cold Relief

Ayurveda is a practice of natural medicine that's been used in India since around 1500 BC. Try this cold remedy that's been passed down through the ages: At the very first sign of a cold, mix 1 teaspoon water with 1 teaspoon raw honey and 1 teaspoon turmeric. Eat it every 30 minutes until symptoms disappear.

Watery Eyes?

If your eyes are itchy, try this quick fix to cut down on your misery: Rub a small amount of baby shampoo on your eyelids. It should reduce your symptoms dramatically.

Goodbye, Swimmer's Ear

If your children are prone to swimmer's ear, a bacterial infection of the ear canal, take this precaution when they've been in the pool: Dab a solution of one part vinegar and five parts warm water into each ear three times a day. The vinegar will ward off bacteria and keep your kids' ears pain-free.

Index

for meat odor removal, 61
for nosebleeds, 465
for odor removal, 17, 21, 299
for pies, 98
for shower curtain cleaning,
265
for stainless steel sink cleaning,
243
for stove cleaning, 245
for toilet bowl cleaning, 263
for vases, 421
for wood floor cleaning, 227
Vodka
for flowers, 422
for label removal, 258
for potpourri, 225
for stainless steel sink cleaning,
243
V-rack, 61, 62

W

Waffles, 47, 52
Wallpaper
cleaning up, 229
hanging, tip for, 324
Wall stud, 330
Wasps, elimination tips for, 356
Water
adding to cooking vegetables,
40
for nut shelling, 42
for sausage shaping, 66
for scrambled egg clean up, 50
Wax paper, 36
WD-40 spray, 298, 305–306, 333,
431
Wedding gift, 117
Windows
blinds dusting, 231
sealed, opening of, 335

stuck , tip for, 231
washing tip for, 231
window screen, 331, 336
Wine
bottle cork, 112–113
bring your own in restaurants,
401
cooking with, 23
freezing of, 176
glass rings, 112
leftover, 113
red wine sediment removal,
176
for roaches elimination, 349
for shower door cleaning, 265
stain removal from, 284
Wine bottles, as bookends, 368
Wine corks, 323
Wish list, keeping of, 439
Wood, sanding of, 330
Wood floors
cleaning tip, 227
homemade cleaner, 228
Wood supplies, shopping for,
439
Wool cleaning, 277
Wool pads, 248
Wrinkles, 288

Y

Yard torch, 319
Yeast, 29
for dough making, 133–134
for drain maintenance, 267
storage of, 131
Yogurt, 35

Z

Ziplocs, homemade, 174
Zipper fix, 287